# SAN FRANCISCO AS YOU LIKE IT

## 20 Tailor-Made Tours

### for

### Culture Vultures, Shopaholics, Neo-Bohemians, Fitness Freaks, Savvy Natives,

### — and — Everyone Else

## BONNIE WACH

CHRONICLE BOOKS
SAN FRANCISCO

Printed in the United States of America.

ISBN 0-8118-1641-9

Library of Congress Cataloging-in-Publication Data available.


Book and cover design: David Albertson Design, SF
Composition: DAD
Cover photography: David Albertson


Distributed in Canada by Raincoast Books
8680 Cambie Street
Vancouver, B.C. V6P 6M9

10 9 8 7 6 5 4 3 2 1

Chronicle Books
85 Second Street
San Francisco, CA 94105

Web Site: www.chronbooks.com

*To my mom,*
*who thought San Francisco would be a nice place to settle down.*
*And to Pete, who lit a fire under my butt.*

# Contents

## Acknowledgments

*Thanks to Karen Silver and Joni Owen at Chronicle Books for their patience and understanding. Thanks to Carole Terwilliger Meyers for her input on the Weary Young Families chapter; and to Autumn Stephens and Leslie Crawford for being great sounding boards. Big thanks to Peter Callahan for all the Nitty Gritty information. And most especially, thanks to Rob Farmer for his insight and contributions on architecture and yuppie hangouts, and for showing me San Francisco for the first time, again.*

As we all know, living in the Bay Area is not without its little sacrifices. Summer, for instance. And the fact that you have to share your living quarters with a lot of people. People with cars. People with cars who always manage to get the parking spot in front of your house. People with pets who fail to uphold the sacred pooper-scooper mandate.

# Introduction

And of course, living here naturally dictates that you will have to spend a lot of time playing tour guide to all the friends, relatives, and relatives of friends who have been waiting for just this sort of an excuse to visit San Francisco.

On the whole, these are sacrifices we make gladly, because, like millions of other people, many of us moved to San Francisco after first coming here as tourists ourselves and falling under the city's mysterious, intoxicating, and slightly damp spell. It's a spell that I've been under since I was old enough to look over the balcony of my parents' house and see the red horns of the Golden Gate Bridge peeking out through a downy halo of white fog in July. Paris of the Pacific, Athens of the West, Baghdad by the Bay. It is all those things and Brigadoon too, emerging shimmering out of the mist on summer mornings like a half-believed, half-dreamed Olympus.

But living here for any length of time also tends to generate a certain kind of complacency. We humans are creatures of habit, and having already searched and found the perfect cafe (usually within a few blocks of our house), we are perfectly content to return to that spot week after weekend with our Sunday *Chronicle,* and read about the latest restaurant openings and theatrical debuts with all the well-intentioned (if short-lived) enthusiasm that a double cappuccino can produce.

So when old college chums from Wisconsin announce that they're coming for a visit, the response is fairly predictable. The mind draws a complete blank, followed immediately by some variation on the phrase "Where the —— am I gonna take them?" succeeded shortly thereafter by a series of desperate, anxiety-driven forays into outdated guidebooks and old newspapers. The thing about San Franciscans is that even though we may not want to play tourist ourselves, we take a peculiar pride in being able to show friends a peek behind the postcard that is most people's perception of the Bay Area. That's essentially what this book is about.

Having personally experienced the agony of dealing with bright-eyed, expectant houseguests, and having on occasion failed miserably to meet those expectations, I wanted to help others in the same predicament.

(It's still painful to talk about that weekend with the company president, whom I nearly bored to death at an ikebana demonstration, then managed to find not one, not two, but three restaurants where the only thing she could stomach was a salad.)

The problem is, what's good for the grandma is not necessarily good for the grad student. Probably, your grandmother would not enjoy the Persian Aub Zam Zam Room—even if she were Persian. Being thrown out of a place for politely inquiring about the wine list just violates some basic tenets of common courtesy to which she's grown accustomed. However, entry into Bruno's private martini parlor might be just the ticket for your old college roommate-turned-yuppie—to whom you feel compelled to prove (due to latent feelings of inadequacy over his skyrocketing Wall Street career) that you've got your finger on the pulse of the city.

It's a grown-up game of show-and-tell, and the prize at stake is that mixed expression of envy and joy that people get when they have an only-in-San-Francisco epiphanic moment. It's at that point that we say nonchalantly, and with only a tiny hint of smugness, "Yeah. It's pretty cool."

Parents. Can't live with 'em, can't take their credit cards with you when you move out. But no matter how many times you've woken up surrounded by pizza boxes and dirty laundry and smiled with contentment when you realized that it was just the cat using your plant as a litter box and not your mom's clicking tongue, you still want

# Tour 1 Parents

to impress them when they come to visit. And it doesn't matter if they only live as far away as Palo Alto. Because this is your town now—your neighborhood, your friends, your beat-up futon, your stack of unpaid parking tickets—and for once you get to be the one with all the presents under the tree.

A couple of things to keep in mind: most parents want the *Sunset* magazine version of San Francisco, not the underground guide, no matter how young and hip and "with it" they pretend to be. They want the San Francisco where people are polite and pick up their trash, where there are brochures and interesting historical markers to read, and where there are plenty of conveniences (read: necessities) such as clean bathrooms and, of course, parking. Second, you'll want to find a good place to put them up *that is not your apartment*. Frankly, you don't want your parents getting too familiar with the contents of your bathroom cabinets or the strange messages on your answering machine. Most important, if they're staying for longer than a weekend, you're going to need a break so you can get back in touch with your real personality. Otherwise, you might find yourself locked in the bedroom with the music turned up real loud, and all those years of hard-won independence will be down the toilet.

Last, try to throw your parents a bone at least once during their stay: wear the damn birthday shirt, let your dad map out the best route even though you've been there a hundred times, tell them how much your friends like them. You've got nothing to lose but some emotional baggage.

## MORNING

Even if you've taken an oath never to do anything this bourgeois, make an exception for **brunch at the Ritz.** Besides scoring major points with the 'rents, you'll probably be surprised (and maybe just a tad disappointed) at how much you yourself get into it. This is the Zsa Zsa Gabor of Sunday brunches—a seriously classy (and pricey) affair served on a sunken rooftop terrace amid an *Alice in Wonderland* rose and hedge garden. The unbelievably lavish buffet begins with a bottomless champagne glass, then segues into fresh-chilled prawns and oysters on the half shell, a complete caviar bar, smoked meats and fish of every imaginable variety, lamb carved off the rack, a half-dozen hot entrees, and a table featuring nothing but muffins, breads, and other baked goods. Just figuring out which courses you haven't tried can be an all-day affair, so it's a good thing they provide entertainment (a jazz combo performs all day). But wait. Don't pop the top button yet. There's more. Inside the dining room is a dessert spread that would make Willy Wonka blush.

Other parent-pleasing brunch spots include:

**Tuba Gardens**—If the Terrace is just a tad too Ritzy for your blood, Tuba Gardens is a half step down on the formality scale. It's tucked in back of a stately Pacific/Presidio Heights Victorian, and parents will love the outdoor patio and gazebo.

**Doidges Kitchen**—This brunch spot has been popular for years with parents, tourists, parents who are tourists, and the crowd of affluent, clean-cut white folk who live in Cow Hollow. Excellent pancakes and French toast.

**The Courtyard**—And you thought there weren't any fern bars left. The Courtyard, in the Outer Richmond, is a bar and grill straight out of the '70s, complete with raw-redwood paneling, ferns, brass accents, a salad bar, and skylights—the basic look of every house you've ever rented in Lake Tahoe (minus the shag rug). For parents whose ability to keep up with fashion gave out somewhere around 1978, and for grown-up kids who miss the old days at Perry's, this is the perfect brunch spot. The food's mediocre, but safe—eggs Blackstone and Benedict, western and Spanish omelets, and fresh-baked jalapeño corn bread. Don't forget the Raimos fizzes. Far out!

**Clement Street Bar and Grill**—This is a really "nice" place, with all that that implies. Noisy without being raucous, hanging-plant homey, but with classy darkwood paneling and white tablecloths. The menu is a happy balance of foods you eat at home and stuff you eat only at fancy brunch restaurants: bagel and lox platters, grilled red snapper with salsa, fried eggplant torta, sourdough French toast, grilled citrus-marinated chicken salad, baskets of warm muffins and fresh breads (oh, and the requisite spicy Bloody Marys and strong coffee).

# NOON

For some strange reason, after parents reach a certain age, they become obsessed with parking. It's a time in their lives when you can expect more than 40 percent of any conversation to include such phrases as: What's the parking situation there? Do the meters take dimes and nickels? Is there a parking lot? How much does it cost? Is that a safe neighborhood to park in? Do you have to parallel park or can you go nose in? They become experts at discerning the color of curbs from great distances and, in certain extreme cases, gear

---

**JUST LOOKING, THANKS**

When I was younger, one of my favorite mother-daughter activities was walking around on Sundays pretending we were house hunting, so we could look inside the big, expensive homes in the ritzy neighborhood that bordered ours. We'd sigh with envy over the astounding views, the master bathrooms with gold sinks and Jacuzzi tubs, the Miele dishwashers, Wolff ranges, hand-painted Italian tiles, and Oriental rugs. We'd make silent gagging noises over the bearskin rugs, the rooms encased in white-marble, and the collections of Leroy Neiman paintings.

Even if this isn't your family tradition, it's still a great way to get your cheap architectural thrills while seeing how San Francisco's better half lives. Don't waste your time on small potatoes; head directly to Pacific Heights, Presidio Terrace, or Sea Cliff, where the most modest of mansions hits the market at a million plus. Homes are generally open for public viewing from 2 p.m. to 4 p.m. on Sundays; they're listed in the real estate section of the *Chronicle*.

entire outings around the fact that they've found a free, all-day parking spot. My friend Heather's mom has become so preoccupied with the issue that she has canceled entire vacations for fear of not finding a place to park (Heather and her siblings have vowed that mom's headstone is going to read: "Finally found a place to park").

San Francisco is not exactly a parking friendly town—and certainly it's a huge adjustment for parents who are used to the embarrassment of parking riches in the suburbs (take a spot—take three). Couple this with the fact that gas stations in the city are disappearing faster than Starbucks are proliferating, and you have a parental nightmare. There are several things you can do to allay their fears:

1. If they insist on driving the Cadillac here, scope out a parking spot ahead of time (or give up yours), deposit the car, and take alternate means of transportation the rest of the time.

2. If they're flying in, pick them up from the airport before they've had a chance to peruse the car rental agencies.

3. Before you go out to a restaurant, research the street parking situation. If it's bad, make sure there's valet parking, or a nearby parking garage. Do not circle for hours like you usually do, praying to the God of Parking Karma. This is guaranteed to drive parents into a paranoid frenzy from which they may never recover.

## Making Nice-Nice with Mom

When faced with an impending visit from mom, and the inevitable dilemma of how to make up for all the Mother's Day/birthday cards you forgot to send over the years, kids in-the-know head to **Rod McLellan.** Sadly, at the time of this writing, the 100-year-old company's huge facility in South San Francisco (known as "Acres of Orchids") had just closed and relocated to San Mateo and Watsonville (the gift shop and spa to the former, the greenhouses to the latter). Rod McLellan tends, sells, clones, pampers, and even babysits every variety and hybrid of orchid ever invented (plus a smattering of gardenias, roses, and eucalyptus plants). The visitors center and garden gift shop is like a tropical Oz with orchids of every hue and style cascading from pots. Here you will also find botanical watercolors, gardening books, decorative planters and furnishings, crystal and silver vases, and cachepots. All the plants are for sale, and come with easy-to-tend instructions (hint, hint). Most importantly, don't miss a visit to the cloning lab, where scientists create new varieties of orchids, and be sure to watch the video of how they make those high-society corsages (they're on sale here and at the greenhouses, HUGE hint). Rod McLellan also features the Bay Area's only orchid spa and daycare center, where you can drop off your ailing plant or board your favorite orchid when your on vacation.

If you're already doing the flowers, why not seal up the inheritance with chocolate? And in this town, no one does chocolate like **Joseph Schmidt.** Purveyor to all the finer stores, Schmidt also keeps a tidy little shop on Sixteenth Street below Church, where you will find his heavenly truffles, along with his trademark sculptured chocolate bowls, white- and dark-chocolate tulips, champagne bottles, golf balls, and other objects of his confection.

## Bonding with Dad

Fishing with Dad is a time-honored ritual that is part of nearly every fatherson bonding movie ever made. Does it work? Who knows. But it's worth a try. Rent a boat and go trout fishing in **Lake Merced,** which isn't exactly Montana's Big Blackfoot, but it's well stocked, and if you catch one that's been tagged, you get prize money for it. Bonus.

If that sounds too strenuous, you can just practice the art of the fourcount fly cast at the **Casting Pools** in Golden Gate Park. Talk about the weather, the war years, the time you sneaked back into the house at five in the morning (oops).

Afterward, take Dad to drinks and dinner at the **Big Four** bar and restaurant in the Huntington Hotel, a place steeped in the cigar smoke of San Francisco's four original Old Boys—railroad barons Collins Huntington, Charles Crocker, Mark Hopkins, and Leland Stanford. While he sips brandy in front of the fireplace and revels in the etched-glass panels, the huntergreen color scheme, and the bounty of dark oak that bespeaks Old Money, work up the courage to ask him for that loan.

The Drinking of the Beer is another father-son tradition that must not be overlooked. At ballgames, in front of the TV, or at the local tap, nothing says "Don't worry, I haven't turned into a freak" better than the sound of a hissing bottlecap. And if you can combine The Drinking of the Beer with a historic landmark and an only-in-San-Francisco experience, you're gonna win some kind of normality award. Aside from making damn good ale, the **Anchor Steam Brewing Company** offers an interesting perspective on a time when San Francisco boasted more breweries than coffeehouses. Tours are offered by appointment only, and you'll need to book a reservation about two weeks ahead, but you'll learn tons about our famous homebrew, and at the end of the tour, samples of Anchor's many fine ales await you. Savor the flavor as you discuss the real reason why it's called "steam" beer (hint: there's actually no steam process involved).

# A Family Outing

Commune with the spirits of San Francisco's founding fathers at the **Neptune Society Columbarium**, one of the city's truly hidden gems and a great way to show your parents that you still respect your elders. The gorgeous 1898 belle epoque building, with its soaring stained-glass dome and windows (one of which is thought to be the work of Louis Comfort Tiffany), houses the ashes of some of San Francisco's foremost citizens. It stands alone now in all its neoclassical glory, tucked behind the Coronet Theater, where once it marked the gateway to the Odd Fellows cemetery. All the bodies were moved out of San Francisco long ago, but the columbarium remained and was eventually restored to its turn-of-the-century glory. Amid the urns of alabaster, copper, and more unusual shapes and substances (there's a silver martini shaker, a tree stump, a baseball, and even a Johnny Walker bottle), lie the remains of the Folgers of coffee fame, the Magnins, Kaisers, Eddys, Shattucks, Hayeses, and Brannans. Definitely take a guided tour from caretaker, ad hoc historian, and storyteller extraordinaire Emmitt Watson, who's spent the last decade making sure our city elders are kept in the style to which they were accustomed.

# Getting Out of Town

Daytrips play a key role in maintaining good parent-child equilibrium. And Sonoma is perhaps the best of the daytripping options, for a number of reasons:

1. It involves getting out of your neighborhood and reducing the number of times your mother shakes her head at the local crazies and says, "So this is how you live."

2. It involves a moderate but not-too-long scenic drive through pastoral Marin County.

3. It's quaint and charming and has lots of nice shops (for your mom), and it's full of juicy war stories about early California (for your dad).

4. If all else fails, you can drink a couple of bottles of good wine—and the fact that you can never please your parents won't seem quite so tragic.

Once you arrive, park at the town plaza, and head directly to the **Sonoma Cheese Factory** to pick up a picnic. If you weave your way to the back of the store, you can watch them slap and drain big balls of Sonoma Jack and Cheddar through cheesecloth. Then work your way back to the front to sample the finished product from the numerous tasting bins, while you decide which variety you want. I prefer my cheese a bit stinkier (they carry a limited selection of more pungent flavors like Cambozola and Schloss), but the housemade hot pepper or pesto Jack should pack enough of a wallop to satisfy most tastes. Next, take your cheese, your bread, your garlic-stuffed olives, and your petulant little chardonnay directly to a picnic table in the park, and nosh (remember to save a few breadcrumbs for the ducks and chickens). Afterward, while your mom goes nuts in the arty knick-knack stores, steer your dad to **Mission San Francisco Solano de Sonoma,** where he can indulge in tales of the Bear Flag Revolt of 1846. A few doors down from the mission is the **Old Swiss Hotel,** which, if you're within twenty miles, is a must-detour on any parental tour. The old adobe building was built in 1850 as a wing to the large residence of General Vallejo's brother Salvador. It's been the Swiss Hotel and restaurant (owned by the Marioni family) since 1926. First stop: the bar—a small, cozy, darkwood affair that spills out onto sidewalk tables, with bartenders who've been there longer than some of the scotch. The thing to order is the Glariffee, a very tasty, cold Irish coffee created by owners Ted and Helen Dunlap (née Marioni) with a recipe so secret, not even the bartenders know how to make it. Helen still lives in a house at the very back of the property and concocts and delivers a batch of Glariffees every day. The recipe is stashed in a safe-deposit box and upon Helen's death will be passed down to one of her nieces. While you sip, make sure to point out the wonderful old photos along the wall, which offer a mer-chant by merchant tour of Sonoma in the '20s and '30s.

The restaurant here is extremely parent-friendly, too: there's a big garden patio, red-checkered tablecloths, and hearty Italian fare that includes housemade seafood ravioli with lobster-basil cream sauce and roasted rosemary chicken (plus gourmet pizzas from a wood-fired oven). If you have a few too many of those Glariffees, this is also a nice place to park for the night (rates are in the $120 range).

Should you decide to throw a few wineries into the mix while you're up here, these are the spots to hit:

**Buena Vista**—Where that wild Hungarian Agoston Haraszthy planted the first zinfandel grapes in California. The old stone building is beautiful (there's a guided history tour of the property every day at 2 p.m.), and there's a nice gift shop inside. During the summer months, Buena Vista hosts a lovely, outdoor concert series, where you can bring a picnic and enjoy music ranging from classical to light jazz and pop.

**Bartholomew Park**—Owned by the folks who brought you the Gundlach-Bundschu winery, this one is part of a lovely hillside park that overlooks the valley. Inside, in addition to some tasty reds, there's a small-but-fascinating wine museum, with artifacts such as Haraszthy's handwritten letters, and dishy historical trivia about the building, which once served as a hospital for women of ill repute.

**Ravenswood**—Great setting, even greater wine—especially the Alexander Valley zinfandel and the merlot. Parents (and okay, kids, too) usually get a kick out of the winery's slogan: Nulla Vinum Flaccidum (No Wimpy Wines), which is available on everything from bumper stickers to T-shirts.

**Chateau St. Jean**—Located off Highway 12 a short drive out from town, this place looks like it could double for the summer estate of Louis XIV. Yards of sybaritic green lawn, a sun-dappled fountain and fish pond, and a breezy collection of light white wines put this on the top ten list for moms.

Though it's closer to home, you can achieve a similar equilibrium on a visit to **Muir Woods, Muir Beach,** and the **Pelican Inn.** If your parents are convinced that San Francisco is merely Sodom and Gomorrah with a few extra hills thrown in, this trip will make them see the light. First, stop at Muir Woods, where one minute spent at the base of any of the 200-foot-high, 1,000-year-old redwoods will save you months of explaining why you got arrested at a "Save the Headwaters Forest" rally. Then proceed to Muir Beach to watch the surf crashing against the craggy rocks and contemplate the vast expanse of Big Blue. You'll see their eyes moisten at the sheer aching beauty of it all (I'm welling up just thinking about it). Have a catch with your dad; stroll along the shoreline picking up shells with your mom. Tell them about your hopes and fears and bad love affairs, because they're not going to be around forever, and there isn't anyone else in your life who's genetically programmed to understand you the way they are.

At the end of the day, walk up the road to the **Pelican Inn** for a pint and some bangers and cottage pie. The cozy Elizabethan-style country inn, restaurant, and pub, with its rough-hewn, darkwood beams, brick fireplace, honeysuckle vines, and Tudor bar, is a popular watering hole for seasiders and hikers, and a nice bit of Olde England in the midst of earthy Marin. The bar serves ales, sherries, ports, wine, cider—and even real mead. If you get warm and sleepy, book a room and spend the night beneath a down comforter in an old-fashioned canopied bed, next to a decanter of sherry (rates are in the $140 to $165 range).

You don't need me to tell you about taking the ferry to Tiburon. The question is not whether to go, but where to sit once you get there.

After you've walked around the shoreline taking pictures of the San Francisco skyline and nosed in all the trinket and expensive doodad shops, you'll need to pick a restaurant with an outdoor deck. For parents, Sam's is probably too young and inebriated; Guaymas might be too spicy and ethnic (unless they love margaritas); but **Tutto Mare** should be just the right speed. The Italian seafood restaurant is a bit more grown-up than its neighbors, with white-tablecloth service upstairs, a trattoria atmosphere downstairs, and a large glass-enclosed deck (so Mom's hair doesn't blow all over the place). The menu features lots of fresh fish and pasta dishes, plus the requisite fried calamari and oysters on the half shell.

# NIGHT

So maybe before dinner or after the show, the parents like to tip back a few scotch and sodas or a white wine spritzer and reminisce about what it was like when they were young. The **Redwood Room** was invented for precisely this occasion. The marvelous 1933 art deco cocktail lounge, with its twenty-two-foot fluted columns, enormous Gustav Klimt reproductions, and gorgeous mahogany bar, will make this inevitable conversation all but painless. Settle into a table near the piano player—usually a tuxedoed fellow who plays oldies and show tunes and reminds me of Sam from Casablanca—order the good stuff, and charge it on your dad's corporate card.

If they love the oldies, and you know they do, take them to the **Plush Room** for a little Cole Porter and Gershwin in an atmosphere of decidedly plush red velvet and stained glass. A relatively small cabaret, it attracts big names in the torch singing business, among them Michael Feinstein, Andrea Marcovicci (she got her start here), Weslia Whitfield, Jackie & Roy, and Paula West. This might actually be a good place to send Mom and Dad for a romantic evening alone, while you order out Chinese and watch *Saturday Night Live*.

A visit to a fancy rooftop cocktail lounge with a sweeping panoramic view of the city should be on every parental itinerary at least once. It almost doesn't matter which one. For nostalgia, the **Top of the Mark** is your best bet, a starlit room that hosted the last dance for many a sailor shipping out to sea during World War II. These days the refurbished room plays the standards for a new wave of youthful swing dancers. The **Crown Room** at the Fairmont is considered by many to have the best skyline view in town (it's the city's highest public observation point), plus your folks will probably get a kick out of the fact that this was the hotel in the TV show *Hotel* and the place where the bulk of the United Nations charter was written. If it's not occupied, ask the concierge if he or she can arrange for you to see the Fairmont's famous penthouse suite, where presidents, sheikhs, and other dignitaries have stayed during the hotel's storied ninety-year history. The penthouse boasts three bedrooms, a dining room, a game room, a library, a patio, and—as you might imagine—a view to end all views.

Picking a dinner restaurant can be tricky. You might not want to overwhelm them with one of those raging of-the-moment places that still have a wait at 11 p.m. On the other hand, you might not want to under-whelm them with a place so obscure or on-the-fringe that they feel ill at ease.

A few restaurants tread a happy middle ground, among them **Harris',** the city's classiest steakhouse, replete with plush, king-size booths; potted palms; a long menu of prime-cut, dry-aged red meats; and gracious owner/former rancher Anne Harris at the helm to make sure everything goes right. Of course you get baked potatoes with sour cream and bacon bits; naturally there's Caesar salad and fried zucchini.

At **Albona,** the staff will make you feel like you're one of the family (minus all the arguing) by suggesting their favorite dishes, making sure your water and wine glasses are always full, and telling stories about the homeland. The restaurant's location—halfway between Fisherman's Wharf and North Beach—is another bonus; it somehow manages to avoid the crowd and parking hassles of both. Plus, your parents will feel like they're doing something daring by trying Istrian cuisine (from the Istrian Peninsula, just below Trieste), a blend of Italian and central European sensibilities.

## WHERE TO STAY

Modest neighborhood inns are a good compromise between your house and a hotel that's clear across town. The **Stanyan Park Hotel,** on Stanyan and Waller Streets across from Golden Gate Park, is a homey, informal place with an air of suburban refinement. The rooms are spotlessly clean but not fancy, and the hotel serves a nice conti-nental breakfast in the downstairs dining room.

If you live in the vicinity of the Mission or Noe Valley, definitely check the folks into the **Hidden Cottage Bed and Breakfast.** Longtime city residents Dave and Ginger Cannata have transformed the top floor of their house at Twenty-fifth and Noe into a charming, airy aerie that feels like home away from home. The room comes complete with hardwood floors, VCR (the kids will go rent you movies), its own fenced-in sundeck, and a private backyard entrance. Mom will love the enormous bathroom and the yards of closet space. In the morning croissants, muffins, and coffee come delivered in a basket to your door.

Everybody's grandparents are different. Some spend hours in the kitchen making perfect gnocchi; others have perfected the art of the microwave waffle. Some impart pearls of wisdom; others impart fruitcakes and hideous, multicolored sweaters with geometric patterns. Some are spritely and engaged and keenly aware of developments

# Tour 2 Grandparents

of the past decade; others think service station jockeys should still wear bow ties and wash windows, and that rock and roll is the devil's work.

My grandmother was a walker. Rain or shine, she loved to take the grandchildren out for a stroll in the woods or down the street, often leaving us in the dust. She was of the Old World—a woman who insisted her French students call her "Madame Dufer" and never "Julia," and who firmly believed children should be seen and not heard (my most vivid memories of her always involve the phrase "schrei nicht so"—"don't scream so"). And though she generally appreciated good food, in her later years, she was most content sitting in a corner booth at Lyon's twenty-four-hour diner with a ham sandwich and a cup of soup.

All this personal reminiscing is by way of saying that grandparents can be difficult people to plan activities for. Sometimes a full day means taking them to a hairdresser and the duck pond, or simply letting them stay at home to cook you strudel/tamales/gnocchi. However, there are two or three universal truths about grandparents: they tend to tire easily, so going places where they can sit down is essential; their day is often centered around meals, so plan those ahead of time and work your activity schedule around them; and they live to hear about your achievements, big and small, so don't whine when you have to trot out that story about the time you appeared on *Oprah*. They're your grandparents. They've earned the right to embarrass you. Get over it.

## MORNING

This is a tough time slot for grandparents, because what they consider morning, you probably consider prime sleeping time. No one knows why, but for some reason when you hit the golden years, your meal schedule begins moving incrementally backwards, until you're eating breakfast at 5 a.m., lunch at midmorning, and dinner at four in the afternoon—hence the origin of the Early-Bird Special. Considering that most cafes aren't open at 5 a.m., and that by the time they are, Grandpa will be ready for lunch, you might want to stock up on Zwieback and waffle mix, and use the morning hours as your prime sightseeing time. If you do have a chance to go out for breakfast, think Old School:

It's not fancy, but all the pastries are made with real, honest-to-God butter and sugar, and you can always find a good coffee klatch at **Star Bakery** in Noe Valley, one of the last holdouts of this once working-class Irish neighborhood. Their authentic Irish soda bread will warm your emerald heart, and the place is filled with the kind of homey, familiar smells that will make grandparents feel like they're back in the old neighborhood.

Nearby **Herb's Fine Foods** on Twenty-fourth Street kills two birds with one stone. You'll enjoy hobnobbing with the Noe Valley "in" crowd and various local celebrities who make a pilgrimage here each weekend (no doubt attracted by the red-leather booths, formica countertops, and crummy coffee). Your grandpa will appreciate the fact that this is a genuine, eggs-and-bacon diner from the 1940s. Grab the sports page and talk Yankees over a plate of bangers and flapjacks.

A sense of family and neighborliness are old-fashioned virtues that seem to have gone out with our grandparents' era. You know what I mean—the local baker who always gave the kids a treat; the butcher who always shared some words of wisdom. Even though **Katz Bagels** has only been here since 1993, Burt Katz and his son, Mike, are two from the old mold. Lining the walls of their shops are hundreds of wonderful photos of all their friends and neighbors, from babies to bohemians (a hobby of Burt's). Grandparents from New York will appreciate their traditional boiled bagels, which aren't too chewy ("We wouldn't be able to look at ourselves in the mirror if we made them any other way," says Burt). Bring your bubby, have a sit, a bagel, some lox, and a little over-the-fence chatter.

**Art's,** at Irving and Ninth, is a classic counter-and-stool joint for eggs any style and hash browns. Huge portions at rock-bottom prices.

**Manor Coffee House** is another haven for the blue-haired set—both young and old. This place hasn't changed decor since it was picked up circa 1955 by a tornado in some tiny Midwest town, and plunked down on this deliciously frumpy stretch in the inner Sunset. Crowning touch: they still have diet plates consisting of hamburger patties, cottage cheese, and sliced tomatoes.

## The Great Benches Tour of San Francisco

To my mind, good benches are worth their weight in wood. From the right perch, you can sit and contemplate city life without having to actually go somewhere. Not to mention the plethora of additional activities you might consider while perching—eating, letting others join you, taking in the views, feeding the ducks, reading the paper, taking a nap. Which is why, for grandparents who want to see it all, but maybe don't have the stamina to get there, benches are perfect observation posts on the world. Here is my list of the top ten benches in San Francisco:

1. **Lyon Street at Broadway:** Situated at the end of the toniest block in all of San Francisco, the landing near the top of the Lyon Street steps affords

spine-tingling views of the Palace of Fine Arts, the waterfront, and the bay. This bench gets bonus points for friendly joggers (occasionally of the celebrity variety) who wave as they sweat by and for the surrounding flower pots and manicured gardens, which make you feel as if you're in a Merchant Ivory film.

2. **Marina Green kite-flying field:** For sheer volume, there's nothing like the Marina Green. It's a place where sitting on a bench is actually a participatory sport. Aside from the obvious attractions (the views of the Golden Gate Bridge, Alcatraz, and the harbor), there are kite flyers, volleyball players, rollerbladers, and the hoi polloi coming and going from the St. Francis Yacht Club.

3. **Strybing Arboretum in front of the duck pond:** On a sunny Sunday afternoon, the duck pond is a small island of tranquility in a sea of activity. Around you, toddlers chase squirrels, Frisbees fly, couples fight and make up, trees carry the whispers of a hundred years of dangling conversations. While you toss breadcrumbs to the all-knowing swans and mallards (or better yet, get a bag of those wonderful sesame cookies from the Japanese Tea Garden), settle in for a long chat about the old days and all the bad things your father did as a child. (The pond is a short walk north from the main entrance.)

4. **Palace of Fine Arts eastern benches:** This is the best bench in the city for vicarious wedding crashers. On weekends in the spring and summer, limos frequently pull up and disgorge happy visions in white lace and bow ties for picture taking. One Saturday afternoon, in a total Annie Leibowitz moment, I saw five bridal parties posed by the banks of the lagoon at the same time. Of course, the other overwhelming reason to bide time here is Bernard Maybeck's magnificent, melancholy pavilion, which begs quiet contemplation. If it's not too cold, try to stick around for sunset, when the palace is lit in all its Panama-Pacific Exposition glory.

5. **Thirteenth Hole at Lincoln Park Golf Course:** The view from the parking lot of the Palace of the Legion of Honor museum is pretty good, but it's even better just below the railing, where a strategically placed bench lets you be part of the golf gallery at the thirteenth hole tee as well as privy to one of the most amazing panoramic vistas of downtown San Francisco anywhere. When you get hungry, mosey up the path to the museum cafe for a tarragon chicken salad or some homemade potato-leek soup.

6. **Dolores Park at the top of Church and Twentieth Streets:** For some reason (maybe because of its proximity to Mission High School or its reputation for being a drug dealing area), people forget about this great sunbathing/dog walking park with its even greater views of the downtown skyline. The drug situation has improved drastically in recent years (it's non-existent during the daytime), and you can't beat the benches at the southwest corner for a bird's-eye view of the rolling grassy expanse where the neighborhood's doggie elite meet for playtime, scantily clad Castro habitués laze in the sun, and the city spreads out below like the backdrop of a movie set.

7. **Montgomery and Filbert Streets (below Grace Marchant Gardens):** This bench, perched midway up the Filbert Street steps, requires a bit of hiking, so it's not for invalid grandparents. But if they're feeling fit, and you take it slow, you'll both be rewarded with a sweetheart of a bench, tucked into the overgrowth and looking out over the Embarcadero waterfront to Treasure Island. You can eliminate some of the hike by driving to the top of Montgomery Street, which transects the stairway at about the halfway point—right at the base of **dalla Torre,** a nice Italian restaurant. There's actually a great bench here, too, where you can sit among the roses and lilies and gaze out onto the '30s art deco and streamline moderne apartment houses perched on the hillside. Convenience of location and a bright, airy dining room make dalla Torre my preference for dining, over neighboring Julius' Castle. Both have knockout views, but Julius' Castle is a major magnet for visiting anniversary couples from Iowa.

8. **Aquatic Park:** The benches just past the steps of Aquatic Park, below the Maritime Museum, were made for grandpas. From here, you can sit and be inspired by the over-sixty crowd from the Dolphin Club swimming by you in the bay, or stroll over and take in a game of bocce ball with the elderly Italian gents, or hear how Gramps got his medal of valor as you gaze at the USS *Pampanito,* the WWII submarine docked at Pier 45 next door. The view from here isn't half bad, either.

9. **Tiburon waterfront:** If your grandparents are up to it, take the ferry here. Otherwise, the drive is also perfectly lovely. After you hit the village and stop for a pastry at the Swedish bakery, stroll a few yards past the ferry landing on the waterfront promenade to one of the benches that looks out over the harbor. Sit, relax, and enjoy the spectacle: Tiburon's well-heeled (in the latest Nikes) jogging by with their Jack Russell terriers; tanned, long-legged gals walking off brunch at Sam's; and in the distance, the familiar outlines of San Francisco's skyline etched against the horizon.

10. **Market Street F Line:** A bench seat inside one of these lovingly restored vintage street cars is a grandparent's E ticket—a bona fide piece of rolling

nostalgia in patent leather and picture windows. The colorful fleet that toddles up and down Market Street originally hailed from places like Hamburg, Blackpool, Philly, and Paris, with each still bearing the markings and unique design details of its native city. It's like a rolling history lesson in early twentieth-century transportation. Grandparents will no doubt enjoy riding the rails they remember from their youths, plus they'll get a tour of downtown—from Castro to the Ferry Building—all for the old-fashioned muni fare of $1.

# NOON

The Bay Area isn't exactly England, with its myriad garden clubs and flower shows, but we have a few places that will delight the retired green thumb. Filoli, down in the sylvan enclave of Woodside, is a perfect day outing. A pretty, forty-minute drive down Highway 280 to Cañada Road, the **Filoli** estate (a name cobbled together from the words *Fight*, *Love*, *Life*) was once the residence of water magnate and gold millionaire William Bourn II. The Georgian-style manor house, designed by Willis Polk in 1916, is definitely worth a visit, but the formal gardens—divided by hedges and patterned borders into a series of unique, separate "rooms"—are the real ticket. You can stroll leisurely for hours over the sixteen acres of roses, tulips, English cottage flowers, Irish yew trees, and immaculately sculpted shrubbery. Afterward, have a cuppa and a muffin or biscotti in the tea shop (on Fridays and Saturdays they also have box lunches with half-sandwiches, fruit salads, lemonade, etc.). And make sure to nose around the carriage house gift shop. Spring, of course, is the best season to visit, when the gardens are a riot of color, but if you happen to get a grandparents visit around the holidays, Filoli does a wonderful Christmas celebration the week after Thanksgiving (reservations for high teas, luncheons, and concerts are a must). Regular, docent-led tours ($10) are conducted February through October.

We used to visit with my grandmother nearly every weekend when I was growing up, and it became a tradition to go out and have lunch—me, my grandmother, my mom, my aunt, and my cousins— somewhere proper and ladylike. The **Allied Arts Guild** seems as if it were invented precisely for this sort of occasion. Tucked off a quiet residential street in Menlo Park, a stone's throw from El Camino Real and the Stanford Shopping Center, the guild is a time capsule of gentility and quiet, old-fashioned graciousness. A Spanish colonial villa, with sand-washed buildings daisy-chained together around a serene Mediterranean courtyard, fountain, and gardens, the complex houses a series of artists' studios and homespun crafts shops, as well as a wonderful little restaurant run (on a volunteer basis) by the sweet little

**dalla Torre**
1349 Montgomery Street,
296-1111

**Aquatic Park**
On Beach Street between
Larkin and Van Ness

**Filoli**
Cañada Road
Woodside, 650-364-2880

**Lawn Bowling**
In Golden Gate Park, near
the Stanyan Street entrance

**The Allied Arts Guild**
75 Arbor Road
Menlo Park, 650-325-3250

old ladies of the Woodside-Atherton Auxiliary for the Lucile Packard Children's Hospital. The restaurant serves one set meal every day for $10.95, which includes soup, salad, an entree, rolls, and dessert. The portions are just perfect—not too big, not too small—and all the menus are based on home recipes from auxiliary members, who also do all the cooking and serving (proceeds benefit the hospital). As you sit in the warm, terra-cotta-tiled dining room with its cozy fireplace, munching on turkey pot pie or chicken Monterey, rhubarb apple crumble or lemon crisp, the volunteers walk around in green smocks, pouring lemonade and tea, and offering motherly advice. The whole thing takes you back to the days of PTA bake sales. To complete the effect, you can purchase guild recipes for seventy-five cents; they're all neatly filed, grandmother-style, on three-by-five index cards on a rack by the entrance. Afterward, take a turn around the garden, browse for garden ornaments or glass animals in the quaint shops, and be sure to take note of the frescoes inside the studios on the east side, which were done by a student of Diego Rivera in the 1930s.

## Tea Time

No grandparents' visit would be complete without a good, old-fashioned heart-to-heart (the kind you never have with your parents, because, well, they'd think all that angst, lack of motivation, and inability to commit was because of something they failed to do as parents). And there's no better setting for it than at tea—real, late-afternoon English tea with all the trimmings. **Lovejoy's Antiques and Tea Room** in Noe Valley is a small, dainty parlor where you can drink Yorkshire gold tea out of real, china teacups, served to you by an authentic Englishman in a starched white shirt and bow tie. The whole place is exquisitely "pinkies out"—from the antique velvet settees and lace doilies that look like they're straight out of Grandma's front room, to the silver teapots. Grandmas go ga-ga over those soft, white, crustless sandwiches made with things like cucumber and cream cheese and bay shrimp and mayonnaise. If she's not watching her cholesterol, also order up a helping of crumpets or scones served with double Devon cream. Gramps will no doubt pooh-pooh the whole idea until he gets wind of the Ploughman's Platter, which involves thick, crusty bread, English cheeses, pickled onions, oak-smoked Finnan haddock, and a bunch of those other weird side dishes that you only hear about when grandparents are around. The best part about this place is that if you really get comfy in one of the overstuffed Victorian armchairs, you can take it home. Lovejoy's doubles as an antiques shop and most of the furniture is for sale.

A little less cozy (and a little more blue-blood) is the **Sheraton Palace Hotel**—which is nonetheless worth an excursion with or without the tea. It's served in the magnificent Garden Court, which is one of the most beautiful rooms in all of San Francisco. The historic stained-glass dome ceiling casts the nostalgic light of yesteryear over the gilded, marble-columned ballroom, calling to mind an era of white gloves and dance cards, and gentlemen with waxed moustaches. No place else serves as elegant a tea—perfect, dainty finger sandwiches, pristine little pots of tea, and the kind of deferential service that grandmothers long ago chalked up to fond childhood memory.

## A Little Lunch

Chances are, if your grandparents live nearby or have visited San Francisco over the years, they have fond memories of places that no longer exist, such as the City of Paris store, which stood on the site of what is now Neiman Marcus. The **Rotunda** restaurant on the mezzanine level of Neiman's manages to recapture some of that old magic—when "going Downtown" was an outing you looked forward to for weeks. The restaurant sits beneath the historic stained-glass dome that was the hallmark of City of Paris, and encircles the inner atrium of the store like a balcony at the opera house, with most tables looking out over bustling Union Square. This a favorite haunt of the Ladies Who Lunch: hats and gloves (and lots of Chanel jewelry) are still the protocol. The lobster club sandwich is the thing to order, but if that's too heavy, perhaps a nice chicken salad, or high tea service (after 2 p.m.).

Seafood places out in the avenues are not like the new wave of haute seafood restaurants—like Aqua, Farallon, or Plouf—where you might take your parents, yuppie friends, or a date. These are, you know, *Avenue* places—bastions of nontrendy neighborhoodiness, havens for the unhip—but boasting big menus of every variety of fish, cooked every way you can think of. With its pink tablecloths and napkins folded formally into fans, **Jonny Nipon's** on Irving is the pinnacle of Avenue seafood eateries. No barely seared tuna, no pan-Asian preparations—just fresh fish: broiled, poached, grilled, sautéed, or fried. There are also a handful of traditional favorites such as sole Florentine (stuffed with shrimp and creamed spinach); fish stew; and shrimp and crab Louie. An added bonus: Jonny Nipon's still does Caesar salad the old-fashioned way—tossed tableside for two (or more).

The Mission district seems the most unlikely spot for an old-time soda fountain, but the **St. Francis**—bless its heart—has been here since 1918, churning out homemade ice cream and Brach's-style candy, and dishing up the kind of classic 1940s diner food that makes grown grannies weep. Ideally, grandparents should come here with their blasé children and not-yet-cynical grandchildren. Sit at one of the straight-back wooden booths and order a double-decker liverwurst, cheese, and tomato sandwich, or cottage cheese topped with pineapple, or a frankfurter plate. Then, after you've dispensed with the nutritional formalities, let the old-timers do what they do best—spoil their grandchildren. The hard part will be deciding between the banana split special, a double-dip soda, a scoop of strawberry shortcake ice cream, or pie à la mode (even better—topped with cheese).

# NIGHT

A night on the town for many grandparents might be a brief affair. If they're tired, settle down to a cup of tea and *Charlie Rose,* and don't complain (it's not like you would have gotten in to Elroy's anyway). If they've still got some energy left, keep in mind that loud, crowded places aren't very conducive to those with hearing aids and bad hips.

Though you gave up on organized religion years ago, you should make an exception for Evensong at **Grace Cathedral** Thursday evenings (5:15 p.m.) For one thing, the men's and boys' chorus is truly exceptional and uplifting; for another, the concert is free. Your grandparents will get to enjoy the city's most impressive neo-Gothic structure, which was modeled on Notre Dame, and you won't have to tell them you don't actually go to church anymore. Recovering Catholics, agnostics, and those of various other faiths can be reassured by the fact that this is a "House of Prayer for All People." (If you miss Thursday, there's another Evensong service Sunday at 3:30 p.m.)

## Silence Is Golden

Take in an early picture show at the **Castro Theatre,** which frequently offers excellent grandparents material—reissued classics, Frank Capra fests, old MGM musicals—plus a preshow performance on the mighty Wurlitzer. If they're visiting in June, keep an eye open for the Silent Movie Festival—an annual ode to the time before talkies, when Gloria Swanson and Mary Pickford ruled the silver screen. Most of the films are shown to organ accompaniment, but occasionally there's a complete live orchestra that sits in the pit the way they did in the old days.

## Pröst

A nice drive is always a safe bet with grandparents, and while I recommend the town of Sonoma as a place to take parents, there is one spot up there where grandparents rule: **Little Switzerland.** Located about two miles west of town, this Swiss restaurant/bar/beer garden is a retirees paradise, but also an absolute gas for younger folk who have forgotten that old people know how to have fun, too. I came here one weekend with some friends and ended up eating sausage and sauerkraut, drinking Jäegermeister, and dancing the polka with some seventy-five-year-old guy who had better moves than John Travolta. I had to retreat to the beer garden out back for a breather, while he just kept on going. Most weekends, Little Switzerland transforms into a small

Oktoberfest, with live German polka and oompah-pah bands, and a family-style buffet meal (usually consisting of hearty dishes like pot roast and potato salad, bratwurst and sauerkraut, roast chicken, or spaghetti) served at long tables with red-checkered tablecloths. Elderly types from all around come and sit and eat and then enjoy a spin (or a slow two-step) around the room. Maybe you could even set your grandma up with some nice elderly gentleman.

## Eating Out

Grandparents grew up in a time when vegan wasn't even a word, so cut them some slack. Take them to an old-fashioned place with white tablecloths that still speaks surf and turf. Here's a quick run-down of suggestions.

**Alfred's**—Not too much has changed (except the location) in sixty-odd years at this traditional, clubby steakhouse, where pre-dining cocktails are a must. Go for a fat T-bone, New York, or porterhouse steak—dry-aged and mesquite-grilled—and of course the requisite baked Idaho potato on the side.

**La Felce**—One of the anchors of the North Beach family-style restaurants of yore, La Felce still serves the full-on six courses—antipasti; salad; soup (probably minestrone or pastina in broth); pasta; a hearty chicken, veal, or beef dish; and spumoni ice cream—and does it with some style and flavor. After dinner, take a slow stroll around Washington Square Park and admire Saints Peter and Paul Church—if not for its magnificent spires, then for the fact that Joe DiMaggio went to school here.

**Fior d'Italia**—A half a block away from La Felce, Fior d'Italia has the unique distinction of being the oldest documented Italian restaurant in the country (opened in 1886). Though its old-style touches—tuxedoed waiters, double-spoon service, private dining rooms—might be considered hokey by some, those people are not your grandparents. Think how many points you'll score by reserving the Tony Bennett Room—a tribute to the crooner who used to make this restaurant his home away from home.

**Joe's of Westlake**—Though it's not related to the venerable Original Joe's in the Tenderloin, Westlake Joe's has been around almost as long, serves many of the same dishes, and is in an area that your grandparents won't be frightened by. Plus, there's plenty of parking, and while the atmosphere is nice, it's not overly dressy. Huge hamburger-steaks are the ticket here, served on sourdough rolls; there's also a variety of steaks, chops, and surf and turf combos.

# Eating In

If she wants to cook, let her cook. Besides, when was the last time you sat down at your own kitchen table for a nice home-cooked meal that you didn't have to make yourself (and Safeway barbecued chicken doesn't count)? Or maybe Grandpa is tired of that fancy California cuisine, and just wants some familiar comfort food. Some suggestions on where to find supplies:

**Lucca Ravioli Co.**—Key items include wonderful homemade ravioli (if Nona's cooking, it'll give her more time to perfect the sauce) and cannoli, great coppa and prosciutto, and dozens of imported Italian goodies.

**Haig's**—A mecca for Middle-Eastern edible imports, including hard-to-find items like halvah, kefir, and Turkish coffee. Haig's also makes some of the best baba ghanoush I've ever had—just the right amount of garlic and fire-roasted aroma. There's also a good smattering of gourmet packaged items from India and Indonesia—including sambal oulek, a wonderful Indonesian red-pepper paste that beats Chinese chili sauce, hands down.

**Speckmann's**—Unfortunately, there hasn't been a good place to get fresh-baked German rye bread since Heidi's on Irving Street closed. But Speckmann's Deli, next to Speckmann's restaurant, does a brisk business in fresh Bavarian farmer's bread, along with herring in cream sauce, smoked pork chops, German potato salad, six kinds of sauerkraut and cabbage, and other specialty items.

**Cinderella Bakery, Deli, and Restaurant**—The bakery that's attached to this small Russian restaurant is like your babushka's own kitchen—Russian wheat bread fresh from the oven, piroshki fried or baked, stuffed cabbage rolls, and hamand taschen (cookie popovers filled with prune or poppyseed filling). Be forewarned, the smells are so tempting you may find yourself sitting down to a meal of borscht and syrniki (cottage-cheese fritters). You'll also be happy to learn that the mystery of the name "Cinderella" has finally been solved. One of the Russian regulars informed me that Cinderella is actually a character from Russian fairy tales as well, where she is known as the "Snow Maiden."

**Shenson's Jewish Deli and House of Bagels**—Pick up the onion sticks and New York corn rye at House of Bagels (Noah's has got nothing on these guys); then go down the street to Shenson's for your gefilte fish, chopped liver, smoked whitefish, and pastrami.

# WHERE TO STAY

Let me begin with the following disclaimer: no self-respecting grand-child shuffles his or her grandparents off to a hotel if he or she can at all help it. Grandparents get the bed; you get the sofa or the floor. That's the protocol. Of course your grandparents may very well prefer a hotel to a house full of screaming toddlers and a bathroom shared by four other people. In the event of the latter, I suggest putting them up at an old-fashioned hotel that still knows how to hold doors and coddle eggs.

A luxury hotel out of another era, **Campton Place** offers the kind of meticulous attention to detail and deft little touches that you thought went out with the Eisenhower era. The rooms are lovely, but more important, the staff here (there are 178 employees for 117 rooms) will make sure your grandparents are comfortable—that they can get what they want, exactly when they want it, exactly *the way* they want it. The house car or limo will be waiting for them when they get to the front door; the on-site laundry and drycleaner will have their suits cleaned and pressed (with loose buttons fixed) in as little as two hours; their special dietary needs will be accommodated without even blinking (the full five-star restaurant menu is available for room ser-vice); and the hotel is literally steps from Union Square, so they won't have to schlepp all over town to shop. For grandma, though, no doubt the biggest advantage is that they allow cats and small dogs in the rooms—and they'll even walk them for you. It's like having your own private San Francisco pied-à-terre.

Grandparents will revel in the history of the **Palace Hotel,** where the likes of Oscar Wilde, Rudyard Kipling, Enrico Caruso, Lillie Langtry, and just about every president from McKinley to FDR have stayed. The fabulous stained glass–domed Garden Court and Pied Piper Bar with its enormous Maxfield Parrish painting are reason enough never to leave the premises.

**Lucca Ravioli Co.**
1100 Valencia Street,
647-5581

**Haig's Delicacies**
642 Clement Street,
752-6283

**Speckmann's**
1550 Church Street,
282-6850

**Cinderella Bakery, Deli, and Restaurant**
436 Balboa Street,
751-9690

**Shenson's Jewish Delicatessen**
5120 Geary Boulevard,
751-4699

**Campton Place**
340 Stockton Street,
781-5555
Rates: $230–$345

**Sheraton Palace Hotel**
Market and New
Montgomery Streets,
392-8600
Rates: $215–$330

They bring you their tired, their weary, their toddlers yearning to be fed. And it's up to you to show them a good time. No pressure. It's only their first real vacation since they had the kids, and they've only been looking forward to it like felons look forward to parole. So now you have to come up with an itinerary that will be fun

# Tour 3 Weary Young Families

for grown-ups and also accommodate cranky babies, feeding schedules, nap time, and short attention spans.

Not having kids myself, I asked my mother-in-law, parent of seven, to impart a few insightful words of wisdom. "My advice," she said as the grandchildren shrieked in the background, "is to leave the little ones at home."

Next I turned to my colleague Carole Terwilliger Meyers, author of several guidebooks on family fun. She offered these basic rules:

1. After you plan an itinerary, cut it in half. Kids (and sleep-deprived parents) just don't have that much gas.

2. Confine your energetic outings to the morning and early afternoon. Save the late afternoon for more mellow stuff. Do not plan to visit museums in the

afternoon, unless there's some kind of sit-down activity for the kids.

3. If you're going to visit grown-up places (and you are, because let's face it—this vacation is for Mommy and Daddy), make sure they're places where screaming babies won't be a problem.

4. Make sure parents pack a goody bag filled with "distractions"—toys, crayons and coloring books, Cheerios, stuffed animals, hand puppets, etc. You never know what little children are going to find fascinating, or more importantly, boring.

5. Don't expect to expand the children's palates with weird, ethnic cuisines, unless you don't mind getting sushi spit all over the front of your shirt. It is the rare kid that appreciates "interesting" foods. They want familiar things—peanut butter and jelly, McNuggets, macaroni and cheese, pizza.

## MORNING–NOON

They'll be up at the crack of dawn, so grind the beans the night before and set the coffeepot timer on "stun." One cup won't be nearly enough, so after you've propped your eyelids open, pack up the pram and head down to Noe Valley, where you can join in the **Twenty-Fourth Street Stroller Derby** while you sip a double half-caf latte. These days, you can't say the words "Honey, don't touch that," without half the population of Noe Valley turning around to see if you're talking to their kid. The neighborhood is positively crawling with babies and new moms and dads, all socializing, sunning, and jockeying for stroller position on the benches in front of Posh Bagel, Spinelli, Starbucks, Martha & Brothers Coffee, Phoenix Books, and the playground at Alvarado School.

Berkeley's Fourth Street offers a similar, baby-friendly scenario, only with better kids' stores, including **Sweet Potatoes,** a great children's wholesale (mostly cotton) clothing outlet. Sign up on the list outside **Bette's Ocean View Diner,** then stroll the boulevard for a half hour or so while you wait for a table. Parents will enjoy the blintzes, omelets, scrambles, and bagel and smoked salmon plates; kids will probably stick to the pancakes or cereal. The '50s patent-leather booths and jukeboxes are fun for everyone.

## Trains, Cable Cars, and Great Big Ships

For little kids, something as simple as riding BART constitutes entertainment. An acquaintance of mine has spent entire weekends taking his grandson to no particular destination on buses and trains and streetcars. My nephew has dawdled away a day climbing on a single fire truck. So when you're thinking about your grown-up destination, factor in getting there in a kid-friendly way.

Start off with a streetcar or bus ride to **Union Square.** Take in the sights and the shops until the kids start to get fussy, then make a detour into the **Disney** or **Warner Brothers Studio stores,** where big-screen cartoons and trailers for the next Disney animated classic will keep them occupied while you shop for Daffy Duck polo shirts. Another great shop stop for kids is **Sanrio,** home of the popular Japanese character Hello Kitty and her friends Spotty Dotty and Kerokeroppi (little girls love to look at Hello Kitty's fairy tale castle).

And of course, no child or child-at-heart should miss a trip to **F.A.O. Schwarz**—if only just to browse. The West Coast outpost of this New York toy emporium has all the stuff you've seen in the movies: a toy soldier or ballerina who greets you at the door, a giant animated clock that winks at you, the larger-than-life-size keyboard that was in the movie *Big*, Barbie World, Steiff stuffed animals, and every kind of toy imaginable—from Nintendo to Thomas the Tank Engine.

Next, tour the lobby of the historic **Saint Francis Hotel** and settle in for lunch or tea at the beautiful **Compass Rose.** The restaurant is equipped with high chairs and booster seats, and kids (especially girls) usually love the idea of a tea party—complete with little sandwiches and pastries, and if you ask, warm milk or hot chocolate instead of tea. Don't leave the St. Francis without riding the famous **outdoor glass elevators** to the top of the hotel— an E ticket for the short set; a fabulous bird's-eye view of downtown, the Bay

Bridge, and Coit Tower for adults. (The other great glass elevator ride is at the **Hyatt Regency** in the Embarcadero Center. The architecture of the hotel is unique, in that the hallways and balconies look inward, with plants cascading down the sides of a seventeen-story lobby atrium. The high-speed elevators face the atrium and the ride up feels like what would happen if they turned a high-rise building inside out.)

You might want to make this part of day two's itinerary, but if your guests are not too tired, catch the **Powell-Mason cable car** heading to Fisherman's Wharf, and get off at Washington and Mason Streets, home of the **Cable Car Barn and Museum.** Kids could probably spend the whole afternoon standing on the observation platform watching the cable wind around the giant wheels. But if they lose interest, there are also a couple of restored, vintage cable cars to climb on while parents watch the movie about the history of the cable car and how it works.

From here climb back on the cable car and take it to the end of the line. Then make your way down to **Hyde Street Pier** where the kids can climb through a ship galley, raise a sail, or pretend they're Captain Hook as they spin the steering wheel on the square-rigger *Balclutha* or the *C.A. Thayer.* In the spring and fall the park hosts sea music concerts and chantey singing; in September, there's the annual **Festival of the Sea,** with boat rides and all kinds of hands-on maritime activities for children.

Before nap time (theirs, not yours), indulge in a little chocolate decadence at the **Ghirardelli Chocolate Manufactory and Soda Fountain.** While you wait for your Emperor Norton (a hot fudge banana split) or your Alcatraz Rock (rocky road ice cream in a shell of hard chocolate), go to the mini-production center at the back of the room and watch melted milk chocolate slosh around in big vats.

And if you're already down here, you can't bypass Pier 39. Best bets for the attention-span-challenged include the **carousel,** the **sea lions,** and **UnderWater World,** a people-mover that transports you "under" the ocean through two clear, acrylic tunnels, where you're surrounded by hundreds of fish. (As entertaining as it may be, consider that the price for this twenty-minute excursion is about $13 for adults, $6.50 for kids.)

Afterward, if you haven't had lunch yet, head to the **Bubba Gump Shrimp Company,** a loud, touristy restaurant inspired by the movie *Forrest Gump.* The place has great bay views and all kinds of cool stuff on the walls. In addition to kid fare such as pizza, corn dogs, and burgers, more advanced palates might dive into barbecued shrimp or the Bucket of Boat Trash—deep-fried shrimp, lobster, and other undersea goodies.

## Museums They Can Handle

So okay, this isn't exactly stimulation for adult minds. Once in a while you gotta give in.

**Bay Area Discovery Museum**—The museum's located in east Fort Baker, on a picturesque site on the waterfront at the base of the north end of the Golden Gate Bridge. If the kids are still in snuggle sacks or strollers, make this an all-morning outing by parking in the south end parking lot, walking across the bridge and down Alexander Avenue to the complex of historic army buildings that house the museum. Kids can crawl through an "underwater" tunnel that simulates marine life in the bay, build a house, pretend to develop photos in a lab, or walk through the Maze of Illusions—a hall of mirrors, holograms, and optical tricks. The Bay Area Discovery Museum is designed for kids ages one through ten.

**Fire Department Museum**—This is the place to take boys, like my aforementioned nephew, who are entranced by that dump-truck video (or anything to do with trucks, for that matter)—and who go ballistic at the sight of a fire engine. The collection of historic fire-fighting memorabilia includes an 1850 hose cart, an 1897 steam fire engine, and an old hook-and-ladder truck. Plus, the museum is attached to a firehouse with a real working fire pole. Mom and Dad might enjoy reading about the glory days of San Francisco's fire department, especially the volunteer units that operated from 1849 to 1866.

**Randall Museum**—Kids will love looking at and petting the museum's resident animals; grown-ups can take in the astounding views from the top of Corona Heights.

**Wells Fargo History Museum**—An authentic nineteenth-century Pony Express stagecoach (that you can climb into), real gold nuggets from the gold rush, and stuff belonging to the notorious stagecoach robber Black Bart are the main attractions at this small Financial District museum, located inside the bank.

## Shanghai Surprise

With all the funny little toys and colorful candies in open bins at the shops along Grant Avenue in Chinatown, you'll be lucky if you get from one end to the other without a temper tantrum. Fortunately, most things in the sidewalk stands go for pocket change. My favorite "must have" items from childhood include the rice-paper candies wrapped in paper that melts in your mouth, and the Chinese versions of those Russian babushka dolls, the ones that you open up to find another, smaller doll inside.

Most Sundays throughout the year, you can get an abbreviated version of the Chinese New Year parade at the weekly **Lion Dance** down Grant Avenue. Light firecrackers or pop those little gunpowder caps as the colorful, thirty-foot lion with the blinking eyelids bobs, weaves, and snakes its way down the street. Afterwards, take the gang to the **Far East Cafe,** where you can sit in mysterious, curtained, wooden compartments and pretend you're in a Charlie Chan movie. The restaurant, which dates back to 1920, offers all the classic, safe Chinese-American dishes that kids like: sweet and sour pork, sizzling rice and won ton soup, chow mein, and chop suey (a hash of beansprouts, noodles, pork, and sauce which was allegedly invented in San Francisco).

For dessert, definitely pay a visit to one of Chinatown's fortune cookie factories. At the tiny **Golden Gate Fortune Cookie Company** on Ross Alley you can watch little old ladies sitting at ancient-looking machines pick up flat cookie disks and fold them around a metal peg into their familiar shapes. Then buy a big bag of sesame, almond, or traditional fortune cookies to munch on.

The family-owned **Mee Mee Bakery** on Stockton Street is a bigger operation, producing dozens of different kinds of daily-fresh Chinese cookies, including ginger, walnut, sesame, and macaroons. Plus, the bakery offers the added allure of fortune cookies that contain your own, personal fortune. If you buy the prepackaged kind, just make sure they aren't the ones with the racy messages (save those until after the kids are asleep, when sex-starved parents can really appreciate them).

## Parking It

Kids and parks are a natural, if for no other reason than because they allow children room to run around while parents get to enjoy the greenery and the sights. But before we get to Golden Gate Park, let me sing the praises of the **Presidio.** It's big, it's green, it comes equipped with a children's playground; a great, cheap, uncrowded bowling alley; cannons and other cool things to climb on; and its very own Burger King—which boasts the most spectacular views of the Golden Gate Bridge this side of Coit Tower. Start out with a tour of the **Presidio Museum.** Kids love the old cannons in front, and the earth-quake cottages out back, which have been furnished just like they were back in 1906. The **bowling alley** next to the parade grounds was, up until fairly recently, a pretty well-kept Presidio secret—just like the hidden tennis courts, the gym and swimming pool (now part of the YMCA), and the wonderful old theater. Though prices have gone up, the bowling alley is still a bargain, plus it's clean and relatively uncrowded; there's plenty of free parking, and after you're done throwing two-handed gutter balls, you can walk down the road to the **Burger King** and drown your sorrows in french fries. Tucked away on a vista point overlooking Crissy Field, this is probably the only fast-food joint in the country where you can sit and eat a Whopper while simultaneously sightseeing.

At the southern end of the Presidio, nestled at the base of Pacific Heights, is the **Julius Kahn Playground.** While there are plenty of kiddie parks in town where you can fritter away a pleasant afternoon, not many of them offer an architectural survey of the city's most extravagant and glamorous mansions.

**CHINA BEACH**

If it's warm enough (you know, that one day during the year), and you want to visit the ocean, the beach to take little kids to is China Beach, located in the refined confines of Sea Cliff. The small, sheltered cove has (relatively) clean bathrooms, a small enough stretch of sand that kids can't run completely out of sight, picnic tables, a pier, and in summer months, a lifeguard. Very civilized. Afterward, walk up Seacliff Avenue past the mauve house flying the flag with the blue wolf on it—that's where Robin Williams lives.

If the kids don't eat fast food (?!), go out the Lombard Street gate, past the Palace of Fine Arts, to the Marina Green, where you can sit and enjoy a healthy picnic lunch. Afterwards, push the stroller down to the end of the walkway along the road that skirts the Golden Gate yacht harbor until you reach the **Wave Organ.** A unique musical instrument composed of some twenty granite pipes that sit at various depths in the breakwater, the organ creates harmonic sounds when the ocean hits the pipes. The best concert is at high tide.

**Golden Gate Park** is basically a three-mile playground. Important kid stops include:

**Children's Playground and Carousel**—Built in 1887, this was the first children's playground in the United States to be constructed in a public park. The swings and slides have been augmented over the years by a geodesic climbing structure/jungle gym and other modern playground fare, but the most popular attraction here is still the historic Herschell-Spillman Carousel. Built in 1914 and still boasting its original band organ, the restored carousel features hand-carved and hand-painted horses, as well as a pig, a gazelle, an ostrich, a tiger, and an old-fashioned sleigh (the carousel currently operates from June through September).

**Asian Art Museum**—No, not for the fine art, but for the Indian storytelling on Sundays at 1 p.m., where the kids can learn about ancient myths and the lore of the Indian gods and goddesses. While the storytellers spin their tales, browse through the art galleries, or shop in the de Young Museum bookstore and gift shop—a great place to pick up original SF souvenirs like sushi earrings and Chinese coin purses.

**Stow Lake**—This is another great late-afternoon activity. Pack a couple of peanut butter sandwiches and some juice boxes and rent a pedal boat (the row boats are too much work; the motor boats are not very PC). Let the kids work the rudder—that is, until you crash into Strawberry Island. Boats rent by the hour, and the lake's not that big, so take your time. And don't forget to bring breadcrumbs for the ducks. If you're feeling ambitious, hike up Strawberry Hill for the views of the city and the top of sparkling Huntington Falls.

**Buffalo Paddock**—It still seems weird to me to see real, live buffalo walking around in Golden Gate Park, but there they are at the western end of the park. You probably won't get close enough to pet one, but little ones might find those horned, shaggy heads a little intimidating anyway.

**Spreckels Lake**—Just west of the paddock is this popular model boat pond, where little boys have been known to go into hyperactive sensory overload while watching the remote-controlled sailboats and yachts cruise the lake.

# Get Outta Town

Though parents may have lofty ambitions to try it, wine tasting with small children is no fun—not for the kids or the other wine tasters. A nice compromise is the **Rouge et Noir Cheese Factory,** located nine miles southwest of Petaluma, off of the D Street extension. The Thompson family has been making seriously wonderful and wonderfully stinky French and Austrian cheeses (Camembert, Brie, Schloss, breakfast cheese) for five generations. The factory sits on five acres of lawn dotted with picnic tables, surrounding an idyllic duck pond. Get your cheese, your bread, your garlic-stuffed olives, and your nice bottle of wine, plunk yourself down at one of the tables or on the grass, and let the kids run around or feed the ducks while you kick back and live the life.

## Great Kids' Tours

**Basic Brown Bear**—All my friends with little children rave about this small Potrero Hill stuffed-animal factory and store, where kids can select a teddy bear from among dozens of styles, and then stuff it themselves. Tours of the factory are offered on Saturdays. And it's conveniently located across from the Anchor Steam Brewery, so that later, grown-ups can enjoy a refreshing malt beverage (tours of Anchor Steam must be prearranged; see the Parents tour).

**Jelly Belly Factory**—This factory in Fairfield is where the Goelitz Candy Company, the inventor of those gourmet bubble gum, pina colada, and (yuck) popcorn jellybeans, makes its sweet, chewy creations. Tours take you through the production rooms, and include—at the end—lots of free samples (note to gummi bear fanatics: they also make a full range of gummi candies).

**Hershey's Visitor Center**—If Yosemite National Park is on the sightseeing itinerary, the Hershey's Chocolate Factory in Oakdale is a mandatory pit stop. Tours, offered Monday through Friday, take you on the journey of the Hershey's Kiss, from gooey mixing vat to mold to wrapper. Afterwards, take your coupon to the visitors' center for a free chocolate bar.

**San Francisco Zoo**—All kids love the zoo; nothing new there. But if your friends are here in July, you should definitely take them on the Night Tour, when kids get to feed giraffes, watch the nocturnal animals prowl around, and see what animals do after dark. Plus, there's entertainment and a barbecue picnic dinner. During the rest of the year, the zoo's greatest hits include the Primate Discovery Center, the Lion House (where you can watch the big cats feast on raw meat), and the children's petting zoo.

## Make*A*Circus

In the summer, there's a ton of fun events for kids, but probably my favorite one is Make*A*Circus, a circus in which children get to learn tricks and be part of the show. The troupe clowns around in parks all over the Bay Area all summer long; their schedule usually includes a couple of stints at Yerba Buena Gardens.

## DINNER

## Good Children's Menus

Not every meal out has to be at Pizza Hut or McDonald's. There are several grown-up places where parents can enjoy actual cuisine and also find kid-friendly food. It's all about compromise, says Carole Terwilliger Meyers. Here are some of her suggestions (for more ideas, see the Nieces, Nephews, and Other Pesky Kids tour):

**The French Room**—The venerable Clift Hotel has always catered well to children, and their French Room restaurant is no exception; it features a great decorated menu with special children's items at prices parents are willing to pay, and elegant food for grown-ups. The waiters seem to be particularly attentive to small children, bringing out little extras such as hot chocolate with milk and offering coloring books and baseball cards upon arrival. While Mom and Dad dine on rack of lamb or seasonal wild game, kids can choose from such specialties as chicken noodle soup, peanut butter and jelly sandwiches, mac and cheese, chicken fingers, gooey cheese pizza, quesadillas, and sautéed filet mignon with veggies.

**Garden Terrace**—The restaurant in the Downtown Marriott is particularly welcoming to young families, with menus designed by kids who have also named some of the items. For breakfast there's scrambled eggs, "San Francisco Mint" silver dollar pancakes, waffles, cereal, and a half-price kids' buffet. Drinks are served with curlicue "Lombard Street" straws (free soda refills). For dinner, there are hamburgers with Frisco fries, cheesesteaks, hot dogs, and spaghetti with tomato sauce.

**Cafe Pescatore**—Despite its location near the wharf, this is a very good Italian restaurant, rivaling (and surpassing) many North Beach eateries. The pasta dishes are exceptional, and the seafood is very fresh and not oversauced. For kids, there are simple dishes like spaghetti with butter, spaghetti bolognese (unadorned meat sauce), penne pasta with fresh veggies in light cream sauce, and wood-fired cheese and cheese and sausage pizzas. And they have ice-cream sundaes for dessert.

**Garden Court**—The sumptuous, stained-glass-covered dining room at the Palace Hotel is a very grown-up place, and accordingly kids seem to put on their best white-glove behavior when they're there (except when they don't). During the holidays, the palace hosts a traditional tea for parents, grandparents, and wee ones.

**Hornblower Dining Yachts**—I have visions of seasick three-year-olds, but Carole swears that Hornblower cruises are great for kids. At the very least, parents will enjoy a morning or afternoon of sightseeing around the bay and a nice meal. There aren't any high chairs, but you can (and should) bring strollers (with locking wheels), and maybe crayons and coloring books. If sailing the high seas turns out not to be their thing, at least the kids cruised for half price.

**Mel's**—I've eaten here with friends who had two fidgety little ones crawling all over the place, and the waiter never even blinked an eye. The menu of mostly comfort food—meatloaf, turkey and mashed potatoes, triple-decker BLTs—seems to bridge the generation gap. Kids get theirs served inside a cardboard car, and they'll honor requests like a scrambled egg with "no things in it."

**El Mansour**—Moroccan food may be iffy for little ones, but there's always rice and bread. And they'll love sitting on cushions on the floor and eating with their fingers while the belly dancer clangs her finger cymbals and shimmies around the room.

## WHERE TO STAY

The grande dame **Clift Hotel** still commands the respect of its newer, luxury upstarts. High ceilings, marble bathrooms, gilded walls, and the art deco Redwood Room are just a few of the glamorous touches grown-ups will like. For kids, there are free toys, miniature plush bathrobes just like the ones Mom and Dad get, games delivered to your room, and milk and cookies before bed.

The **Mansions Hotel,** an eccentric and beautiful Queen Anne Victorian, was built in 1887 by Senator Richard Chambers and is said to be haunted by the ghost of his niece, Claudia. Way cool. Each of the twenty-one rooms and suites are decorated with Victorian memorabilia and antiques, and named after a famous San Franciscan. But the biggest draw for kids is the magic show ($10), performed nightly. Later, dinner is offered in the formal dining room, where kids eat for half price.

You know her, you love her. She's in all the Woody Allen movies. She's your slightly eccentric, wild-haired, flowy-skirt-wearing aunt—the one who always gave you those "interesting" Christmas presents. You loved her the best of all the relatives because she was fun, and kinda kooky, and knew stuff about rock music, and let you have puffs

# Tour 4 Avant-Garde Aunts

of her cigarette when your mom wasn't looking. Her apartment (she'd never do anything so bourgeois as own a house) was always a marvelous clutter of lamps draped in fringed Chinese shawls, incense, dried roses, and old record players spinning Piaf or Jacques Brel or *Madama Butterfly*.

In my case, my avant-garde aunt was actually an uncle from England. A playboy of the Western world, he seemed to live a terribly glamorous life that was always just the gray side of shady. And when he came to visit, we went to new places and tried unusual things that we never would have on our own. Though at first we were always a little skeptical, we invariably ended up enjoying ourselves immensely.

## MORNING

No enlightened aunt worth her weight in empowerment will want to miss a trip to "Feminist Avenue," aka Valencia Street. Though the anchors of the area, Old Wives' Tales bookstore and the late, great lesbian bar Amelia's, are both gone now, there's still a strong female vibe in the neighborhood. Begin with a cup of coffee and a muffin at **Red Dora's Bearded Lady Dyke Cafe,** which is actually a few blocks away from the Valencia hub, on Fourteenth Street. Though it's a lesbian gathering place, straights won't feel out of place. The atmosphere is homey, warm, vegetarian, and accepting—and the sandwiches and housemade soups are tasty. Proceed from here to the **Women's Building** on Eighteenth Street and find out where to catch an all-women's comedy night, or a lecture by Susan Faludi. Then head off to **Osento,** the women-only spa located in an old Victorian on Valencia Street, for a soak in the communal hot tub, a sauna, a dip in the outdoor cold plunge, and a massage. This low-key spot has been a gathering and relaxing place for women for almost twenty years, and though most of the clientele is lesbian, it is by no means exclusive.

No visit to Valencia Street would be complete without a stop at **Good Vibrations,** the sex emporium. Unlike porn shops or most mail-order catalogs, Good Vibrations is a place that constantly reinforces the notion that sex shouldn't be a dirty little secret. There are no dark rooms, no sectioned-off bookshelves, no items wrapped up in brown butcher paper. Sex toys of every shape, color, variety, and flavor line the walls, and the no-nonsense staff is only too happy to explain their uses. The selection of erotic and self-help literature is extensive, and there's a full calendar of events ranging from the silly to the sensual to the serious. At first you might find yourself looking around to see if anyone's watching you surreptitiously thumb through *The Joy of Sex*— they're not. And before you know it, you'll be shamelessly perusing the display of antique vibrators. (This is the most erotic fun you can have in town without a cover charge.)

After you've worked up an appetite, head west to outer Noe Valley for a bite at **Valentine's Cafe,** where you may be all the way through a hearty omelet brunch before you realize that this place is vegan. A gay couple (who named the restaurant after their scotty dog, Valentine) turned this sleepy corner on Church Street into a hot spot several years ago with creative vegetarian cuisine that will entice even the most dedicated carnivore.

# NOON

New age mysticism is hardly fringe anymore, but chances are you don't have your charts or chakra read on a regular basis, because somehow it still seems a little bit out there. Your wacky auntie is the perfect excuse to pass the buck and indulge in a little inner-self-analysis and psychic exploration. Spend an afternoon down in Hayes Valley, where the razing of the Central Freeway seems to have sparked a small spiritual and artistic renaissance.

Begin at the **Psychic Eye Book Shop,** a fascinating emporium of meta-physical merchandise—a sort of mainstream mart for all your new age needs. Wander through the aisles of tarot cards, Egyptian cat icons, new age musical instruments, incense, herbs and roots, candles, talismans, Chinese health balls, crystals and stones, self-discovery books, and meditation tapes. Then have your palm, your chakras, or your astrology chart read by any number of on-site astrologers and psychics; most services cost about $10.

Over on Hayes Street at **Mad Magda's Russian Tea Room,** you can have your tarot cards or tea leaves read by a modern-day gypsy woman while you sup on a bowl of borscht, or sip a cup of divine Masala chai (a blend of black teas infused with coriander, cardamon, ginger, honey, and warm milk). The funky, folky atmosphere is like some sort of synthesis between Rasputin's den and a bike-messenger hangout. If it's sunny, head to the outer sanctum in the backyard, making sure to pay your respects to the shrine/art exhibit in the windowbox as you pass.

The sisters who do it (creatively) for themselves are ensconced across the street at the **SF Women Artists Gallery,** a wonderful space run by women, exclusively showing women's art. The organization was actually founded back in 1925 to help women artists find a forum for their work and to give exposure to emerging artists. The shows are wonderfully eclectic, ranging from painting to sculpture and photography, and the space is a soothing, light-filled nook with a sweet little cobbled courtyard out back.

Next, zigzag down the block to **Star Classics,** where you can peruse the bins for an obscure recording of Garland singing "The Man that Got Away," or of Piaf at Carnegie Hall. The store specializes in show tunes, great song-sters of yesteryear, and classical music.

## Pottery and Crafts

Every avant-garde aunt has a wild, artistic streak. And even though she may have evolved through her raku pottery and beaded lampshade phase, she's always on the lookout for unique handmade crafts or that sensuous figurative work. Take her directly to **La Tienda,** the retail shop in the Mexican Museum at Fort Mason, where you'll find crafts from all over Latin America, including painted masks, Day of the Dead figurines, tree of life dioramas, tin ornaments, wall hangings, and embroidered textiles. There's a similar selection a few build-ings over at the **San Francisco Craft and Folk Art Museum,** but supplemented with African carvings, Turkish rugs, handwoven clothing, and furniture. In the Mission, **Galeria de la Raza** is a local institution. On one side is an art gallery featuring revolving exhibits by Chicanos and Chicano-Americans; on the other is a small shop with a colorful array of folk art, painted furniture, figurines, paintings, shrines, and books on Latin American culture.

If she's here in December, definitely find time to attend the **Celebration of Craftswomen,** an annual sale and celebration of fine crafts by women from all over the country. Items range from hand-made quilts to jewelry and ceramics. In October, the main event is **Open Studios,** when artists all over town open up their private domains and sell directly to the public. On each of four weekends, different neighborhoods are showcased, including the underdiscovered artist enclave of Hunter's Point Naval Shipyard. To get an idea of who does what, go to the Open Studios exhibit at **Somar Gallery,** where each artist has a representative piece on display. Then pick up a map of the studios and go nuts.

If your aunt wants to get into the act, take her to the **Sharon Art Studio**—that curious, stone, castle-like building atop the knoll next to the carousel in Golden Gate Park. This lovely little aerie offers drop-in drawing, brush painting, and stained-glass making classes for all skill levels. Take your sketchpad and spend an afternoon capturing the bucolic splendor of Sharon Meadow on canvas, while the '90s flower children dance around the drumming circle, and little kids roll like barrels down Hippie Hill.

**Terra Mia** in Cow Hollow is really more a place for *Friends* groupies than for your hip aunt, but the one in Noe Valley may be just her speed. If you haven't heard of it, this is the place where you paint your own pottery, and it's a great way for erstwhile artisans to while away an afternoon or evening. The studio provides the bisque-ware (everything from toothbrush holders and pasta bowls to candlesticks and cafe au lait cups), as well as the glazes, brushes, stencils, etc. You simply paint. When you're done, you hand it over, and they'll fire it within a couple of days. (A word to the wise: Terra Mia charges about $7 an hour, so come in with a design idea; otherwise, between your pottery purchase and studio time, you could end up spending upwards of $50.)

## Dressing the Part

Every flowy-frock-wearing aunt needs to restock her wardrobe once in a while, and Indonesia or Guatemala is an awfully long way to go for a batik or something in natural cotton. For simple-yet-elegant tunics, drapey raw-cotton dresses, and ensembles you might wear to a wedding on Mount Tam, head to **Alaya** on Ninth Avenue. The small boutique usually has just the right look for someone not interested in anything form-fitting, midriff-baring, or lycra-infused.

**Joshua Simon** on Twenty-Fourth Street offers a slightly more youthful look, with an ethnic bent. This is a great place for exotic scarves and shawls; batik and ethnic-print tops; crinkly, gathered-waist skirts; funky dangley earrings; and 100 percent cotton leggings and tees. Sort of modern-day earth mother wear.

A pioneer of washable rayon and velvet, **CP Shades** makes gathered-waist pants and long baggy vests look positively glamorous. Your aunt will love the brocade-trimmed velvet jackets and pant sets—funky, loose, and as comfortable as a pair of pajamas.

## AND FOR JUNIOR . . .

I don't know why, but when I think of eccentric aunts, I always think of small, handbag-size dogs with names like Percy, whom Auntie treats like the child she never had. Wherever she goes, she must seek out gifts for him. Take her to **Cool Doggy-o's,** a kind of beatnik bowwow store where she can get home-baked doggie cookies, tie-dye doggie T-shirts, and hand-painted Indonesian dog food bowls. It's billed as a store to get "pet parafurnalia," but the merchandise is really more reflective of pet owners' personalities.

If Percy is a poodle (God forbid), **Ken Grooms** in Presidio Heights may be more her style. This is Neiman Marcus for haute hounds—a shop where you can pick up a pooch-size Burberry raincoat, sirloin tip doggie treats, and diamond-studded collars.

## Grace Cathedral

Some aunties might find a visit to a sanctum of organized religion terribly "establishment," but Grace Cathedral is such an unconventional hybrid of traditional belief systems and new age spiritual searching that you'll be instantly forgiven. At the east entrance, just past the magnificent Ghiberti bronze-relief doors (which are cast from the same mold as those that hang in the Florence cathedral), is the **Labyrinth**—a mystical maze of meditation. Carved in a geometric swirling pattern in the floor of the cathedral, the labyrinth is a replica of the one at Chartres Cathedral, which was laid in stone in 1200. Those who participate in this ancient rite are supposed to find inner peace and "become attuned to the potential of the spiritual self." Labyrinth walkers are asked to remove their shoes, clear their minds and hearts, and follow the path at the pace their "bodies want to go." On the way in, the idea is to free your mind of thoughts and emotions; at the center, stop, meditate, "and receive what there is to receive"; on the way out, become empowered with "the energy, vision, and courage to meet the demands of the twenty-first century." (For those who want to try this in a less formal, less conspicuous setting, there's a labyrinth outside, too, just to the north of the front doors.)

## Daytripping

The town of Freestone, located, appropriately, on the Bohemian Highway between Sebastopol and Bodega Bay, is really not much more than a picturesque bend in the road punctuated by a couple of beautiful, historic Victorian houses, a serene nursery, and—oddly enough—**Osmosis,** America's only enzyme baths. Why the founders picked Freestone is a mystery, but for the last eleven years, avid spa-goers and curiosity seekers have been flocking here to enjoy the benefits of a soak in a giant vat of heated cedar fiber, rice bran, and more than 600 enzymes. The Japanese apparently originated this treatment, which is supposed to break down toxins, relieve stress, and soften the skin. If you and Auntie have already gotten up the nerve to try this, go ahead and do the works. Begin with a cup of enzyme tea, to be drunk while sitting on a futon on a small veranda overlooking a tranquil Japanese garden. Next immerse in the enzyme bath, followed by a shower, and either a half-hour blanket wrap accompanied by "Metamusic" (designed to balance the left- and right-brain hemispheres) or a seventy-five-minute massage (throw in a couple of extra bucks, and you can have it in an outdoor pagoda). Afterwards, amble across the street to the **Wishing Well Nursery,** which seems to be part garden, part quail habitat, and part art gallery. As you wander through rows of fuschias, begonias, and roses, fuzzy little chicks scurry underfoot. In the back of the garden is a giant urn and a choir of Greek maidens—salvaged relics of the 1915 Panama-Pacific Exposition (crafted by Bernard Maybeck, who built the Palace of Fine Arts), which were discovered by the owners in a field in Petaluma. Inside the house is a small shop-cum-art gallery filled with vintage and vintage-looking curios—dried roses, cameos, flower pots, trinkets, sachets, and so on.

On the way back to town, take **Highway 116** through Sebastopol, otherwise known as Antiques Avenue. A dozen or so collective antiques markets and shops line the road, some with genuine antiques, others with interesting collectibles that are not terribly old. Stop and pick up an iron door knocker, a Russian avant-garde poster, a turn-of-the-century lunchbox, or an old church pew.

# NIGHT

If she wasn't an *artiste*, she was definitely a *danseur*—an ephemeral wood nymph in the mold of Isadora Duncan. Take her to a performance at **Project Artaud,** an art and performance space that hosts everything from the wonderful, innovative Lawrence Pech Dance Company and Kronos Quartet (who do regular seasons there) to quirky, occasionally strange theater productions. The live/work complex is divided into Theater Artaud, which features primarily dance; a Traveling Jewish Theater (self-explanatory); Theater Yugen/Noh Space, where you can see such productions as *A Christmas Carol* done as a traditional Japanese Noh drama; and Southern Exposure, an alternative art gallery. Plenty to groove on, and when you're done, head over to the **Slow Club** for a drink, a smoke, great fire-roasted vegetables and Caesar salads, and the companionship of the city's young Avant Guard.

In the York Theater, just across Potrero Avenue, you can take in a little thought-provoking drama while supporting the women's movement at **Brava! For Women in the Arts.** The multicultural theater group stages works by women playwrights.

## Far Out, Man

The **Audium** is one of those quirky '70s things that refused to go the way of Roots shoes and peacock feathers and is definitely the kind of happening that avant-garde aunts will delight in. The "concerts" have actually been going on since the '60s, when composer Stan Shaff and equipment designer Doug McEachern, both musicians interested in "new musical vocabularies," began performing at SF State and other venues. The permanent theater on Bush Street was built in 1975 and designed specifically for "spatial composition" and sound movement. Shaff mans the foyer, takes the tickets, then leads you into a theater where chairs are positioned in concentric circles, surrounded on all sides by hundreds of speakers. The lights lower until you're immersed in pitch blackness, and then, from a console on one side, Shaff begins to weave taped sounds in an intricate aural sculpture. Ambient sounds both familiar and strange—snatches of music, conversations, marching bands, parade noise, drums, rushing water—wash over, under, and around you at various tempos and levels of intensity. Somewhere midway into it you find yourself losing sense of time and place. When you return to the here and now, you might have an overwhelming urge to call your parents, eat Hostess HoHo's, or pull out the Beatles' *White Album*. Trust your instincts.

If your chakras aren't quite rung out, head directly to **Karma Moffett's Tibetan Bell Experience,** where you can dispel bad karma and bring on wish fulfillment in a kind of wild musical Zen experience. Richard Bruce "Karma" Moffett—artist, musician, harp maker, gallery proprietor, Zen guy—has amassed, over the course of about twenty years, a wonderful collection of old Tibetan instruments, all of which he uses during his weekly candlelight ceremonies. His Castro district studio looks like a garage sale at the Dalai Lama's house—dragons and Tibetan symbols dangle from the ceiling, paintings of tranquil waters hang on the walls, the floor is awash in kilims and cushions. Karma sits at the center of it all, surrounded by handmade bells and harps, *Wizard of Oz* dioramas, conga drums, prayer beads, long horns, conch shells, Tibetan singing bowls, candles, and cymbals. At 8 p.m. most Friday, Saturday, and Sunday nights, Karma performs a musical wish-bestowing ceremony—a convergence of bell harmonics and synthesizers that takes you on a symbolic journey to Tibet, granting your most fervent desires along the way. Chant your favorite mantra and be one with Karma.

Finish off your weekend at **Kabuki Hot Springs,** a traditional Japanese spa. Begin in the communal hot pool (there are separate days for men and women), and spend a half hour or so jumping from here into the cold pool and back. Next a steam, followed by a cool shower, followed by a stint in the dry sauna, and another plunge in the cold pool. For the finale, a shiatsu massage, performed in a room full of massage tables—making it all the more community-oriented and exotic. You will be a wet noodle by the time you're done, so it's only fitting perhaps that you go around the corner to **Mifune,** Japantown's great (cheap) little noodle house, for a bowl of ramen or udon.

## WHERE TO STAY

Artistic types of all kinds will feel at home at the **The Art Center Bed and Breakfast,** a low-key (there's no sign out front) inn carved out of an 1857 French provincial–style apartment building in the heart of Cow Hollow. The owner, Helvi Wamsley, is an artist who will offer pointers for amateur painters and is always eager to engage in salon discussions on art and culture—though she's nearly eighty years old by now. Wamsley's art pervades the inn, which features five units—two small studios with fireplaces, two large suites with private street entrances, and a three-room apartment. In back is a sunny skylit garden room—the perfect place to paint that still life. Full breakfast is served.

The **Victorian Inn on the Park** on the Park itself is not particularly avant-garde, but it's located along the Panhandle, in a quiet, mostly residential neighborhood that's destined for hipness any minute. Storyville, the righteous jazz club, is just around the corner, as are the Western Addition and Haight-Ashbury, and the blocks around the inn are already starting to bud with groovy new cafes and restaurants. This B&B is housed in an absolutely gorgeous (and enormous) historic 1897 Victorian that was once the residence of the Clunie family. It was restored about fifteen years ago to its turn-of-the-century splendor, though modern amenities (including private bathrooms) were added for guests' convenience. There's a continental breakfast in the morning, and sherry or wine is served evenings, in front of the fire in the front parlor.

Being a kid in San Francisco can be both a liberating
and a confining experience. Back when I was growing
up, while my suburban friends rode their bikes around
the orchards, I was riding the bus down to the Castro
Theatre to watch Gene Kelly musicals and having herb
tea with my friends at the Owl and the Monkey.

# Tour 5 Nieces, Nephews, and Other Pesky Kids

Definitely cool. But on the flip side, I never saw a drive-
in movie until I was in college.

Certainly there's plenty for the average adolescent or
pre-adolescent to do in San Francisco, but sometimes
doing it with parents (or worse, parents' friends) can be
downright excruciating. Compromise is the key. Find
places that are fun for both adults and kids, or places
where adults can do one thing and kids can do another.

## MORNING–NOON

For most kids (and even for most adults), taking a ferry *anywhere* constitutes
an outing. But taking one to the most notorious prison in American history
is payday. If your friends have a mind to take a tour while they're here—
especially if the kids are along—**Alcatraz Island** is the one to take. It's got
history, it's got Hollywood sex appeal, it's got a boat ride, and it's got views
to end all views. Start out at Fisherman's Wharf with a walkaway crab or
shrimp cocktail (that is, unless you have a tendency to get seasick), then
walk over to Pier 41 and catch a Blue and Gold ferry to The Rock. Once

there, you can take a ranger-led and/or a self-guided tour of the old cell house (definitely do the audio tour—it's narrated by former Alcatraz guards and inmates, who talk about life behind bars in a way no outsider ever could). Along the way you'll get to see where such notorious criminals as Al Capone and the Birdman of Alcatraz did time, and even sit inside a solitary confinement cell. (A note to the uninitiated: these tours are very popular; call ahead for reservations, especially in the summer months. And wear warm clothes.)

For older kids, the other common ferry destinations—Larkspur, Sausalito, Tiburon—don't really hold that much appeal beyond the actual boat ride. But lots of people overlook the black sheep of the ferry family, the **Alameda/Oakland Ferry,** which leaves from the Ferry Building and Pier 39 approximately every two hours and zips you across the bay on an air foil to **Jack London Square**—a warmer, funkier version of Fisherman's Wharf. Kids will have fun following the wolf tracks through the square to learn about the Oakland waterfront's most famous resident, Jack London. The historical markers lead to the Jack London statue and museum, and eventually end up at the **Potomac,** President Franklin D. Roosevelt's yacht, once known as the "floating White House." The yacht offers tours and cruises. In the surrounding complex, there's a small Museum of Children's Art; an enormous Barnes and Noble bookstore (one of the largest bookstores in Northern California); great family restaurants, including the Old Spaghetti Factory, Pizzeria Uno, and Scott's Seafood (which sits directly on the water looking out over the bay); and in the summer, concerts performed dockside. The first Saturday of every month there's an antiques and collectibles show along Water Street; and every Sunday there's an open-air farmer's market from 10 a.m. to 2 p.m. (For adults, the best thing in Jack London Square—and maybe in all of Oakland—is Yoshi's jazz club, which attracts the biggest names in the business. See the Impressionable Dates tour).

# Graves, Ghosts, and Ghouls

So maybe it's a little morbid to take kids to a cemetery for entertainment, but probably no more so than going to a ghost town or watching *Night of the Living Dead*. Besides, how often do you get a chance to see **Wyatt Earp's grave?** The legendary gunslinger and sheriff who made Tombstone, Arizona, and the OK Corral the stuff of Hollywood movies is laid to rest at the **Hills of Eternity**—a Jewish cemetery on El Camino Real. Earp died in 1929 and was buried in the family plot of his wife, the one-time actress Josephine Marcus (she was Jewish), from whom he was rarely, if ever, separated. Also buried at Hills of Eternity is blue jeans inventor Levi Strauss.

While you're in the neighborhood, you should also take a little lesson in San Francisco history over at **Cypress Lawn,** where half the city's hoi polloi are buried, including publisher William Randolph Hearst, firebrand and tower namesake Lillie Hitchcock Coit, cable car inventor Andrew Hallidie, and arts patron Charles de Young. The cemetery, built in 1892, offers tours of the mausoleums—some of which (like the Flood Family's) are enormous architectural monuments. Also of note are the stained-glass windows in the chapel, which were designed by Louis Comfort Tiffany.

Last stop on the Colma graveyard tour should be **Olivet Memorial Park,** where Ishi is interred. Perhaps it was only required reading on the West Coast, but *Ishi: Last of His Tribe* was one of the most memorable books of my childhood—the true story of the last Yahi Indian, who came out of the forest and spent his final years in Berkeley. His ashes are in the columbarium at Olivet.

## BAY MODEL

I take back part of what I said about Sausalito. The Bay Model (located there) is a fascinating feat of engineering that's definitely captivating for older kids. Built by the Army Corps of Engineers, the two-acre hydraulic scale-model of the San Francisco Bay and Sacramento Delta shows the flow of the tides and currents of the Bay at 100 times their speed (an entire cycle takes fourteen minutes). There's also a small museum, and a good self-guided audio tour that explains about the bay environment. The tide test schedule is erratic, so call ahead.

## Good Sports

I may get into trouble from a few parents and Muni bus drivers (not to mention my mother) for bringing this up, but the thing is, they're teenagers and they're gonna do it anyway, so . . . I'm talking, of course, about the **6 Parnassus ski lift** (what did you think I was talking about?). Skateboarding is a dangerous sport in the best of circumstances, and the streets of San Francisco are certainly no place for novices to get their feet wet, but those hills also make for some exciting terrain. And nowhere can you get a better run for your money than down the Ninth and Tenth Avenue slopes in Golden Gate Heights. I grew up on Tenth Avenue, so I know. My mother spent many a weekend constructing elaborate barricades in an attempt to prevent these same teenagers from cutting bank turns into her driveway.

Here's how it works. Pick up the 6 Parnassus bus at Ninth Avenue and Judah, pay a buck, get a transfer, and ride to the top of Tenth Avenue and Cragmont. From there it's a long, glorious, steep (but not too steep) skate back down to the bottom of the hill, where for the next hour and a half, the ride up is free. No doubt there are safer places to skateboard (such as the park) but the added thrill of the hill makes this one of the greats.

Other popular local skateboarding zones (courtesy of *Slap* magazine):

**The Dish**—Sadly enough, the cement bowl in a somewhat dubious part of Hunter's Point is the only place in the city specifically designed for skateboarders.

**Fort Miley**—A monument and abandoned artillery base near the VA hospital with pyramid-shaped bumps.

**Embarcadero/Pier 7**—When the cops started cracking down on skateboarders in Justin Herman Plaza, the thrasher crowd moved farther north. These days you'll find them jumping ledges, gaps, and steps and creating obstacle courses out of art objects along the waterfront near the Ferry Building and Pier 7.

**Kezar Pavilion**—Steps and handrails on the Lincoln Avenue side.

**Playground at Wallenberg High School**—Two levels with ramps, slopes, rails, and ledges.

**DMV Parking Lot**—Curbs, flat handrail (very popular).

**Hubba Hideout**—At the top of the grassy area at Maritime Plaza there are several sets of stairs and handrails—oh, and also a twenty-foot drop.

**China Banks**—Brick banks, benches, and a bridge over Kearny Street.

**Union Square (at night)**—Ledges, metal benches, steps.

**Moscone School**—Stairs, sidewalk gaps, low ledges, and wooden benches.

## Baseball

Okay, okay, so you've already thought about taking in a Giants or an A's game (until the new stadium's built, I'd say go to an A's game—better seating, lots more sunshine—the food's not as "gourmet," but honestly, do you really go to the ballpark for cuisine?). But what if it's the off-season, or the team's on the road? Then what? Head to **Big Rec field,** the baseball diamond in Golden Gate Park at Seventh and Lincoln, where you can catch a semipro game nearly every weekend. First though, go to Ninth Avenue and pick up some supplies—a hoagie or a hot dog from the **Submarine Center No. 2,** or maybe a burrito from **Gordo Taqueria.** Then settle in on the bleachers for a few innings of serious hardball. If the game isn't as intriguing to grownups as to aspiring shortstops, adults can wander off to the solitude of the Shakespeare Garden or sign up for a few sets of tennis at one of the twenty or so courts located right behind the field.

# In-Line Skating

In places like San Francisco, where "icing" generally refers to cake topping and not hockey penalties, in-line roller hockey has become the hottest thing since sliced sourdough. **Bladium** in China Basin, just over the Third Street bridge, is part of a new wave of in-line arenas dedicated to the sport, which—unlike ice hockey—is played equally by competitors of both genders (sometimes on the same team). This is not like those roller derby arenas of the '70s (although someone should think about bringing those back); this is a serious sport—with sponsors and fans. And it's almost as exciting to watch as it is to play. Bladium offers league play at all levels, with special times designated for high schoolers and younger kids. Plus, several afternoons are reserved for "open skate," which is your chance to cut the kids loose while you suck down a beer at the Penalty Box sports bar. For visiting bladers, there are skates for rent at the pro shop.

# Shopping

Teenage girls love to shop. There's no denying it. So suck it up, put on your best face, and pretend you're impressed by four-inch platform tennis shoes (*hello*—we had platform tennies with live goldfish in them, remember?).

**Esprit outlet store**—Get there early, or expect to wait in long lines at the register. The China Basin warehouse has been selling flirty slip dresses, midriff tops, and whatever the kids are wearing these days for going on twenty years. The outlet carries overruns, past season and irregular clothing, mostly for girls and juniors. Prices are less than retail, but not astoundingly cheap, unless you hit a special sale day or dig through the $10 bins.

**Urban Outfitters**—Trendy slacker clothing, home furnishings, and pop culture merchandise for the generation that falls somewhere between X and Y.

**Buffalo Exchange**—One of the best (and cheapest) of the used-clothing emporiums, mainly because of the constant influx of new merchandise. The selection usually includes old Levi's, '50s housedresses, bowling shirts, tight polyester blouses, leather jackets, and a good smattering of last year's Gap-wear.

**Downtown Limited and Express**—The downtown store just off Union Square is probably the company's largest—three enormous floors of young, fad fashions—practically all made of microfibers and rayon (with the occasional cotton and silk items). Express Campagnie Internationale, with its thumping Euro-radio soundtrack, offers a slightly younger, lower-priced, and more sporty look. The Limited carries everything from nice dresses and skirts to khakis and shorts.

**Virgin Megastore**—The prices at Tower are cheaper, but they don't have the multimedia entertainment value of Virgin: video walls, listening stations, lots of in-store appearances by hot, new artists, a huge selection of CD-ROMs, a cafe, a bookstore—oh, and they also have about a million compact discs.

After your shopping spree, take the gals to **Planet Hollywood,** where they can ogle Sylvester Stallone's form in a block of ice à la *Demolition Man*, contemplate *The Terminator*, and admire gowns from *Gone with the Wind*. Like Hard Rock Cafe, this celebrity-owned theme eatery is big with tourists, and the lines can get silly. But it's fun to look at all the movie memorabilia, and the T-shirts, etc., always make good souvenirs. Foodwise, stick to the basics here—sandwiches, burgers, and salads.

Though shopping isn't usually a passion for adolescent boys, there are two places that might get them to take off the headphones for a few minutes. The **Rock Express Outlet** on Spear Street sells left-over and flawed rock concert T-shirts for as little as $6 (if you hit it on one of their blowout sales weekends, usually around Christmas time, you can get them even cheaper). Rifle through the racks for that coveted Megadeth or Beastie Boys tour shirt; then check out the posters, buttons, programs, caps, and other stuff that sell for quadruple the price if you buy them at the show.

**NikeTown** is the other big draw—more multimedia entertainment center than retail outlet. They do have all the latest "swoosh" gear—logo jackets, sweatshirts, caps, duffel bags, and of course, "The Shoes," but the boys come here almost more to see the video walls and the displays of Michael Jordan, Grant Hill, et al., basketballs, shoes, etc.

# NIGHT

## Tactile Dome at the Exploratorium

Amazingly, this sensory funhouse (conceived by August Coppola—Francis Ford's brother, Nicholas Cage's father, and an erstwhile SF State professor) has been in operation for nearly twenty years, and it's still going strong. That's probably because adults love it just as much as kids do (maybe more). This is a great thing to do at night, preferably before dinner, because all that crawling around can work up a serious appetite (and being upside down and sideways with a belly full of pizza may not be such a great idea). The idea of the dome is to help you expand and explore your sense of touch. It's completely black inside, a factor which has been known to frighten some younger children (the supervising "dome guy" has speakers in each room with which he monitors everyone; and he'll come and get you out if you're feeling scared or claustrophobic). You enter in groups of two or three and are instructed to feel your way around each room for openings and interesting tactile experiences—identifiable household objects, unusual shapes and textures (if you find the keys, you may proclaim yourself a Dome Master). Sometimes you crawl; sometimes you walk; sometimes you slide or bounce. Be open to losing your sense of direction and distance and to allowing your other faculties to compensate for sight. It's a major giggle fest that gets more fun each time through.

## Basketball

My friend Jon thinks this is one of the coolest and best ways to entertain teenage boys (and their dads), and I'd have to agree. Every summer from June through August, college basketball players and pros play in a Pro-Am League at Kezar Pavilion and **Potrero Hill Recreation Center.** In addition to getting to watch your favorite hot college players sharpen their skills, you might get to see three-pointers made by the likes of Rex Walters, Jason Kidd, Gary Payton, Joe Smith, and other pros. Games are played Monday through Thursday nights at 8 p.m. and—the best part—it's free.

## Japantown

It seems an unlikely place to entertain out-of-town guests, but bowling can be a surprisingly San Francisco thing to do—particularly in the Presidio or Japantown. At the **Japantown Bowl,** take kids glow-in-the-dark bowling at "CyberBowl XLS." Tuesday, Saturday, and Sunday nights, they turn off all the lights, turn on lasers and fog machines, hand out glow-in-the-dark balls, and turn the alley into a bowler's laserium. There's a flat lane fee rather than a per-frame charge ($45–$60, up to six people per lane), and shoes are included.

Afterwards, cross the street to the Japantown Center, check out the shops, and stop off for dinner at **Isobune**—a great place to introduce youngsters to the undersea wonders of sushi. Chefs stand on an island behind a moat, rolling and slicing their seaweed-wrapped rice creations. Then they place the finished products on little floating plates that circle around the sushi bar like boats in the harbor. Diners pick up selections that look appealing. (The entertainment value of the sushi boats often distracts kids—and some adults—from the fact that they may be eating eel or sea urchin.)

If salmon roe won't fly, just next door is old standby **Benihana**—which has somehow retained its popularity where other gimmicky chains have failed (witness Chuck E. Cheese and Victoria Station). That's probably because the gimmick still works. Zany, wisecracking chefs, trained in the art of cleaver juggling, kamikaze slicing and dicing, and shrimp-to-plate tossing, make cooked-to-order surf and turf at your table. Though the jokes may have become a little stale, the high jinks are still pretty fresh, and the food is surprisingly decent.

## Minor Setbacks

Teenagers are at that painful age when they're listening to a lot of rock or rap music, but they're not old enough to get into nightclubs to see their favorite bands. **Bottom of the Hill** gets between the rock and that hard place. This underground, shabby-chic Potrero Hill club showcases up-and-coming local bands, and on Sundays, becomes teenager heaven, with a $4 all-you-can-eat barbecue and a music line-up that welcomes all ages. The cookout starts at about 4 p.m.; the bands about 5:30 p.m. Grab some chicken, sit on the back patio, and bond over power pop.

The **Palladium** is the city's oldest (and only) under 21 all-night dance club, located just off Broadway in North Beach. Tosca Cafe regulars no doubt curse the club's longevity, since they get the cocktail-rattling bass boom almost nightly through the floorboards. But for eighteen-year-olds, it's an introduction to the club life that's fun and relatively harmless (unless you count staying up all night dancing as dangerous). Deejays spin house, techno, and dance mixes from 9 p.m. til 6 a.m. Fridays and Saturdays on "the world's largest circular stainless-steel dance floor" (till 4 a.m. Thursdays and Sundays; they're closed Monday through Wednesday).

For serious thrash, garage band, punk, and other sweaty, head-banging music in a safe and sane atmosphere, there's **924 Gilman Street** in Berkeley, an all ages, no alcohol, cooperative nightclub whose motto is "Doing it for the kids, not to the kids." The club features bands with appropriately antisocial names, but it has a policy of not booking homophobic, ageist, or racist groups. The $5 cover is supplemented by a $2 membership fee for first-timers (good for one year). It's a place where parents can comfortably send kids into the mosh pit, without having to worry that they've stumbled into a lion's den.

## More Kid-Approved Restaurants

**Mel's**—The original '50s *American Graffiti* diner actually stood on the very same Geary Street spot where the modern-day version now resides. It was brought back to life with an eye to all the old details—tableside jukeboxes, a long soda counter, American flags, gum-snapping waitresses, patent-leather booths, blue-plate specials such as meatloaf and open-face turkey sandwiches, and huge milkshakes.

**Max's**—The South of Market diner is a hybrid between Mel's and a Jewish deli, with good food served in huge portions (along with a heaping pile of tongue-in-cheek attitude). Best bets include Reuben sandwiches, chicken pot pie, Chinese chicken or Cobb salad, and anything in the cake or pie department. Make sure to read the menus front to back; they're a scream, especially Max's rules, which promise a meal on the house if a waitperson ever asks you, "Is everything all right?"

**Johnny Rockets**—Less of a diner than a glorified soda fountain, this local chain serves all the usual nostalgic fare—hamburgers, fries, shakes—and it's open late.

**House of Prime Rib**—I'm not sure why, but meat-eating teens seem to really like this place, a bar and grill out of the 1970s mold, with big booths, and big slabs of prime rib carved tableside (growing boys can even get seconds).

**Barney's Hamburgers**—I recommend this place to vegetarians eating with nonvegetarians; it's also a great place to go with teens, many of whom seem to adopt the vegetarian lifestyle in their high school years. The menu features a variety of beef burgers with all sorts of toppings, plus a big selection of chicken sandwiches, tofu burgers, and garden burgers—oat patties mixed with shredded carrots, zucchini, cheese, and other goodies.

**Bill's Place**—A San Francisco institution since 1959, this family-owned restaurant features more than twenty-five kinds of burgers, many of them named after local celebrities. The burgers are big and juicy, and the prices are incredibly reasonable.

**North Beach Pizza**—There are so many places to eat in North Beach, you could write an entire book on just that. But not that many of them are appealing to kids as well as adults. North Beach Pizza scores on both accounts. Probably the most popular pizza delivery restaurant in the city, the two eat-in locations on Grant Avenue (one at Union, the other at Vallejo) are loud and boisterous and steamy and fun, especially late at night. It's the kind of place that makes you feel like you're part of the scene. (And don't even think about ordering anything but pizza.)

**The Gold Spike**—Family-style Italian restaurants, once all the rage, are getting harder and harder to find these days, but you can still get the full six courses (including spumoni ice cream for dessert) at the Gold Spike, a North Beach staple since 1920, run by three generations of the Mechetti family. The small dining room is covered from floor-to-ceiling with tchotchkes and bric-a-brac, and the tables sport red-checked tablecloths. Go on Friday for the $13.95 cacciucco feed (a robust Italian seafood stew made with prawns, clams, crab, and calamari).

**Zachary's Pizza**—Always packed, and always worth the wait. The deep-dish Chicago-style pies are simply the best (my favorite is the basil-tomato, but many people swear by the smoked chicken and mushroom).

**Hard Rock Cafe**—The granddaddy of theme restaurants, this bastion of rock-and-roll memorabilia packs in the tourists like it's a roach motel. The thing is, it's still fun. Sit under the front end of the Cadillac or beneath Huey Lewis's gold records and scan the room for beautiful people while you shout your order over the blasting music.

## Weird Museums

In my family, no vacation came without a visit to at least one museum and one old church. And though later in life I was grateful for the cultural exposure, at the time I think I would rather have had my gums scraped. The key to making museums attractive to kids is to find a subject they can relate to, or a collection that's just weird enough that they'll think it's neat. Here are some favorite oddball museums:

**Cartoon Art Museum**—Past exhibits at this comic strip and animation cel bastion have included art from *The Tick* and *The Flintstones*, a survey of *MAD* magazine drawings, a *Peanuts* retrospective, and work by tons of cult and underground comix artists.

**Musée Mechanique**—This is not technically a museum, but a collection of great, vintage carnival arcade games—all restored and fully functional. Parents will wax nostalgic over the mechanical gypsy fortune teller (like that one in the movie *Big*), the baseball game with the painted wooden players and the spring-wound bat, the hand-crank nickelodeons, and the miniature mechanical carnival that has trains and Ferris wheels and shooting galleries that spring to life with a coin deposit. Kids will get a glimpse of life before Nintendo. Be sure to peruse the old photos of the Cliff House and Sutro Baths along the wall, and don't forget to say hi to Laughing Sal, the chuckling fat lady who used to grace the entrance to Playland-at-the-Beach back before they built those godawful condos. For the complete San Francisco experience, run down to Safeway at the bottom of the road and pick up some **It's It**s. The quasifamous chocolate-dipped, ice-cream cookie sandwich was invented in 1928 at Playland. Stand on the balcony overlooking Seal Rocks and the Pacific and savor the San Francisco flavor. (Note to adults: if you get bored, arm the kids with quarters for the arcade and head upstairs to the Cliff House for a cocktail and a fabulous view of the sunset.)

**Barbie Hall of Fame**—Mrs. Evelyn Burkhalter's enormous personal compendium (some 20,000 pieces) of the perpetually perky blond doll and her cars, pets, playhouses, purses, etc., lives here. The museum contains everything in the Mattel catalog, from the first Barbie (issued in March 1959) to the present day—the largest Barbie collection in the world open to the public. Viewing hours are Tuesday through Friday 1:30 p.m. to 4:30 p.m., and Saturday 10 a.m. to noon and 1:30 to 4:30 p.m.

**Behring Automotive Museum**—For car freaks, this East Bay museum is worth the hour or so drive from the city. It features more than 100 classic and one-of-a-kind cars in several large showrooms, including a 1935 Mercedes-Benz, a 1936 MG Model PB, and a 1968 Bizzarrini Spyder.

**Pez Museum**—A whole museum devoted entirely to dispensers for those little rectangular candies—way cool. There's Tweety heads, Batman heads, and even Japanese characters—some 300 in all.

**Santa Cruz Surfing Museum**—Located in a lighthouse overlooking Steamer Lane, which is Santa Cruz's most gnarly surfing spot, this one-room museum displays old surfboards (including one bitten in two by a great white shark), surfing memorabilia, wetsuits, photographs of famous surfers, and a brief rundown of the history of the sport. After you're done looking at the stuff inside, find a perch at the cliff's edge and watch 'em ride the waves live and in person. It's teenager nirvana.

**San Quentin Museum**—Unlike Alcatraz, this is still an operating maximum security prison, which may make the museum here that much more appealing. It has old tools of incarceration, like a ball-and-chain and an Oregon boot, a gun collection, and a re-created 1913 prison cell.

**Museum of Ophthalmology**—Some of the things in this tiny museum—diseased eyeballs; glass eyes; strange, creepy surgical devices used in early eye surgery—might put you off your lunch, but the kids will probably think it's great. The museum, located near Fisherman's Wharf, is open Monday through Friday 8 a.m. to 5 p.m. by appointment only.

# The Usual Suspects

It would be impossible to write about kids' activities without mentioning some of the tried-and-true places that are givens on any tour of youthful San Francisco.

**Academy of Sciences/Steinhart Aquarium/Laserium**—To my mind the best attractions at the academy are the scale where you can see how much you weigh on different planets; the earthquake simulator; the Shark Roundabout; the glass case with the giant python; the gem and mineral hall; and (for grown-ups) the Far Side Gallery of Gary Larson cartoons. Laserium is a great activity for adolescents (the Lollapalaser show), or for adolescents and their ex-rocker dads (the Pink Floyd show).

**Japanese Tea Garden**—Certain rituals must be observed here. Climb the Moon Bridge and throw a penny into the wishing pond. Have tea and cookies at the tea house; pick out the almond and sesame cookies and save them for last. Play with the funny little Japanese dime-store toys and ogle the origami papers at the gift shop. Leave a rice-cracker offering at the giant Buddha.

**Exploratorium**—The giant spirograph, the tree that lights up when you clap, the device where you hear yourself on a split-second time delay, the giant bubble-blowing machine, holograms, and the two-way mirror where you can put your head on someone else's body—all these are only a tiny sample of the exhibits at this enormous hands-on science playpen. Sure it's for kids, but you'll have a hard time dragging adults out of here at the end of the day.

**Monterey Bay Aquarium**—If you have time, a trip south to this remarkable living aquarium is a must. From the two-story neon-jellyfish tank to the outdoor sea otter habitat and the walk-through tour of the Monterey Bay that starts underwater and works its way up in elevation to a shorebird aviary—there's nothing quite like it anywhere else. The surrounding Cannery Row area is basically Fisherman's Wharf South, but fun for an afternoon of walkaway crab cocktails, factory outlet shopping, arcade games, and taking a portrait of yourselves dressed up like Old West gunslingers.

**Paramount's Great America**—Our version of Disneyland has more rollercoasters and thrill rides. Worth the long waits are the Vortex stand-up rollercoaster, the Top Gun inverted coaster (your legs swing free), the giant-screen IMAX movies, and—for those can stomach it—the Drop Zone Stunt Tower, in which you free fall some 200 feet.

## WHERE TO STAY

The hip, high-tech decor and celebrity handprints in the cement in front of the entrance to **Hotel Diva,** plus its location directly across from the Geary and Curran Theaters and next to the California Pizza Kitchen make this a good compromise for families.

The few years that I was a Bay Area expatriate, I learned something that a lifetime here never taught me. You can take the city for granted. Hard to believe, I know. But there I was sitting in House of Woo, somewhere in Milwaukee, Wisconsin, in the middle of February, staring at what was supposed to pass for a plate of cashew chicken

# Tour 6 Cynical Natives

(for which I had graciously paid $10) when it occurred to me: I wasn't in San Francisco anymore. And like one of those movies where the girl has amnesia, and then gets knocked on the head and all her memories come flooding back to her in a whirlwind montage sequence set to the tune of "I Left My Heart...," I suddenly ached for San Francisco in a way I hadn't known was possible. I yearned for the sight of the late-afternoon sun streaming down California Street in October; for steaming bowls of Thai lemongrass coconut soup from Thep Phanom; for old Italian men playing bocce ball in Aquatic Park; and for movie watching as a participatory sport.

The following spring, when I came back for vacation, the light and the fog and the intoxicating goofiness of the city overwhelmed me. I got out my camera and went to the top of Russian Hill and snapped away like some kind of lovesick suitor. And I knew at that moment, as I sat on the steps near Macondray Lane—flower boxes overhead, Alcatraz dancing in the bay like an island paradise—that I had to come home.

Not everyone has this volatile a reaction. For some, this city is more like a chronic addiction, except without all the bad side effects (unless you count the shakes). Others may need a little reminding—something to stir the old embers, to rekindle the romance, to make 'em hug a total stranger and say, "Can you believe it? I *live* here!"

## MORNING

As a populace, San Franciscans tend to be generally disdainful of anything that smacks of bandwagonism. We don't bound up to movie stars in restaurants for an autograph; we refuse to do the wave at sporting events; and we definitely don't do anything as obvious as ride a **cable car** (you might as well ask us to eat Rice-a-Roni). But if you haven't ridden the rails down Hyde Street (and I'd hazard seven out of ten residents haven't), you're cheating yourself out of the best E ticket in Friscoland. The problem is how to accomplish this without being mistaken for someone who's completely lost his or her sense of propriety. Best advice: set the alarm for 6 a.m., grab a trench coat and a pair of sunglasses, and head down to the Hyde Street turnaround at Ghirardelli Square. There, while the camera-toting, plaid-shorts people are still sleeping off those Buena Vista Irish coffees, you can indulge in this guilty pleasure without losing face. Buy the gripman a cup of Peet's best and he might even let you hang off the running boards Doris Day–style (because you know you've been dying to do it). As you swing in the sea breeze, soak up the city at dawn: the Pavlovian smell of roasting coffee and Chinese barbecue pork buns, the glint of dew on the tracks, the sultry harmonies of fog horns and seagulls punctuated by the thump, thump, thump of *Chronicles* being thrown at doorways. Don't forget to turn around at the top of the hill for the cynicism-melting view of the wharf and the waterfront. All this for the low, low price of $2.

After you've worked up an appetite, head up Market Street to **Zuni Cafe** to recharge your spirits as well as your batteries. (If you've got your old college buddies in tow, dinner is the meal to come here for; if you've got no one to please but yourself, breakfast is definitely the Zuni meal of choice.) The menu is simple and soul-warming, just like the early-morning ambience. All around you, deliciously urban Hayes Valley starts to pick up the pace. Savor a steaming bowl of au lait and read the paper over a plate of toast, a soft-boiled egg, and some steel-cut oatmeal.

**Alternative #1:** On weekends, lots of people opt for a glamorama brunch at Sam's or Guaymas in Tiburon. Which is great if you're with your parents or first-timers. But there's something sublime about sitting in the morning sun, watching the ships roll in, and watching 'em roll away again at the **Mission Rock Resort.** (Okay, so Otis Redding was in Sausalito when he wrote "Dock of the Bay." He should have been here.) Mission Rock is a working man's port, where giant tankers sit rusting in dry docks and ramshackle boats are tied by frayed ropes to splintering wooden piers. Formerly the ugly stepsister of its dockside neighbor, The Ramp, the Rock (aka Poor Man's Sam's) was bought out in early '98 by the folks who brought us Pat O'Shea's. At the time of this writing they had closed the doors for remodeling and promised (threatened?) to put a new sparkle in the old girl's step. More's the pity. While no one could dispute that the pier was falling apart, the charm of the Rock was that it never tried to put on airs to attract a more refined clientele. When it reopens, no doubt the old soul-nurturing jukebox that filtered Patsy Cline and Otis Redding onto the sunny top deck through somebody's older brother's hand-me-down speakers (for that wonderful, scratchy vinyl effect) will be gone. But hopefully, they'll keep the Ramos Fizzes by the carafe, and that recipe for Bloody Marys. And they certainly can't take away that gritty industrial ambience. So, who knows? Best-case scenario, you can snuggle up to a pitcher of beer, listen to the blues, and find yourself still "sittin' when the evening comes."

**Alternative #2:** At the opposite end of the city and on another waterfront is another one of San Francisco's fast-vanishing institutions, **Louis'** at Ocean Beach. Never mind that it's right next to the Cliff House. None of that cheese rubbed off on Louis, a classic diner that has been overlooking the ruins of Sutro Baths since 1937. Your corn-beef hash will probably be delivered to you by original waitress Rachel, a spry old thing with owl-eyed specs who's watched the world turn through Louis' steamy windows for more than fifty years. As you would expect with every good diner, the coffee's weak, but the cup is bottomless—leaving you lots of time to contemplate the mysterious cargos of those enormous barges as they head in and out of the Golden Gate. Try to get a table in the back corner, so you can truly appreciate your precarious position on the edge of the planet.

# NOON

San Francisco long ago banished its dead to burial blandness in Colma, leaving only two cemeteries within the city limits—Mission Dolores and the **National Military Cemetery** in the Presidio. You wouldn't think a graveyard was the kind of place you'd go to fan the flames of a wavering love affair, but then again, you probably never thought you'd find yourself sobbing during those AT&T commercials either. Graveyards are peculiar little time capsules—microcosms of a city's history distilled into a poignant shorthand of names, dates, and one-sentence epitaphs. But they tell volumes about a place: of battles fought and won, of love affairs gone awry, of family scandals and tragedies. Mission Dolores is more noteworthy for those who are not commemorated there (namely hundreds of Native Americans; see the Politically Correct tour). The Presidio's contribution is more subtle. Secluded on an enchanted sylvan stretch that gazes out over the Golden Gate Bridge, the cemetery, built in 1884, makes you look at the city's love-hate relationship with the military in a new light. Follow the stone fences along the rows of gravestones and monuments and you'll be swept up in tales of Civil War spy Pauline Cushman Fry, of Generals Funston and Kearny, of union busters and Indian guides, of Spanish-American war heroes, American war mothers, and the 15,000 young men (including thirty-five Medal of Honor recipients) who died in World War I. Most important, if you let the hush and solitude of this place seep into your overstimulated urban brain, you'll become one again with the gentle and noble underbelly of San Francisco.

It seems only fitting in San Francisco that just below this somber tribute to human war heroes lies a burial ground devoted to our fine four-legged friends. If you didn't need a hanky before, you'll need one now. Only the stone-hearted wouldn't melt at the sight of fresh flowers resting against the gravestone of Skipper, the "best damn dog we ever had." The **pet cemetery** (originally reserved for animals of military personnel, but usurped over the years by the general populace) contains the remains of loved ones ranging from Afton the boxer to beloved rats Chocolate and Candy. There is something so endearing and so very EssEff about all these crooked little handmade markers with their poems and pictures that even the most blasé among us will be moved to wag a tail. (Note: Due to construction and a toxic soil threat, the pet cemetery is less accessible than it used to be. But it's definitely worth the extra effort.)

From here head down toward the waterfront and the **Golden Gate Promenade,** a name which always makes me envision big-busted ladies in feathered hats and lace-up boots carrying parasols and pushing prams. But as you know if you've walked it, this 3.5-mile path is actually a lovely little slice of open space smack dab in the middle of the metropolitan maze. To truly appreciate the promenade, you must walk the entire trail, not just a piece of it, because there are various stations along the way that are essential to revitalizing your sagging civic spirits. Start out at **Aquatic Park,** where you can watch members of the **Dolphin Club** don cheery orange swim caps and do the backstroke in the bay. Some of these folks are in their seventies and eighties, and have been treading these waters for forty-odd years. (If you're doing this walk in the fall, or on New Year's Day, try to catch the Alcatraz Island to Aquatic Park Swim.) Follow the path around to **Fort Mason,** where you must make a mandatory stop at the bakery at Greens restaurant for a loaf of Acme sourdough, and at the public library's bargain **Book Bay** for a quick browse through the quality paperbacks before you stroll down the path through the sailboat marina. Next comes **Marina Green,** which has become a curious and blissful cross-section of sunbathers in Speedos, gay volleyballers, East Coast private college grads on rollerblades and mountain bikes, and Old Money spillover from the St. Francis Yacht Club across the way. Five-star people watching. Proceed down the road to **Crissy Field,** and plant yourself on the beach to watch the windsurfers brave the whitecaps, while you take in the entire span of the Golden Gate Bridge (it's one of the few spots in all the city and Marin where you can actually see the entire bridge). Then continue walking the trail past the Gorbachev Foundation and the dormitories and offices for NOAH (what other city in the world offers primo beachfront property as housing for environmental research volunteers?), until you reach **Fort Point.** Here you'll likely be joined by a number of tourists. Don't let that deter you. Walk along the iron-link guard rail to the spot where the waves crash on the rocks and spray the parking lot. Then reenact the scene from Hitchcock's *Vertigo* when Jimmy Stewart jumps into the bay to save Kim Novak (except maybe without the jumping in part). Next, walk across the parking lot until you're directly under the bridge, look up, and marvel at the awe-inspiring underside of one of the Seven Engineering Wonders of the World. Inside the fort, make sure to check out the cannon that was cast in Peru in the 1600s and brought here by the Spanish in the late 1700s, when Fort Point was an adobe compound called El Castillo de San Joaquin. And absolutely don't miss the film about the construction of the Golden Gate Bridge (complete with great old newsreel footage) that's shown daily in the bookstore.

## Zing, Zing, Zing Went My Heartstrings

I think nostalgia and sentimentality are extremely underrated. When I was in Milwaukee, and San Francisco seemed but a distant dream, just hearing the whistling part of "Dock of the Bay" was enough to send me over the edge into slobbering sentimentalville. Living here, you have to work a little harder to get that tear-jerk reaction. But there are places that can help the process along.

Just a block from the dreaded Land-o'-White-Shoes (aka Fisherman's Wharf) is the **San Francisco Art Institute,** a place that will restore your faith in the notion that not everything down here comes with a built-in ticket vendor. Walk up Chestnut Street from the big Tower Records store and you'll come to the entrance of this beautiful old Spanish colonial revival building, designed in 1926 by Brown and Bakewell (the same architectural team that gave us City Hall and the War Memorial Opera House). The doors open onto what was once a stately tiled courtyard and fountain. These days it has taken on the genteel, slightly melancholy air of an abandoned nineteenth-century Spanish villa, which somehow makes it all the more charming. On the west side of the courtyard is the skylit Diego Rivera Gallery, which houses a large mural Rivera painted in 1931 as a tribute to the American laborer. Sit on the bench in the center of the room, in the stillness of the fading afternoon light, and contemplate Rivera's backside—truly sublime. Then make your way to the roof deck and **Pete's Cafe,** where you'll find one of the best wharf views you've never had to pay a quarter for. (Residents with neobeatnik types in tow take note of the cafe sign that reads "Pseudo-Bohemians Welcome.") The cafe and surrounding sunny concrete pad are walled-in castle-style, allowing you to gaze out through the trees and over the apartment houses, to smell the crab pots, to listen to the seals barking and the fog horns blowing, and maintain complete, blissful anonymity.

# Dago Mary's

On the opposite end of the waterfront spectrum, we have **Dago Mary's,** which, considering its location amidst the splendid squalor of the Hunter's Point Naval Shipyard, is not the likeliest place to relight the old SF Duraflames. But this is one of the great ghosts of San Francisco's reckless youth. Sally Stanford's den of inequity is gone, you can't visit Tessie Wall's parlor house anymore, but you can still have lunch at Dago Mary's.

"Dago Mary" Chiorizio was an Italian madam who ran a posh brothel out of these digs in the 1930s, just after the repeal of Prohibition. The restaurant doesn't look like it has changed much since its shady days. Highlights of the ornate Victoriana decor include gold-flocked wallpaper, plush red velvet drapery, and gilded chandeliers (apparently Mary's tastes ran a bit to the gaudy side). In one of her more acquisitive moods, Mary also picked up the marble fireplace from the Flood Mansion in Menlo Park and deposited it in the lobby. Don't let your fear of Hunter's Point prevent you from coming out here—at least during daylight hours. This is a nice, white-tablecloth restaurant, serving large portions of basic Italian food, and catering to the business suit, shot-and-a-beer crowd.

## Shaken and Stirred

The 1906 earthquake hit San Francisco at an impressionable age, when the city was still struggling to prove it wasn't merely a flash in the gold rush pan. But disasters have a funny way of bringing out the best in people, and San Francisco proved to the world she was a real scrapper, triumphing against the odds and rising like a phoenix from the ashes bigger and better than before. Visit some of the shrines of the 1906 quake and you'll feel a swell of pride and a renewed sense of that can-do San Francisco spirit. Set the tone by renting (or re-renting) *San Francisco*, the 1936 classic film starring Clark Gable, Spencer Tracy, and Jeanette MacDonald. Between the earthquake scene (a chandelier-swinging tour de force long before there were computer-enhanced special effects), and the scene in which MacDonald sings a soul-stirring version of "San Francisco," to win a contest and bail out her rogue gambler boyfriend Blackie Norton, you'll find yourself cheering for the Little City That Did. Next, head over to Twentieth and Church Streets and pay homage to the **fire hydrant** that saved the Mission district. Now painted gold and commemorated with a plaque from the city, the brave little hydrant was the only one that kept pumping during the great fire, and is the reason the Mission still has so many fine specimens of Victorian architecture.

From here, swing over to Golden Gate Park and the shores of Lloyd Lake, where perhaps the most poignant memorial to the old city lies moldering. Christened **Portals of the Past,** the stately marble portico is the only remains of one of the grand Nob Hill mansions (and maybe the reason they always tell you to stand in a doorway in the event of an earthquake).

## Swan Oyster Depot

Locals would rather call it "Frisco" than go to the wharf for a crab fix, but there's nothing like fresh-from-the-ocean Dungeness crab or Tomales Bay oysters to remind you that in some places, Mrs. Paul's is top shelf in the seafood department. Swan's not only satisfies your seafood jones, it'll cure your hankering for talking with some unpretentious, honest-to-God San Franciscans. This fish market-cum-lunch counter was opened in 1912 by the Lausten Brothers, but has been run since 1946 by an assortment of members of the Sancimino family. Swan serves up fresh, no frills seafood—filleted, cracked, and shucked before your eyes—along with healthy portions of friendly banter. Belly up to the marble counter and start with a bowl of clam chowder, served with a hunk of fresh sourdough and all the oyster crackers you can stomach (adventurous types will want to try one of the assortment of wacky hot sauces, which boast names like Ass in Space, Ultimate Burn, and Vampfire). Then move on to a plate of fresh-cracked Dungeness crab, thinly sliced smoked salmon, a half-dozen Miyagi oysters, or mixed seafood cocktail/salad. Jimmy, Mike, or one of their brothers will pile on crab, prawns, bay shrimp—whatever's exceptional that day—and top it off with a dollop of cocktail sauce or homemade horseradish. Wash it down with a pint of San Francisco's own Anchor Steam.

## Center for the Arts and Yerba Buena Gardens

San Francisco is one of those rare cities where "good" doesn't automatically translate as "old." Case in point: the TransAmerica Pyramid, which despite a rocky reception back in the '70s, is now San Francisco's second most-celebrated skyline icon (the Golden Gate Bridge, of course, being the first). The Center for the Arts and Yerba Buena Gardens are not nearly so controversial. In fact, they are a place that gives you hope that urban renewal can really work. And there is no better spot for viewing San Francisco's eclectic downtown architecture.

On a sunny afternoon, begin your stroll through the galleries for an eye-opening introduction to the diversity and talent of local artists. Next, grab a sandwich at the top of the esplanade, sit at one of the outdoor tables, and look east, where you'll be treated to a vista that includes the Bay Bridge; Timothy Pflueger's magnificent Pacific Telephone Building (the city's first downtown skyscraper); the dramatically striped skylight of Mario Botta's Museum of Modern Art; the "jukebox" Marriott Hotel with its seashell windows; and a hodgepodge of other buildings—historic and modern—all thrown together in a happy architectural jumble. From here, head down to the Martin Luther King Jr. Memorial waterfall, and read the "I Have a Dream" speech, which never gets cliché and never fails to remind me that we live in a town that tolerates all kinds with good grace and humor. Finally, settle down in the grassy area for some peaceful R&R. If it's a summer weekend, chances are there'll be some kind of ethnic fair, Make*A*Circus, or other group offering a free performance on the outdoor stage.

## Last Stop

Wander through the Hearst Court, past the children's gallery and the Art of the Americas corridor at the de Young Museum, and you'll happen upon one of the most delightful cafe finds in all the city. **Cafe de Young** has managed to escape the standard attraction eatery stereotype—usually some sort of formica-infested cafeteria catering to busloads of chattering tourists who are more interested in $10 mayonnaise sandwiches than art. The quaint dining area opens onto an idyllic sunlit spot in a serene enclosed courtyard, surrounded by alabaster cherubs, a bird bath, and a Victorian arbor. Order a couscous/veggie or a warm goat-cheese salad—always made with impeccably fresh-from-the-farm produce.

# NIGHT

Okay, so maybe it's a tad cliche, but there's definitely something heart-warming and refreshing about seeing San Francisco through the wide eyes of a neophyte. A year ago I would have sent you straight to Lefty O'Doul's, but at the time of this writing, the old baseball legend's hofbrau and wonderfully schmaltzy sing-along piano bar was fighting a losing high-rent battle (if it's still open, make sure to go in and sign one for the gipper, as you gaze at Marilyn Monroe's USO license and all the memorabilia from the old Pacific Coast League). Their closing seemed to leave a gaping hole in the corny-but-sincere San Francisco nostalgia category—until I remembered the **Gold Dust Lounge.** The re-created gold rush honky tonk in the heart of tourist-land doesn't have a sing-along piano bar, but it does have dixieland jazz bands, and some darn good ones at that. Where else in San Francisco are you going to find that old-time Bourbon Street sound now that Turk Murphy is gone? Grab a beer, surround yourself with vacationing couples from Ohio, and see if you don't find yourself wiping a tear from the corner of your eye during the clarinet solo.

Even though Lefty may have gone to that big baseball diamond in the sky, you can still pay tribute to Lefty O'Doul himself, and to the other working-class Irish folk who built this town, at the **Francis "Lefty" O'Doul Drawbridge** on Third and Berry Streets. (For those who aren't familiar with the story, Francis Joseph "Lefty" O'Doul was a phenom for the Yankees before he became manager of the San Francisco Seals—part of the Pacific Coast League—where Joe DiMaggio got his start back in the '40s.) It's one of two remaining drawbridges in San Francisco (the other's on Fourth Street), and the only one that you can still get a rise out of once in a while. Watching the enormous metal-grate roadway loom over Mission Bay, like a giant crocodile opening its jaws, never fails to put a lump in my throat. It somehow harkens to a grander, golden age of industry, when San Francisco worked hard and played hard and was truly the "City That Knows How." Your best chance to see the drawbridge in action is during Fleet Week in October, when boats go in and out of the slips along Mission Bay.

## Castro Theatre

If you haven't gone to a revival or classic film re-release at the Castro, you're missing out on one of the best "only in San Francisco" experiences. The theater itself is worth the trip, designed in 1920s art deco movie palace grandeur by Timothy Pflueger, the same genius who gave us the Paramount Theatre in Oakland, the former I. Magnin building on Union Square, 450 Sutter, and the Pacific Telephone Building on New Montgomery.

For maximum enjoyment, go for a musical like *My Fair Lady,* anything filmed in San Francisco, or a classic Hitchcock flick where great sexist lines like "Change your hair color for me, Judy. It can't matter to you" bring down the house. Make sure you get there early enough to get popcorn—with real butter—and so you don't miss the performance on the giant Wurlitzer organ. It never fails to give me a thrill when I see that thing rise out of the theater pit just before showtime and the organist leads the audience in a clap-along of classic show tunes, followed by a rousing rendition of "San Francisco." I also love the fact that the biggest applause during the opening credits are not reserved for the stars, but for the costume designers. Make sure to look up at the elaborately painted and gilded ceiling and light fixture.

## Top of the Mark

This was the sky room where World War II soldiers danced their last dance and vowed to be true to shapely gals they'd known for hours, before they shipped off to fight the good fight. It's also purportedly the view that inspired Tony Bennett to croon, "I Left My Heart in San Francisco." And though the room has been completely made over, some of that old SF nostalgia still lingers, especially on misty nights when the mournful fog horns blow like the unrequited sighs of a war bride. Order a Singapore Sling, stare out over the "cool, gray city of love," and get dreamy-eyed as the band plays "Isn't it Romantic?"

## North Beach

Old stalwarts argue that North Beach now isn't what it was Back Then. But frankly North Beach has never been what it once was. That's the beauty of it. When it became a predominantly Italian neighborhood in the late nineteenth century, the Irish lamented. When the beatniks moved in in the '50s, everyone complained. And now that the neighborhood is becoming increasingly Chinese, the Italians are shaking their heads. Hopefully a little bit of every culture survives, and in some cases—as with the Irish and the gay communities (it did a brief stint as a gay district in the '40s)—revives.

For locals, the problem is distilling the neighborhood down to its essence. On the Italian side of things, there's a million-and-one restaurants between Broadway and Bay, all of which are run by authentic Italians, and all of which seem to capture the flavor of Old North Beach. For my money, **Buca Giovanni, U.S. Restaurant,** and **L'Osteria del Forno** do it best. Buca Giovanni is tucked below street level in a wine-cave setting that feels at once hokey and hopelessly romantic. Chef Giovanni Leoni's Tuscan-style food is hugely flavorful, hearty, and soul-warming—none of this Italian-lite stuff. The enormous menu offers plenty of meat and game, tons of pasta (all of it housemade) and wonderful vegetable side dishes (many of the greens are grown on Leoni's own ranch).

Down the street, tiny L'Osteria del Forno does a brief, simple menu that hits the spot every time. Choose between the roast or pasta of the day, or the thin-crust pizza, made in the brick-lined oven.

In the category of inexpensive, unpretentious, heaping plates of good food, U.S. Restaurant wins the prize. Go here for lunch and order a huge pile of pasta, a humongous sandwich (with fries), or the red clam chowder, before retiring to a perch at an outdoor cafe for some espresso and people-watching. (At the time of this writing, the U.S. Restaurant was under new management and about to re-open. The new owners promised to preserve popular menu items and that homespun atmosphere.)

## Booster Shots

If Milwaukee taught me anything besides how to tear the blue ribbon off a Pabst Blue Ribbon for a free beer, it's how to find a good street festival. When you first move to a new place (or when you get old enough to appreciate drinking in the streets), you find yourself going to every single one of these things, and they all start to run together—the guy who makes those hand-made rocking chairs, the Victorian house light-switch plates, lemonade slushies—etc., etc., roll tape.

But all street fairs are not alike. And there's nothing quite like a good (emphasis on good), old-fashioned block party to soften the jaded soul. Maybe because of the location, the mix of cultures, or the colorful history, **North Beach Fair** (in July) is one of the best—a glorious, uninhibited, yet spendidly Old World slice of San Francisco life. Where else can you sit on a grassy knoll in the front of the spires of the church where Joe DiMaggio went to school, with a glass of pinot grigio or a cup of espresso, and watch a guy who looks like he just stepped off the set of *The Godfather* dancing to a band playing the "Hawaii Five-O" theme song? Other highlights include street vendors selling calamari with lime-garlic-dill aioli, a fantastic street-painting contest, lots of men in tank-top undershirts and black socks, a street-corner poets tent featuring real, live, genuine Beat poets, and the wafting scent of meatball sandwiches and baking biscotti. It's enough to make you weep.

The other standout is the **Chinese New Year's** fest and parade. If you've never done this, you don't know what you're missing. A guaranteed flame rekindler. Giant dragons and lions dance through Chinatown; sleek Asian beauties wave from elaborately decorated floats; mayors campaign; firecrackers fly; and Grant Avenue is awash in the glow of a hundred tiny Chinese lanterns. After the parade, have a cocktail at **Li Po** or the **Bow Bow Lounge** for a *World of Suzie Wong* meets *Flower Drum Song* experience. It's Chinatown, Jake.

## Enjoy Life, Sleep Out More Often

If you and the city are gonna rekindle the old romance, why not set the proper mood? Leave the laundry, drop off the videos, and head to a hotel. Best bets include the **Seal Rock Inn,** down by Ocean Beach. It's not fancy (in fact it could use a bit of sprucing up), but you get to wake up to the sound of waves crashing and fog horns blowing. Treat yourself to an early-morning walk on the beach, followed by breakfast at Louis'. Then walk on down to the **Beach Chalet** and reminisce among the WPA murals. Play the locals version of *Where's Waldo* and see if you can spot beloved Golden Gate Park superintendent John McClaren, sculptor Benny Bufano, and some of the lights of 1930s San Francisco society in these wonderful frescoes. Afterwards, head upstairs for an amber ale at the microbrewery.

For the more pampered route, park yourself in a bay view room with a window seat at the exclusive **Sherman House** in Cow Hollow. The sumptuous-to-the-point-of-decadent rooms will make you feel like you're the star of a Danielle Steel novel or an extra on the set of *Dangerous Liaisons*. There's a top-notch in-house restaurant that is so discreet, it's not even open to the public (which may explain why people like Robert de Niro find this place so appealing). The only danger of staying here is that you may never want to leave the premises. If you do, the good news is you're only steps away from Union Street, where money does indeed buy happiness (or a very cool pair of shoes).

A weekend at **The Claremont** resort and country club is like a Palm Springs vacation—only better—since you can sit on the terrace and gaze across the bay at the San Francisco skyline. After your spa session and gourmet low-cal lunch, lie poolside and dream of the fairy-tale city that lies shimmering just beyond the horizon.

Scenario #1: You met her in an America Online chat room. You spent hours "talking" about deep philosophical matters—how you hate Starbucks and *Forrest Gump,* that there's no good way to do underlines and italics in e-mail—and of course, expanding your repertoire of clever computer smileys :~). Finally, you decided it was

# Tour 7 Impressionable Dates

time to meet face to face. She's flying out for a visit, and you're nervous. Very nervous. You're determined to impress her with your knowledge of San Francisco and show her that the soft romantic you revealed to her in the private chat room wasn't just a figment of her Macintosh.

Scenario #2: You met riding the 38 Geary each morning to work. He lives in the Richmond; you live in the Western Addition. You both know the city like the back of your hands. You finally got up the nerve to ask him out, and now you're thinking, "If I take him to some place like Julius' Castle, he'll dump me faster than an old transfer." You want romance, but you don't want it wrapped up in a box of truffles, tied with giant corsage bow, and rammed with a drip-wax chianti bottle down your throat. What will you do? What WILL you do?

# MORNING

Granted, most dates don't start out first thing in the morning (unless it's the morning after, and then we're not exactly talking "date" any-more). Morning dates are usually spend-the-day-together-and-see-if-we-run-out-of-things-to-talk-about affairs. They're low-stress in the sense that there's not that "are we, or aren't we" pressure that you get at the end of a night-time date; but they're high stress in the sense that there're a lot more hours to fill with actual, nonnaked activities.

The **Presidio,** I've decided, has something for just about every-one, but this pristine, private, wooded glen is a particularly romantic spot, both on sunny days when the views make you want to dance a jig, and on cool, misty, mysterious ones when you can pretend you're John and Yoko watching the play of light and fog as it sweeps through the Golden Gate. There's nothing to indicate that **Lover's Lane** is an officially designated amorous spot, aside from a small street sign, but just the fact that this little footpath is called "lover's lane" makes you want to hold hands and sing about moon and June and spoon. Pick it up just past the Presidio Boulevard Gate at the southeast entrance, and walk slowly (the whole trail only takes about fifteen minutes), making sure to point out all the silly romantic stuff along the way—squirrels sharing their nuts, the brick footbridge built for two, the huge weeping willow at Tennessee Hollow that's the perfect place to hide love notes or have a clandestine tryst. When you're ready to step up to the big leagues, there's also a spot in the Presidio called **Inspiration Point.** Located near the top of Arguello Boulevard, just past the Presidio Golf Course clubhouse, the spot looks out over the Palace of Fine Arts and the Golden Gate. The Ecology Trail takes you right to it, but if you're already heading for the spot known as Inspiration Point, why not do it properly: drive here and "park."

## Alternative Route

Start by sharing a chocolate croissant at a sidewalk table at the **Tassajara Bakery,** one of the city's coziest cafes, in Cole Valley. Then, walk west up Parnassus Avenue to **Willard Street,** hang a left up the hill, and you'll find yourself on a cobbled lane that time forgot—and your date probably never knew existed. After admiring the Wurster-esque shingle-style houses along Willard and nearby Edgewood Avenue and Farnsworth Lane (a treasure of a secret, cottage-dotted stairway), turn around, head back to Willard Street, and follow it to the end, where you'll find the entrance to **Sutro Forest.** Walk hand-in-hand along the footpaths, through the shady woods, beneath the fragrant eucalyptus trees, until you emerge into the sunlight at a destination that's invariably surprising. One trail leads to the back of UCSF; one to the houses along Stanyan Street; another to tiny Belgrave Avenue, just below Tank Hill. Depending which way you go, you might happen upon a lovely glade, a redwood grove, or a perfect vista point. Half the fun is in the not knowing.

## NOON

There are dozens of romantic spots in Golden Gate Park, none of them completely undiscovered, but the **Shakespeare Garden** is certainly a spot that often gets overlooked in the romantic department. Grab a bottle of wine, some grapes, and a volume of Shakespeare's sonnets, and sit on the grass under a canopy of flowers and plants—every one of which is mentioned somewhere in the Bard's works. If you forgot your Penguin compendium, you can read from the inscriptions on the stone wall at the south end, or hum a few bars of "How Do I Love Thee . . ." and fake the rest.

A dozen roses is always a sure-fire date-pleaser, but also a tad on the cliché side if you ask me. If you really want to impress, take a drive up to the **Berkeley Rose Gardens,** and present him or her with a *thousand* roses—along with a spectacular view of the San Francisco Bay and skyline. The lovely stone-terraced amphitheater, a WPA project of the 1930s, is filled with every imaginable variety and color of rose—like some kind of English grandmother's fantasy run amok. If things are going well, slip your hand in his or hers and stand under the trellis at the bottom, where dozens of couples get married each year.

## Drake's Beach

Sure, you could do the whole oysters-champagne-aphrodisiac routine at a restaurant somewhere, and be one of six other couples doing exactly the same thing. Or you could take a leisurely drive up Highway 1 to Point Reyes in the middle of the afternoon, make your way to romantic Drake's Beach, grab a dozen barbecued Hog Islands, Johnsons, or Tomales Bay boys from the beachside grill, curl up on a blanket, and feed them to each other while swapping swigs from a bottle of decent chardonnay. You make the call. The sheltered beach is surrounded by tall, dramatic, white cliffs—the kind you might imagine Catherine running out across with Heathcliff in close pursuit. In between slugs of wine, gaze out toward the horizon and weave a romantic tale about the *Golden Hinde* sailing into the lagoon with Sir Francis Drake at her helm. The English adventurer purportedly landed here in that ship in 1579.

## Saying "They Do"

In most towns, going down to **City Hall** to get hitched is about as romantic as getting your driver's license. But most towns don't have a City Hall as magnificent as ours. Each year, hundreds of couples—gay and straight—say their vows in the stunning rotunda at the foot of the grand marble staircase, beneath the soaring copper dome of this 1915 French Renaissance masterpiece (ceremonies have been on hiatus during the renovation, but should begin again in 1998). Sometimes the ceremonies are conducted en masse, followed by a formal presentation of the newlyweds, who descend the stairs like they're walking on air. Even if you may be years away from marriage, you can't deny that a good, three-hanky wedding will put you in the mood. Bring flowers and give them to a bride who's bouquetless; be a witness for someone who doesn't have one; or just stand on the sidelines and beam.

## NIGHT

Lots of people come down to the **Palace of Fine Arts** in the afternoon, but for romantics, nighttime is definitely the right time. In the still of the evening, with the dome lit up and casting its shimmering reflection onto the lagoon, the palace looks like something Zeus created for Hera to hold all her earthly treasures. Chances are, unless it's a warm night or there's an event at the theater, people will be few and far between. Take full advantage of this. Walk slowly around the pond and take in the pavilion from all sides. Make sure to ponder architect Bernard Maybeck's mysterious weeping maidens wreathing the top of the pavilion. Then stand under the dome at the very center (there's usually a small circle marking the spot) and clap—for a very cool echo. Frequently, you'll encounter a lone flutist or saxophone player using the ethereal acoustics to great effect. Don't squander this opportunity. Ask your date for a dance.

Dinner and a movie is probably the oldest dating ritual in the book and, in general, is a pretty nice way to spend an evening, except it's not terribly impressive on the creativity front. **The Casting Couch,** though, is an entirely different story. It's a "microcinema," complete with fifty comfy armchairs, sofas, and loveseats, where you can catch all the obscure indie and film fest releases you never knew existed while munching on popcorn and guzzling pale ale (delivered to you seat-side) in a room about twice the size of your den. You may only have to share the theater with a few other people, but if that isn't private enough for you, you can rent out the whole place for a very impressive romantic evening. Begin with dinner at **Pastis** across the street (a very good, upscale, modern French restaurant by the people who also own Fringale) or **Hunan** (perhaps my favorite Chinese restaurant of all time). In between bites of hot-smoked chicken, casually suggest a movie. Your date will no doubt think multiplex at the Embarcadero—and wonder where the hell you're going when you step into an office building, stroll through the lobby, and duck into a curtained doorway at the back. You can almost hear the points racking up. Movies cost $8.50 at last check, or if you really want to go all out, get the Casting Couch to bring dinner in (they did a great Valentine's Day deal a couple of years back that included a five-course dinner, chocolates, and a screening of *Casablanca* or *The Way We Were* for $180).

One of my all-time most-romantic date memories involves sneaking Chinese food into a movie theater and filling the auditorium with the smell of garlic chicken, while we giggled over *Gregory's Girl* and our neighbors salivated. There's nothing sneaky about the reciprocal arrangement between **Giorgio's Pizzeria** and the **Plough and Stars** on Clement, but it's somehow impressive (and therefore romantic) when you've got an insider's edge on the local rituals. The routine goes like this: arrive at Giorgio's about the same time as the live, Irish minstrel music starts up across the street at the pub (between 8 and 9 p.m.). Order a couple of the stellar calzones. Peruse the shop windows for a little while, and then scope out your table at the P&S (the long, wooden tables are designed for conviviality rather than intimacy, but you can usually find a good niche on one of the benches along the wall). After about twenty minutes you can pick up your steaming stuffed popover and bring it back to your table in the bar. Immediately order a perfect, room-temperature Guinness (with a bartending staff that is almost exclusively Irish, you will not find a more perfectly poured pint in town), then sit back and tap your toes as the fiddles and the flutes infect you with their mischievous spirit.

**RECOMMENDED DINING SPOTS**

These places keep coming up on my dating friends' lists of romantic dining spots. Who am I to argue?

**Acquerello,** 1722 Sacramento Street, 567-5432

**Cafe Majestic,** 1500 Sutter Street, 776-6400

**Fleur de Lys,** 777 Sutter Street, 673-7779

**Woodward's Garden,** 1700 Mission Street at Duboce, 621-7122

**Café Jacqueline,** 1454 Grant Avenue, 981-5565

**Cafe Mozart,** 708 Bush Street, 391-8480

**Cafe Kati,** 1963 Sutter Street, 775-7313

**The Meeting House,** 1701 Octavia Street, 922-6733

## Romance in the 'Hood

There are certain concert venues that are so exceptional, for one reason or another, that I'll go to a show there almost regardless of who's playing. The Greek Theatre is one of them (can't beat the views of the stage and the bay); the **Noe Valley Ministry** is another. This little church auditorium provides an incredibly intimate concert experience, and you'd be amazed at the performers they slip in the back door—Gypsy Kings, Box Set, Tracy Chapman, Jonathan Richman, X. For obvious reasons (and even if you're not sure of your companion's musical tastes), this is great place to take a date. Begin the evening at **Elisa's Health Spa** with a dip in a cozy, outdoor Jacuzzi (suits optional) and a sauna or steam. Tucked behind the Star Magic store, this neighborhood spa has been soothing sore muscles for more than twenty years. Next, walk up to **Bacco's,** easily the most romantic Italian restaurant this side of Twin Peaks. Order the risotto or gnocchi—both out of this world—and a bottle of chianti, or ask for the chef's recommendation (sometimes they put together special romantic, prix fixe dinners). From here proceed to the ministry for your living room concert. Unlike the big arenas, if the seats are all taken, they'll often let you sit on the stage behind the performer—it's like having a backstage pass without knowing the bouncer.

## Cruise and Snooze

*Note: this is more of an anniversary date than a first date, as the sleeping arrangements don't leave much room for ambiguity.*

There's nothing like a moonlight cruise to put you in the mood— the ocean breeze in your hair, the lights of the Bay Bridge reflecting off the water, the fog horns calling forlornly to anyone who'll listen. Begin with a sunset ferry ride to **Jack London Square** (the Oakland/ Alameda fleet leaves from Pier 39 and the Ferry Building every two hours or so); ride topside if it's not too cold, so you can see the under- side of the bridge as you pass beneath its vast span. From the Oakland docks, it's a short stroll along the main drag, past shops and restau- rants and wharfy knick-knack parlors, to **Yoshi's,** for an evening of top-notch jazz and Japanese food (make sure to order lots of sake). The club, which moved to the Oakland waterfront in 1997, features some of the biggest and best names in the business—from Joe Henderson to Tito Puente. After the show, when your date is starting to wonder how you're going to get home, lead him or her to the *Voyager,* a 46-foot ketch-rigged sailboat docked in the marina looking out over the bay to the San Francisco skyline. The *Voyager* is one of six yachts that make up the East Bay arm of **Dockside Boat & Bed,** a sort of floating bed and breakfast inn (another seven are moored at Pier 39, but it's hard to imagine a romantic evening shouting over sea lions and dodging instamatic cameras). For between $110 and $270 a night, you can sleep aboard a private luxury yacht equipped with TV/VCR, stereo, sundeck, wet bar, coffeemaker, and continental break- fast. For an all-out mush fest, charter the boat (captain provided) for a cruise and a catered candlelight dinner. Pretend you're Jean-Paul Belmondo and Brigitte Bardot as you dance in the moonlight with the ocean lapping against the hull, letting the waves work their magic.

## WHERE TO STAY

**The Archbishop's Mansion** is a sumptuous, restored 1904 Victorian mansion where you get to have breakfast in bed, take baths by candle- light in a claw-foot tub, and sip brandy in front of the fireplace. It all adds up to the ultimate honeymoon (or popping the question) hotel.

Even though I grew up here and can never fully realize the wondrous revelation of seeing San Francisco for the very first time, I imagine that for many it's a life-changing experience. I mean—if I can still get choked up at the sight of a cable car silhouetted against the sunset, just think what that could do for an impressionable person from Louisiana.

# Tour 8 San Francisco Virgins

Playing tour guide to an SF virgin is a wonderful thing for a number of reasons:

1. It's easy—they've never been anyplace, so everything's new and exciting and amazing—even that lady with the space-alien lights in her hair that plays the accordian and sings "Feelin' Groovy."

2. You're required by the laws of hospitality to go to all those "tourist" places you'd never dream of visiting otherwise (but were secretly dying to see), and you can blame it on your guests.

3. There's nothing quite like seeing your old, familiar haunts through the eyes of a neophyte—a great way to renew your romance with the city.

# MORNING-NOON

With first-timers, itineraries are a little more important than with other types of guests, because there's a lot to squeeze into a day. Tours should be geared around areas where you can park and walk to a number of places, or where there's a logical progression in one direction. If your virgins are fairly fit and not afraid of a little traipsing, start out early Saturday morning in **Chinatown,** when the merchants are setting up shop. The streets fill with the smell of simmering soups and barbecue pork buns; in the windows are hanging roast ducks (heads still attached) and bizarre delicacies (at least to most Westerners) like armadillo, turtle, and pigs' noses; and on the sidewalks are bins of embroidered slippers, wooden toys, and rice-paper candies. At about 10:30 or 11 a.m., scope out a dim sum parlor. The choices are endless, and it's actually hard to go wrong anywhere in Chinatown, but if your friends are not terribly adventurous, try the **Golden Dragon,** where you can get all the standards—pork and shrimp dumplings, roast duck, pot stickers, and sticky rice and sausage wrapped in a lotus leaf.

Location is the prime reason to try the **Hang Ah Tea Room,** which—in the tradition of the American "Breakfast Anytime" diner— serves dim sum until 9 p.m. Billed as the oldest dim sum place in Chinatown (established in 1920—the management claims some of the cooks have been here since then), it's located below street level on a tiny back alley called Pagoda Place, at the junction of even tinier Hang Ah Street. As you descend the steps, you half expect to see old Chinese men with long braids sitting cross-legged on pillows smoking opium pipes. But once you're inside, it's just your basic, no frills Chinese restaurant. For those who don't like weird food surprises, you can get traditional sweet-and-sour dishes here, as well as dim sum such as shrimp toast, foil-wrapped chicken, and steamed pork buns.

For more interesting variety and a Hong Kong atmosphere, try the enormous, three-story **Gold Mountain,** where steaming carts whiz by faster than traffic moves on Broadway, and where it's occasionally hard to hear yourself over the roar of the chattering—mostly Chinese—crowd. Dare your friends to close their eyes and point at a dish, regardless of what may be in it (the waitresses don't speak enough English to tell you anyway). Besides, half the fun is in the not knowing. (Hint to newcomers: if it looks like chicken feet, it probably is.) **Pearl City** is an inexpensive, good bet for the more adventurous palate. The mysterious-looking wrapped bundles are filled with everything from scallops and taro to sweet beans. (To my mind, the two best dim sum parlors in the city are **Yank Sing** and **Harbor Village,** neither of which is located in Chinatown. So if it's just excellent food and not atmosphere you're striving for, then skip the above and make one of these restaurants your morning destination.)

After brunch, wander through Ross Alley, making a gratuitous stop to watch the little old ladies carefully fold bits of wisdom into wing-shaped cookies at the **Golden Gate Fortune Cookie Factory** (more on this in the Pesky Kids tour), and up to Waverly Place. From the street, these apartment buildings don't look too inviting—a little rundown, many with locked gates. But look up and it's a whole different world. Incense wafts from the ornate painted balconies, colorful Chinese paper lanterns swing in the breeze. Out-of-towners might feel apprehensive about going inside, but if they can handle four flights of stairs, they'll be rewarded with an amazing vision of pre-twentieth-century Chinese religious life. **Tin Hou Temple,** dedicated to the Queen of the Heavens and allegedly the oldest Chinese temple in San Francisco, is the one to visit with neophytes. Step inside the gate, and suddenly you're not in Kansas anymore. The ceiling is festooned with dozens of lanterns hung with red prayer papers and gilded miniature dioramas of villages. On one side, oranges, tangerines, flowers, and incense surround photos of loved ones who've passed away; on the other, there's an altar with ornate antique Buddhas and other intricately carved religious figures. On the balcony, an ancient Chinese woman burns incense and folds prayer papers. Encourage your friends to make a traditional offering by stuffing a dollar or two inside one of the small red envelopes at the front table.

From here, wander north along Grant Avenue until you hit the corner of Columbus. Prep your guests for the culture shock by stopping for a photo op at the intersection of Columbus and Broadway. Turn around and the Columbus Tower, in all its patina green flatiron glory is perfectly juxtaposed against the TransAmerica Pyramid, making it seem like they're right next to each other.

As you walk up Columbus into North Beach, start whistling the famous aria from *The Marriage of Figaro* or "That's Amore." If your visitors are literary types, take a quick dip in **City Lights Bookstore** and **Vesuvio,** explaining the whole beatnik/Jack Kerouac connection (more on this in the Neo-Bohemians tour). Then zip across the street and into the **Condor Bistro,** nowadays a fine, upstanding establishment, but once (as you may recall) the site of the first-ever topless club in California—a fact that always seems to satisfy the expectations of small-town folk who like to envision San Francisco as a wild, decadent, anything-goes kind of city. In 1964, dancer Carol Doda made headlines when, with the aid of silicon injections, she went from a 36B to a 36DD overnight. Doda's titillating topless act included descending on the hydraulically operated white piano that now hangs from the ceiling of the bistro. Her original "topless bathing suit," along with the old marquee sporting the famous blinking nipples, are part of a small shrine in the cocktail lounge dedicated to the club's risque heyday. Newspaper clips along the wall give the place historical grounding; you can score extra points with first-timers by filling in the gory details of the incident involving the stripper found one morning in a very compromising position (naked on top of the piano, sandwiched between the ceiling and the club manager, who'd had a fatal heart attack).

Though not nearly as prurient in their connotation, the salamis that swing from the rafters at **Molinari's Deli** up the street are no less an integral part of North Beach's history, and a must-stop for virgins. Opened in 1896, the deli exudes mangia mangia spirit from every pore. Make your way past the jars of anchovies, artichokes, olive oils, pasta, and tomato sauces, past the glass cases filled with coppa, mozzarella, marinated red peppers and mushrooms, calamari et al., and up to the counter. Grab a hard roll from the box, hand it to the nice Italian man behind the counter, and get him to make you a peppersalami sandwich with all the trimmings. Carry your precious cargo as directly as possible to **Washington Square Park** for a picnic (you might need to make a stop on the way at **Biordi,** the wonderful Italian pottery and hand-painted ceramics store). After you get comfortable on the lawn, gaze up at the spires of Saints Peter and Paul Church. Then send your friends on a quick jaunt to **Liguria** bakery on the northeast corner of the park. Probably they're thinking they couldn't possibly pile anything on top of that sandwich, but the smell of fresh, steaming focaccia will change their minds. The small bakery with its old-fashioned ovens was founded on this spot by three brothers from Genoa in 1911. Still run by members of the family, Liguria does nothing but make three or four kinds of focaccia bread every day. Locals line up around the block for it, and when the shop runs out, they close. (If you can't eat it now, save it for a late-afternoon snack.)

This may sound a little weird, but those **self-cleaning French toilets** are a nifty novelty for those who've never tried them (locals included), and there happens to be one located right on the south border of Washington Square, a perfect pit-stop on your way to Grant Avenue. Deposit a quarter in the slot and watch the magic door slide open. Step inside, do your business, exit swiftly (there's actually a time limit of twenty minutes, so don't get caught with your pants down), and then listen as the little machines inside make all kinds of strange sanitizing noises. You'll have to deposit another quarter to admire the sparkling results of their handiwork.

**LEVI'S FACTORY MUSEUM**

For foreign virgins who will often stop at nothing to get their hands on a pair of authentic red-line Levi's, a tour of the old Levi Strauss factory on Valencia Street is a must. Built in 1906, the plant, housed inside a cheery yellow-and-white wooden gingerbread building, still churns out 501s like it did in the old days. Tours are conducted Tuesday and Wednesday mornings by appointment. After a visit to the sewing rooms where piles of blue jeans lie in wait for shipping, stop in at the small Levi's museum, and learn about the history of the famous copper-riveted, leather-label miners' pants.

Grant Avenue has always held a mysterious allure. There's something about the mix of divey bars, impossibly tiny storefronts crammed with assorted bric-a-brac, and cozy European cafes that makes you feel like you've discovered something no one else knows about. I have a revelation each time I walk down this crooked backstreet—a faux-leopard-collar jacket in the used-clothing shop; a vintage poster in Show Biz, the movie memorabilia store; great sangria at the North End Caffè. Let your friends wander aimlessly along the avenue for as long as they want; just make sure they eventually find their way into **Quantity Postcards.** Amid the flying saucers, clowns, and other salvaged spoils from Playland-at-the-Beach are thousands of incredibly strange and wonderful postcards—not a one of them your garden variety "Weather is fine; wish you were here" types. Among my favorites: tacky '50s ads for oil cans, vacuums, and nudist colonies; old fruit and vegetable crate labels; pictures of office buildings and factories in obscure towns in the Midwest; and bad celebrity mugshots. There's even a selection of preowned, already written cards (some from the '20s and '30s), full of details about other people's fabulous vacations in San Francisco—in case your friends can't be bothered. Often the most entertaining postcard is the free one you get with your purchase, selected by the proprietor (if it's a photo of nuclear holocaust, just smile, nod, and make a beeline for the exit).

Not finishing an afternoon in North Beach with an espresso at an Italian *caffè* is tantamount to sacrilege on a virgins tour. With postcards in hand, head down to **Caffè Trieste** and sit at one of the sidewalk tables. Once an arty beatnik hangout (it opened in 1956), Trieste is run by the Giottas, the city's only opera-singing, coffee-making family, who perform popular Italian songs and arias on Saturday afternoons. Get a double latte (fresh-roasted next door and served perfectly—with the dark stuff still separated from the steamed milk in your glass), then settle into a chair and write a missive to Mom, as the strains of "Santa Lucia" waft out the door and the scenesters pore over dog-eared copies of Bukowski.

Just before sunset, stroll down to the opposite end of Grant Avenue (between Chestnut and Francisco) and look for the staircase leading up to **Jack Early Park,** one of those stumble-upon-it spots that never fails to make newcomers shake their heads in delight and amazement. The "park," built by neighborhood resident Jack Early in 1962, is actually not much more than a scenic overlook at the top of a set of zigzag steps, which are flanked by a well-kempt garden. But there's something about the hiddenness and the hush of the square platform, with its old-fashioned lamppost, that feels secret and special. Lean out over the railing and gaze down onto Fisherman's Wharf, as the barges plow through the bay, and the call of the mournful fog horns and barking sea lions drifts overhead. Behind you, the million-dollar mansions of Telegraph Hill look on approvingly. Request a moment of silence and let the sounds of the city seep into your soul. Then watch your starry-eyed friends for signs of a perfect San Francisco moment.

## Filbert Street Steps

Perhaps no single place captures the have-your-cake-and-eat-it spirit of San Francisco better than the **Greenwich and Filbert Streets Steps.** Though they sit smack dab in the heart of the city, they exist almost separate from it—an intimate, magical Eden perched against the precariously steep slopes of Telegraph Hill. The cottages that flank the wooden stairs along Napier Lane and Darrell Place enjoy the rare privilege of an auto-free environment, yet they boast the most coveted views of the bay money can buy. Look to the side and you'll feel like you're in a French village—cats lolling beneath vine-covered walls lapping up tin pans of milk, flower pots spilling over the walkway, watering cans propping open stylishly rusted gates. Look back and you're engulfed by Grace Marchant's beloved terraced garden of baby tears, clamboring roses, and bougainvillea—lush and overgrown, yet all but invisible to the world. Look up and you'll wonder if you're on the right continent—flitting through the treetops are flocks of South American and Amazonian parrots, macaws, and canary-winged parakeets, once caged household pets, now happily undomesticated and breeding in the warm banana trees. Look out and the harbor spreads before you, with the East Bay shimmering dreamily in the distance. If you happen to time it just right, and your friends are here around Halloween, take them down the steps in the evening, when the Telegraph Hill dwellers light up dozens of jack-o'-lanterns for the trick-or-treaters.

On your way up or down the steps, be sure to point out significant sites: the art deco apartment house at 1360 Montgomery Street that was the facade used in the Humphrey Bogart/Lauren Bacall flick, *Dark Passage;* the hole on the hill just before you descend to Sansome Street where a house came crashing down a couple of years ago; the miniature trompe l'oeil doggie park on Montgomery Street just above the steps, with its adorable mural of an alluring poodle and a tempting fire hydrant; and of course **Julius' Castle,** the venerable romantic restaurant with the above-average (and expensive) food, whose views of the bay remain unchallenged in the city.

## Doing the Wharf Thing

When you're dealing with San Francisco novices, there are certain visitation requirements, and Fisherman's Wharf is one of them. It doesn't matter that you'd rather spend an afternoon in Turlock. First-timers want to see what all the hype is about, and as host, it's your duty to deliver them to it. So why not make the best of it? The wharf may even surprise you. If you can weed through the sidewalk sketch artists, the piles of "I Escaped from Alcatraz" T-shirts, the churro sticks, and the wind-up cable cars, you might even find a few things worth seeing.

Begin at the **Maritime Museum** and spend a few minutes studying the nineteenth-century renderings and photos of the old waterfront, when clipper ships graced this C-shaped inner harbor. Then step out onto the back veranda, squint your eyes a little bit, and with the help of the historic ships docked nearby (especially the *Balclutha*, an 1883 square rigger that once sailed around Cape Horn and looks like a giant prop for a swashbuckling pirate flick), you can imagine these waters a hundred years ago. Go down the steps and walk around **Aquatic Park,** making sure to point out the old men in the orange caps (members of the Dolphin Club) swimming in the bay as if it were their own private pool. For some odd reason, not too many people (other than Marina district joggers and fishermen) seem to venture out onto Municipal Pier at the west end. Silly them. The long, curving walkway arcs around to the edge of the harbor and into the bay, where you can hobnob with the fishermen and get show-stopping views of the port and Alcatraz. (Caution: if seen at sunset, this vista may very well cause your friends from Buffalo to put a "For Sale" sign on their front lawn.)

Next, head east through **Maritime National Historical Park,** and board at least one of the boats. Most opt for the *Balclutha*, because it's the most showy, but the *C.A. Thayer*, an 1895 three-mast lumber schooner, and the hardworking tugboat *Hercules* are equally interesting. In the spring and fall, the *C.A. Thayer* hosts the Festival of the Sea and a music series—a tribute to the nautical life in melodrama and song.

From here make your way past Pier 45, where what's left of the fishing fleet delivers its catch early in the morning, and on to the dreaded **Pier 39.** Honestly (and even your trailer-trash cousins from Middle-of-Nowhere, Florida, will agree on this one), this is one seriously tacky tourist trap. But if you can stop struggling and accept that, you might actually enjoy yourself. First off, visit the sea lions on the west-side docks. People invariably seem to forget that these barking, belching, herring-eating buffoons, now considered one of the numerous attractions on the pier, chose to come here *all on their own*, and not as part of some elaborate fake set-up. It's still amazing to see them lying all over each other, fighting for sunbathing space, and bobbing around the harbor like it was Sea Lion Week at Club Med. Probably the only other thing worth checking out at Pier 39, aside from the juggling and magic acts, which are always worth a few chuckles, and the City Store (see the Green Types tour), is the old **Eagle Cafe.** In one of the rare instances where big developers actually listened to the voice of the people, the turn-of-the-century bar and cafe—once a favorite hangout of dockworkers and literati—was saved from the wrecking ball by picking it up lock, stock, and barrel and depositing it on the second level of the pier. Order a Bloody Mary and a plate of eggs and admire the photos and memorabilia that tell a tale of the waterfront before the carnival moved in.

From the outside, **Lou's Pier 47** seems like it might be one of those bars that push expensive cocktails and cheesy disco dancing (à la Houlihan's), but it's not. The second-story bar is one of the few places where you can hear live music—specifically blues—all day, every day. Admittedly, some of the bands are reminiscent of those you hear at high school reunions, but some of them are local favorites and genuine talents (hey—a gig's a gig). Either way, it's a nice little break from the madding crowd.

From Lou's head west to the Cannery and the **Museum of the City of San Francisco** (located on the third floor), a small, charming exhibit of San Francisco artifacts and memorabilia. Virgins will enjoy the photographs of the 1906 earthquake and fire, and fun souvenirs such as Earthquake in a Can. You might get a kick out of the collection of old film projectors, the painted wall map of the original Forty-Nine-Mile Drive, and the trinkets and programs salvaged from the California Mid-Winter Fair, the Golden Gate World's Fair, and the Pan-Pacific Exposition.

Now you're ready for an Irish coffee at the **Buena Vista Cafe.** Sit at the bar (not a table) and watch the deft bartenders line 'em in a long row and pour 'em—creamy and perfect. The cocktail was not invented here, but it was the late *San Francisco Chronicle* columnist Stanton Delaplane who brought the recipe back from Dublin in 1952, and a Buena Vista bartender who re-created it for the first time stateside.

Next: dinner. When a-million-and-one tourists head to a seafood restaurant on Fisherman's Wharf, locals naturally assume it sucks, and run in the opposite direction. It's a matter of personal pride. But you've gotta ask yourself, What keeps bringing these people back? The hype? The enormous cocktails? A lack of imagination? Maybe, just

maybe, there's some merit in the *maré*. I think that's definitely true of
**Alioto's** and **Scoma's.** For first-timers, the fish-receiving station at Scoma's
is a big bonus, a chance to see the wharf actually at work. The building
boasts big windows where you can watch the daily catch being hoisted from
fishing boats onto big tables, where it's cleaned, filleted, declawed, etc. The
famous crab comes in November through May; salmon season is May
through September; and you don't have to get up at dawn to catch all the
action. Local fisherman are notoriously irregular with their deliveries; it all
depends on which way (and how hard) the wind is blowing. The restaurant
is tucked in at the end of Pier 45, on a suprisingly quiet stretch of the wharf,
fronting a small arm of the harbor. Maybe its hidden location is one of the
keys to Scoma's unflagging popularity—who knows? Wharf restaurateurs
have been trying to figure out for years what makes this the highest gross-
ing restaurant in California. On any given day, the menu offers maybe a
dozen kinds of fresh fish and shellfish, including (when seasonal)
swordfish, ahi tuna, halibut, snapper, salmon, sole, sanddabs, oysters, and
scallops. This is also a great place to eat if your virgins have kids (an oxy-
moron?). Besides the fish-handling station (a huge child-pleaser), Scoma's
has placemats kids can color and a special children's menu that offers
nonfishy food.

For sheer historical value, you owe first-timers a lunch or dinner at
Alioto's, where practically everyone is named Nunzio and where authentic
San Francisco cioppino (the Italian shellfish stew made with crab and red
sauce) was first popularized. If you've never been to Alioto's, you're in for a
surprise. The food is good. And it's not just your run-of-the-mill grilled fish
with a pile of sauce on top. The seafood risotto rivals just about any in town,
the seafood sausage stuffed with lobster and other delicacies is made fresh
daily, and the cioppino is hearty and messy and chock-full of fresh shellfish.
Descendents of the original Sicilian family who opened this place as a walkaway fish stand back in the 1920s still run the ship (Nunzio Sr., well into
his eighties, mans the door).

Finish off the evening with a ride on the cable car back to downtown.
At night, when the crowds have died down, your virgin friends can truly
appreciate the concept of riding "halfway to the stars" the way Tony Bennett
described it.

## Other Statutory Stops
You can take 'em or leave 'em, but the first-timers love 'em. In brief:

**Walking across the Golden Gate Bridge**—As the fog buffets you around like
a cat toy and the sailboats disappear into the mist, sing a rousing version of
"San Francisco, open your Golden Gate . . ." or "California Here I Come."

**Cocktails at sunset at the Cliff House**—Go ahead, get sappy. Applaud when the sun dips below the horizon. That's why you come here. A hipper alternative is English ale at the **Beach Chalet** overlooking the schools of hot, young surfers.

**Beach Blanket Babylon**—There's a reason this is the longest-running musical revue in history. It's funny, it's lively, it's clever, it's got ridiculously gargantuan hats. And where else are you ever going to see a chorus line of men in togas, sandals, and bald caps singing "I'm a Yankee Doodle Ghandi?"

**Driving Highway 1**—Doesn't matter how many times you've done it, every time you come over the crest near Devil's Slide it takes your breath away. The precipitously winding road that skirts those sheer cliffs, the sun-bleached beaches, and the wild green surf is nothing short of miraculous. Rent a convertible and do it right.

**Alcatraz Island**—The best tour for your tourist buck. Spend the extra $2 and get the audio narration of the cellhouse, which features tales of The Rock told by former guards and inmates. Sit in the solitary confinement cell. Stare out at the city from the ferry docks and imagine the tantalizing agony of being so close to San Francisco and not ever being able to set foot on her shores.

**Sam Woh**—The food, she stinks. But like the **House of Nanking** (where the food's much better, but the lines are longer), dining here is a San Francisco tradition. In the old days, when the impossibly narrow, rickety restaurant was run by hilarious dictator Edsel Ford Fong, you couldn't beat the place for atmosphere. These days it's tamer, but you still have to walk through the kitchen and up the staircase to get to the dining rooms, the sink is still in the middle of the room (remember to wash your hands), and if chow fun noodles are your bag, you can still get big, sloppy platefuls of 'em here.

**Wine Tasting**—Okay, admit it. You love doing this as much as they do. But not when you have to sit bumper-to-bumper with a bunch of drunks on Highway 29. So do yourself and your novice friends a favor and bypass Napa Valley for the verdant vineyards of the Russian River region, where tastings are free and picnic grounds are plentiful. Head up Highway 101 past Santa Rosa to River Road and follow it to the string of picturesque wineries along Westside Road, in particular **Davis Bynum, Rochioli, Hop Kiln,** and **Rabbit Ridge.** Rochioli makes a great pinot noir and has lovely picnic tables that overlook a vineyard; the Hop Kiln tasting room next door is housed inside a historic stone building that was once used to dry hops for beer making. Rabbit Ridge and Davis Bynum are equally pretty, and they make wines that are simply out of this world.

## Going to Extremes

I like to call this the "-est" tour. It's the one where you get in the car and take your friends who hail from the flatlands down the steep*est* streets and crooked*est* streets, and up to the high*est* summits for the suprem*est* views of the city. Virgins love it because it's the San Francisco they see in all those car-chase movie scenes. You love it because you get to pretend you're Karl Malden in a forgotten episode of *Streets of San Francisco*.

Steepest streets—There are two—**Filbert** between Hyde and Leavenworth, and **Hill Street** at Twenty-Second. Milk it for all its worth. Drive very slowly to the top. Inch the nose of the car over the crest. To the untrained eye, it seems like you're about to drop off the edge of the earth. Wait for the gasps and white knuckles on the back of the seat, then plunge over the edge while laughing maniacally.

Crooked streets—Wait in line and do the requisite serpentine ride down **Lombard Street.** Let the kids hang out the sunroof. Take the photo looking down Hyde Street. Then hang a right at the bottom of the hill and go three blocks to Union Street and take them down **Macondray Lane.** The tiny, tucked-away street, with its rickety wooden walkway and apartments hidden amid overgrown vines, was the model for the fictional Barbary Lane of Armistead Maupin's *Tales of the City* books.

Afterward, go to the back of Potrero Hill and show them the real "crookedest street in the world"—minus all the hype and tourists. The end of **Vermont Street** packs more thrilling twists and turns into its eight switchbacks than Lombard; plus the views are almost as good, and you get the added bonus of landing in the Mission district, home of the best burritos this side of Tijuana.

High Points—Though the city was built around seven main peaks, there are actually forty-three hills in San Francisco, all of them with something to say about the lay of the land.

**Twin Peaks—**The granddaddy of inspiration points, offers a view of the city and environs to the east, north, and south. The only problem with this over-look is the freezing, blowing fog that often engulfs it and obscures views. If that's the case, drive down to the perch just below it, either on Diamond Heights Boulevard just as it rounds the bend to Safeway, or at the top of Upper Market Street, where the the tip of the Pyramid and the lights of the Bay Bridge are just a little more tangible.

Twentieth and Church Streets (Dolores Park)—Sit at a bench at the top of the park and downtown jumps out at you like a children's pop-up book.

Tank Hill—Go up Stanyan Street to the very tip-top, hang a left at Belgrave Park. Hike up the dirt path. Be prepared to gasp. To the left, the Golden Gate Bridge, the Pacific, Golden Gate Park, and Saint Ignatius; to the right, downtown, the Pyramid, the Bay Bridge, and the East Bay.

Nineteenth and Texas Streets—The best point on Potrero Hill from which to survey the downtown landscape. Ironically, the house on the corner was the main setting for the movie *Pacific Heights*.

Marin Headlands—This is *the* postcard view of San Francisco. Nothing beats watching the fog roll in through the Golden Gate. Take the first turnoff after the bridge onto Conzelman Road.

# NIGHT

There are so many restaurants that do California cuisine (or some variation on the theme), that when the uninitiated ask "Where's the best place?" you invariably look at them stupidly and say, "Um, I know this great Thai restaurant. . . ." What they want, of course, is the stuff they've been reading about in *Zagat's* and *Gourmet* magazine. Here's where you should take them:

**Chez Panisse**—Unlike Stars, which rides an ever-dimming reputation, the restaurant that invented California cuisine nearly thirty years ago still makes exquisite food—homey, flavorful, simple, and using the freshest fish, game, and produce from local (mostly organic) farms and ranches. I once had a summer tomato salad with goat cheese there that made me weep with joy. Reservations are not optional at the downstairs restaurant, which serves a nightly four-course, prix fixe menu for (at last check) $68 on weekends, not including tax, wine, and a 15 percent gratuity that's automatically tacked on to the bill. It ain't cheap, and even with your month-in-advance reservations you may have to wait a few minutes (people love to linger), but it's worth it.

If the price isn't right, or you didn't have time to plan in advance, the upstairs casual cafe is a good second choice, pulling its Mediterranean-inspired menu from the same refrigerators, but offering a wide range of à la carte items at prices that average about $20 for an entree. They don't take dinner reservations Fridays and Saturdays (you may go through a bottle of wine waiting at the bar), but they do take a limited number of same-day reservations Monday through Thursday.

**Vertigo**—Nestled at the base of the TransAmerica Pyramid, the dizzying view of the triangular tower through the copper-mesh ceiling and skylights is a huge crowd-pleaser. The fabulous food (lots of innovative seafood dishes) is icing on the cake.

**Cafe Kati**—Kirk Webber creates dishes that are as beautiful as they are tasty—sculptural creations, really—with curlicue vegetables, towers of spun sugar, and hieroglyphic drizzles. Diminutive Cafe Kati was one of the first of a wave of "fusion" restaurants that married the flavors of India, Thailand, the Pacific Islands, and China to California homegrown meats and vegetables.

**Globe**—Meat on the menu, what a concept—and all of it prepared exquisitely. Frankly, I've never had lamb so good. And don't overlook the baked mussels, shrimp, and scallops, which are served on a plate with indentations that coddle the shellfish in their own individual garlic-butter bath. Another great touch: salads and soups served in giant handmade pottery dishes and mixing bowls.

**LuLu**—It's hard to beat this cavernous room for its lively see-and-be-seen scene. Plus, the menu reads like the dictionary definition of California cuisine: wood-fired rosemary chicken, skillet-roasted mussels, thin-crusted pizzettas, garlic-and-olive-oil mashed potatoes, and pasta dishes overflowing with vegetables straight from the organic garden. Who cares if you can't hear yourself think?

**Zuni Cafe**—Judy Rogers's original house of Cal-Med cuisine was doing wood-fired meats long before LuLu was even a blip on the screen. The crowd is Hayes Valley meets Pacific Heights; the decor is neo-industrial meets New Mexico. Lots of attitude and good smells. All in all, pure San Francisco.

**Ristorante Ecco**—The quasi-obscure trendy South Park neighborhood is guaranteed to impress all on its own. Couple that with some great Cal-Ital cuisine, and they'll be talking about you for years.

# WHERE TO STAY

Though I generally prefer to stay in off-beat, cozy boutique hotels, San Francisco virgins will probably get the most from one of the Nob Hill grande dames—the **Mark Hopkins,** the **Fairmont,** or the **Huntington.** Of these, the Huntington is the most personable (it's still family-owned), though not as kept-up as the other two. The Mark really feels like a grande dame, with its venerable skyroom lounge and its sweeping driveway entrance. The Fairmont has its reputation and its stint on TV (as the hotel in the show *Hotel*) going for it, plus all those international flags and plush, red velvet interiors.

On the modern end of the scale, two hotels show off San Francisco's stylish side in the best light. The decor at the **Hotel Triton** is court jester playroom meets Mount Olympus—squiggly-back chairs topped with giant tassles, undulating pillars covered in gold leaf, spiraling floor lamps, walls painted in harlequin checkers, tables that jut out at odd angles, royal blue carpeting emblazoned with stars. Your friends will get a kick out of the hotel's suites, a number of which were designed by artistic celebrities, including the late Jerry Garcia, Joe Boxer, Wyland, and Carlos Santana. The rooms are small, but nice and—a bonus for foreigners—the hotel lies adjacent to a cafe that carries all the international periodicals—from French *Vogue* to *The Tatler*.

Up on Geary Street, just off the theater district, the **Hotel Monaco** blooms larger than life, like an art nouveau poster for the golden age of travel. It's not as wacky as the Triton, but more impressive because of its soaring scale (the decor makes the rooms feel a lot bigger than they are). The front desk, with its colorful luggage labels, looks like a giant steamer trunk. And the **Grand Cafe** next door, with its whimsical iron sculptures and grand light fixture, is like being in an American bistro set in a Paris train station. Don't forget to order the polenta soufflé.

Fellow longtime party animals have complained to me of late that San Francisco just isn't as much fun as it used to be. They say that, as opposed to the City That Never Sleeps, San Francisco has its teeth brushed, its jammies on, and is curled up with a pint of Häagen Dazs by midnight.

# Tour 9 Extroverts

That's just not true. While some of us are becoming less and less inclined to stay up for the third band (and more and more excited by the prospect of watching *Letterman* in bed), at least when we do stay up, we're usually out there with arms flailing and sweat flying. I've been to other parts of the country where a rousing show of appreciation amounts to standing six feet away from the stage, meticulously avoiding eye contact, and simply maintaining a face that's chiseled into an expression of delight.

Californians still know how to have a good time. Historically we're famous for wearing our fun on our sleeves (and our shoes, and occasionally our wet T-shirts). And while perhaps some of us have toned it down a tad—faced with the inevitable burden of two-day hangovers and the Monday morning dreads—there are still plenty of places where an extroverted gal or guy on holiday can dance on a table and not raise an eyebrow.

# MORNING

After that first cup of good, strong coffee, you'll want to take your chatty, outgoing type to a friendly diner, or a place with a good core of regulars and waiters with plenty of attitude. **It's Tops Diner** is one straight out of the books (since 1952), complete with gum-popping waitresses in pink uniforms and cat-eye glasses, who look as if they should have night jobs as back-up singers for Lisa Loeb. Counter seating is essential for maximum conversation with the It's Tops clientele—a motley crew that ranges from twenty-something musicians coming off all-night benders to Castro and lower Haight habitués and Union Local 319 workers. Ordering tip: the eggs are damn good, but the blueberry and banana pancakes are the real ticket. For an Edward (or Dennis) Hopper-esque experience, come here during the wee hours (they're open til 3 a.m. Wednesday through Saturday) and take advantage of $1.75 Anchor Steam pints, or have a slice of lemon meringue pie and a malt made in an authentic, stainless steel 1950s Carnation milkshake machine.

Down in the Castro, nothing rocks at brunch like **The Patio,** an indoor/outdoor tropical greenhouse restaurant tucked in back of the Skin Zone. Highlights of this place include tables strategically placed for maximum eavesdropping on really dishy morning-after conversations, waiters with so much attitude you'd think they were method actors, fun fruity cocktails (some with umbrellas—c'mon, it's nearly noon; you're ready for a drink), and seriously yummy eggs Benedict.

For all-around gregariousness though, **Twenty-Fourth Street** in Noe Valley might just win the prize. With three coffeehouses, two bagel shops, and several bakeries crammed into a four-block stretch, extroverts can turn breakfast into a progressive meal. Best benches and stoops to squat on are outside **Martha & Brothers Coffee,** which is conveniently located next to **Holey Bagel.** The regular coffee klatch here will rope you into a discussion about jogging, El Salvador, or what's in the headlines faster than you can say double decaf nonfat latte. The party continues down at **Spinelli,** which is spitting distance from Holey's classy cousin, the Posh Bagel, as well as Bakers of Paris and the homespun Noe Valley Bakery and Bread Company.

On Saturday mornings, if you're not sleeping off last night's martinis, head down to Fort Mason for the live taping of National Public Radio's **West Coast Live** radio show. Each week, host Sedge Thomson (his name alone is worth the $10 price of admission) interviews a fascinating array of musicians, authors, wits, and wags. Audience members are often recruited to create sound effects, talk about what brought them to the show, and participate in regular segments such as "True Fiction Magazine," a hilarious, created-on-the-spot sketch performed by the show's resident improv players.

If *West Coast Live* is the PBS of local radio shows, the **Johnny Steele Show** weekday mornings on Live 105 would have to be the Fox network. Johnny's predecessor, Alex Bennett, was known for being racy, raunchy, sophomoric, and downright tasteless at times; Johnny has toned it down a bit and brought up the intelligence level. Unfortunately, the show now only features a live studio audience on Fridays. For out-of-towners, Johnny and his daily cast of comedians, columnists, pop culture figures, and downright odd characters offer unique insight into San Francisco life—where, as we know, everyday reality can often be stranger than fiction. Though the studio audience doesn't usually get to do a whole lot (besides whooping it up at the appropriate moments and serving as a sort of dysfunctional laugh track), extroverts will no doubt enjoy the thrill of knowing that their colorful side commentary is being heard from here to Vallejo. One other caveat: the show runs from 6 to 9:30 a.m.—not exactly extrovert hours.

# NOON

## Nude Beaches: Daytime...and the Dipping Is Skinny

Contrary to what some people believe, an extrovert is not what you get when you cross an exhibitionist with a pervert, although you may encounter a little of both when strolling along some of the Bay Area's best nude beaches. Nude beaches are great places to take your uninhibited friends. They're also terrific spots to take repressed friends to whom you want to give a big California slap on the ass.

**North Baker Beach,** the most popular naked spot in the city, has a few drawbacks—it rarely gets warm enough in the city to make lounging around outside in the nude a relaxing pastime (and even the most committed extrovert is helpless against the biological inevitability of shrinkage and high beams). The other possible detraction, at least for some, is that Baker sometimes attracts a largely male (gay) population, particularly at the north end—spillover from Land's End Beach next door. This being said, for the debriefed, Baker Beach still holds an irresistible allure. There's something wildly exhilarating about being able to walk around without clothes on in the middle of the city, sipping a Calistoga, taking in spectacular views of the Golden Gate—and not get arrested.

If you're looking for a more blue-collar nude beach experience in the city, try **Fort Funston.** Mellow nakedness takes place primarily on weekdays, and the beach doesn't attract as many poseurs as Baker. This is a good place to take extroverts who still have some deep-seated privacy issues.

Down the peninsula, where it's warmer, there are a number of places to let it all hang out, but a perennial favorite is **San Gregorio State Beach** (off Highway 1, ten miles south of Half Moon Bay). There are three big advantages to this beach: location, location, and location. The experience begins with the drive down Highway 1—the kind of glorious, sea-spraying, cliff-hanging, sunlight-dancing, so-this-is-what they-mean-by-the-Golden-State journey that makes you want to rent *Foul Play* and sing "Artichoke Fields Forever" at the top of your lungs. The state beach sits just off of the Highway 84 turnoff, wherein lies the **San Gregorio General Store,** or as I like to call it, the Center of the Universe. All trips to the beach here should be prefaced by a stop at the store. The two sand-washed buildings (one of which is a post office) are all that remains of the town of San Gregorio, once a bustling stop on a turn-of-the-century coastal stagecoach route. Whatever you've got a hankering for, it's here—hip waders, Gunther Gräss novels, righteous Bloody Marys, live bluegrass music, fish stew, and a wildly diverse-yet-harmonic convergence of bikers (self-propelled and gas-powered), hippies, yuppies, beachies, moms, philosophers, and cowboys. I recommend that you only leave the General Store after having enjoyed a couple of Bloody Marys, a chat with a few old-timers, and some guitar pickin'. By the time you get to the beach, your last vestiges of inhibition will be cast—like so many boxer shorts—to the winds.

## Life of the Party

No other town I know honors extroversion with its own holidays, and in San Francisco we don't have just one, but several. First and foremost is the **Bay to Breakers Race,** which is also, of course, a foot race, but really—who cares? This annual spring ritual every May is about seeing people running (or walking or getting pushed in shopping carts) dressed up like giant cocktail weenies or blind Venetians or better yet—not dressed at all (ouch). The most amazing thing about Bay to Breakers is that even if you've never jogged down the street for a carton of milk, you'll find that you have the stamina to get to the finish line. The sheer momentum of this massive conga line, plus the hordes of cheerleaders leaning out of windows and doorways along the way and the bands at every intersection, carries you along the 7.5-mile route. While your friends chat with a group of jogging salmon (who keep turning around and trying to spawn upstream), stop at the top of the Hayes Street hill, look back, and let your extrovert heart swell to three times its normal size.

Bay to Breakers is always followed in short order by **Carnaval,** and while it's not Rio, at Carnaval San Francisco the odds of not getting mugged are a whole lot better. This is probably the most multicultural, toe-tapping, hip-shaking festival and parade all year. Samba dancers strut their stuff wearing costumes that put Las Vegas showgirls to shame; enormous stilt-walking puppets undulate down the street. And as Latin rhythms, mariachi trumpets, and Native American chants fill the air, even introverts can't help but shake their backyards. After the parade, steer the conga line over to **La Rondalla** on Guerrero where the cheap margaritas flow like wine. This divey, impossibly narrow Mexican restaurant seems to celebrate Christmas all year-round—twinkling colored lights festoon the bars and windows, piñatas and colorful banners hang from the ceilings, and mariachis stand in the corridors playing traditional favorites in your ear. The food, she's not so great, but the festive atmosphere more than makes up for it.

**COMIC RELIEF**

Stand-up comedy is not for sissies. Frankly, it's not for anyone who has even a shred of vulnerability. But it's great fun to watch and even more fun to heckle. Open mic nights at local comedy clubs were huge in the '70s and early '80s, when a lot of San Francisco's big comedians got their start. These days it's usually confined to one night a week. At the **Punchline,** it's Sundays. Sign up your extrovert friend for a session, or sit back and watch as funny (and not-so-funny) people work out the kinks in their routines. (Fortunately for the audience, but unfortunately for budding comedians, signing up doesn't necessarily mean you'll get to perform.)

Much like the Bay to Breakers, **Halloween** is a day when everyone is given carte blanche to dress for excess, act outrageous, and dance in the streets. But unlike the Bay to Breakers, on Halloween you don't have to exercise to participate (unless you count disco dancing or twelve-ounce curls). Costumes range from clever to campy to downright amazing. A few of my favorites: the group of guys dressed as bridesmaids chanting "always the bridesmaid, never the bride"; a satyr with hoofed rear legs that moved in sync with his human legs; and the Fruits of the Loom. Since the Castro was the birthplace of this annual Born to be Weird party, dressing in drag is always de rigueur. In 1996, the crowds got so big that they moved the official celebration to Civic Center. But the best costumes and characters still roam the side-walks near Upper Market Street. A word to gawkers: real extroverts wear costumes.

# NIGHT

San Francisco's a great town for observing people doing things that you would secretly like to do, if only you had the guts. The beauty of this is that for every person who still clings to a modicum of modesty, there's a whole bunch of crazy, no-holds-barred, Mr. Microphones around through whom you can be a vicarious extrovert.

Take friends-who-would-be-rock-stars to the **Diamond Heights Yet Wah Restaurant** (upstairs, between Safeway and Thrifty Drugstore), where Thursday through Saturday nights karaoke is king. A Chinese restaurant overlooking the Safeway parking lot might seem like an unlikely place to take out-of-towners, but where else, I ask you, can you sing "My Way" in front of a room full of enthusiastic and inebriated strangers while munching on really decent Kung Pao chicken? For my money it just doesn't get any better than this (apparently I'm not alone in my view; celebrity snapshots on the wall attest to cameo appearances by ex-mayor Frank Jordan and other local bigwigs). If this setting is a bit too suburban, you can also follow the bouncing ball to **Pierce Street Annex,** a power bar in the notorious "Triangle" (a Bermuda-esque configuration of drinking establishments) that attracts a seriously college sweatshirt and crop-top Marina crowd. Tuesday night is karaoke night (9 p.m.–1 a.m.), and if you're in the mood to mingle with young bachelors and bachelorettes who are being put up to singing "Like a Virgin" in between shots of tequila, this can be a lot of fun.

For a more serious karaoke experience, the kind where people can actually sing, head down the street to the **Silver Cloud,** which offers this unique form of exhibitionism every night of the week.

If your friends truly enjoy singing in a crowd, and they happen to be in town in December, join the world's largest chorus at Davies Symphony Hall for the **Sing-It-Yourself Messiah.** This is the equivalent of baseball fantasy camp for closet Pavarottis, with the SF Symphony and Chorus providing back-up for an audience of hundreds of wannabes and almost-weres. Lots of people do indeed know the entire score, and can even sing it without cracking too many notes. No need to be intimidated by this. It's all just build-up for the Hallelujah Chorus, a massive choral free-for-all that instantly levels the playing field. May the best diaphragm win.

# Letting It All Hang Out

Several mainstream San Francisco nightspots specialize in extroversion, notably **Julie's Supper Club,** a mostly yuppie power bar and restaurant, serving great martinis and a satisfyingly chic menu that ranges from lamb tenderloin to grilled salmon. But lurking beneath that White Rain–veneer beats the heart of a serious extrovert. This is one of the few places in town where you can dance on the bar and not worry about some yahoo stuffing a dollar in your shoe and expecting more personalized service. The mood is usually boisterous and convivial early in the evening on Fridays and Saturdays, with the rooms equally divided between dinner and cocktails. But by about 10 p.m., after the bachelorette parties have slammed several rounds of tequila poppers and Purple Hooters (and probably opted to skip dinner entirely), things begin to swing. If there's a band, the dancing in the front gets hot, heavy, and sweaty; if there's piped-in house music,

**Carnaval**
Held every May
along Mission Street,
near 24th Street

**La Rondalla**
901 Valencia Street,
647-7474

**Halloween Celebration**
Castro and Market Streets,
October 31 and
preceding weekend

**The Punchline**
444 Battery Street,
397-7573

**Diamond Heights Yet Wah**
5214 Diamond Heights
Boulevard, 282-0788

**Pierce Street Annex**
3138 Fillmore Street,
567-1400

**Silver Cloud**
1994 Lombard Street,
922-0753

**Sing-It-Yourself Messiah**
Davies Symphony Hall
in December
Grove Street and
Van Ness Avenue, 864-6000

**Julie's Supper Club**
1123 Folsom Street,
861-0707

"Brick House" and other assorted flavors from the '70s get the juices flowing. Before you know it, someone's on the bar, and there are stiletto heels weaving in between your daiquiris.

For those who want a bit more XXX for their extrovert bucks, the Trocadero Transfer's **Bondage a Go Go** night (Wednesdays) may be just the ticket. The lines start after 10 p.m. at this fairly tame (by Folsom Street standards) leather and lace party. There are lots of young gals dressed in black latex, an up-all-night industrial dance scene, and a room where you can watch a little whip-and-chain action. Certainly not for the shy or easily scarred.

# Nourishment

Believe it or not, even the life of the party has to eat. Do yourself a favor and take him to a loud, boisterous Thanksgiving-at-the-Waltons kind of place where his antics won't phase anyone. On one end of the cuisine spectrum is **LuLu,** a cavernous interactive party of a restaurant. Sit at one of the tables around the perimeter for a panoramic view of the whole room in stereo sound. Then let your waiter put together a meal of shared plates—maybe the roasted mussels, wood-fired rosemary chicken, and a couple of the truly sublime pasta dishes. Let your ears do the walking on your long strut to the bathroom and you may get the skinny on City Hall, Don Johnson, or any number of intriguing topics.

**Stars,** of course, is practically legendary in San Francisco—not only for the reputation of its food, but for its celebrity clientele and the fabulous flamboyance of chef/owner Jeremiah Tower. Best strategy is to sit at the bar, have a cocktail, and if you get hunger pangs, order something not too messy from the bar menu. It's the San Francisco equivalent of Maxim's or Swifty Lazar's—with all the dazzling, star-studded air kissing you can stomach.

It's practically impossible to avoid interaction at **Cha Cha Cha,** the perennially popular Cuban/Puerto Rican/Caribbean restaurant in the Haight-Ashbury. Share a pitcher of sangria with whoever's nearby as you wait—sometimes interminably—for a table. If you get chummy enough (and you invariably do), maybe your new best friends will invite you to join them at that huge booth. Order up a mess of tapas to share, and don't forget the jerk chicken, or the fried plantains.

If you have a hankering for the dance and a yen for the paella, you owe yourself and your uninhibited friends a dinner at **La Bodega.** While there are definitely better places in town to get Spanish food, at those restaurants you don't get to have a tap-off with a real live flamenco dancer, while the rest of the diners shake tambourines, maracas, and body parts. From what I can tell, it's a lot easier than belly dancing (though the outfits aren't as enticing).

But if in fact the Dance of the Seven Veils is more what you had in mind, you can bare your midriff and do your best Mata Hari impression at **El Mansour,** a Moroccan restaurant located in the Outer Richmond district. As you sit around low-lying tables on large floor cushions, the scent of cardamon, cinnamon, and cumin waft through the air. Suddenly a belly dancer appears, a vision in jingle bells and tiny finger cymbals, rippling her torso in ways most men dream about. Though they probably won't need a prompt, this is the part where you push your extrovert friends forward, encouraging them with banshee cries. Then, still heady from glasses of Moroccan wine, they'll proceed to undulate with the natives whilst others look on enviously (or with great relief).

## WHERE TO STAY

I suppose an ideal hotel for an extrovert would be something like Jamaica's Hedonism II resort—a place that's more like a commune, where everyone jumps in the hot tub naked and shares a giant Mai Tai. There really isn't a San Francisco equivalent, but there are some good compromises. The rooms on the top floors of the very classy **Mandarin Oriental Hotel,** for instance, offer glass-wall bathtubs that look out over the entire city. Soak up the views as you sip a glass of champagne, and for an added vicarious thrill, stand up and see if you can get the attention of that beleaguered business exec burning the midnight oil in the office tower across the way.

If it's a pool party you're after (or an after-hours pool party), there's no place but the **Phoenix.** This tragically hip Tenderloin no-tell motel is where visiting rock bands and avant-garde filmmakers like to stay. The ranch-style rooms, furnished in '50s rattan funk, encircle one of the city's only outdoor hotel swimming pools, where you can plant yourself by a palm tree with a fruity cocktail and imagine you're in Palm Springs or Negril (never mind the goosebumps). Potential Speedo-to-Speedo encounters with the likes of Flea from the Red Hot Chili Peppers or filmmaker Wim Wenders are just the ticket for most brazen conversationalists. If you're having trouble breaking the ice, perhaps expound on your interpretation of the famous swirl mural that lines the bottom of the pool.

In San Francisco, sooner or later, it always comes down to food. Where are we going to eat? What kind of food do you want? Have you tried that new restaurant? Have you tried to get into that new restaurant? How the *hell* did you get into that new restaurant?

# Tour 10 Foodies

Indeed, in this town, eating is hardly ever just a bite before the main event. Eating *is* the main event. And when company comes to town, the value of the food factor grows by exponential leaps and bounds. Because aside from the bridges, the hills, and the cable cars, almost everyone who comes here has heard about the restaurants. It's hard enough choosing the right dining spot when you live here and you've got time to try them all, but when your days are limited and your eating companions are from out of town, picking just the right restaurant can become a paralyzing decision.

So you turn to the guidebooks, which present you with 100 more choices that you hadn't even thought of. And pretty soon you just want to give up and order take-out. What you really need is someone to make the decision for you. Someone to tell you where to go and what to order when you get there. Then if they hate it, you can just blame it on me.

# BREAKFAST

There are three kinds of breakfast people: nibblers, diner and coffeeshop types, and serious brunchers. As you can tell by the number of divey countertops I've described in this book, I'm a diner kinda gal. (If you're looking for a dissertation on breakfast's constant companion, coffee, see the Neo-Bohemians tour and the Politically Correct tour.)

For nibblers of the bagel variety, **House of Bagels** on Geary is where the cream cheese meets the onion stick. There will be many who will disagree vehemently with this assessment. They'll say Noah's makes softer, cushier bagels; they'll argue that you can't get blueberry or chocolate chip bagels here; they'll say that they don't have date-walnut or tofu-dill schmears. Tough toenails. It's not your book. No one can touch House of Bagels's traditional onion bagels or sticks, bialys, or flat-bread bagels (no holes). They're chewy without being mushy, they're not enriched in any way, they're kosher, they're not completely coated with onions or salt or poppy seeds to the point that that's all you taste, and they're so incredibly flavorful (especially right out of the oven), you won't even need any of those fancy spreads. The bakery also makes fabulous pumpernickel, egg twist, and New York corn rye bread. Everything's fresh-baked daily and for cheapskates, whatever's leftover is sold for half price the next day.

I'm not a donut fanatic, but many people I know belong to the Church of the Old-Fashioned Glazed. And they tell me there's one word in donuts in this town: **Bob's.** If you don't believe them, the morning traffic jam on Polk Street in front of this no-frills bakery should convince you. Bob's makes doughnuts from scratch every day; they're baked in small batches that are sold immediately, so they don't sit around and get stale; nothing is over-fried or over-sugared; and they don't use any artificial flavors or colors. When five out of six but-termilk bar addicts agree, who am I to argue?

Italian pastries really fall more into the realm of afternoon coffee break, but if your friends like them with breakfast, the **Italian/French Baking Company** (see the Neo-Bohemians tour), **Danilo,** and **Stella,** on Columbus Avenue, are the places to go. Get your biscotti, your semisweet hard cookies, and your panettone at one of the first two; get your sacripantina (a Marsala-soaked sponge-layer cake topped with zabaglione) and your cannoli at Stella.

On to bigger and butter things. Diner rats have already read in these pages about It's Tops for atmosphere; Art's for big piles of good cheap eggs and hash browns; Herb's for celebrity sightings and parental bonding; and Manor Coffee Shop for a '50s time-warp experience. To these I must add **Tyger's** in Glen Park for the quintessential, neighborhood eggs-over-the-fence encounter. This corner coffeeshop is one of the only diners in town that's full every day—and not just with retirees. People actually spend their days off reading the newspaper and lingering over scrambles and toast here. On par with Tyger's for conviviality and hometown hospitality is **Al's** "Good Food" diner on Mission, and **Hungry Joe's** in outer Noe Valley. Any one of these should satisfy your friends' counterculture itch.

**Kate's Kitchen** bridges that delicate gap between a diner and a full-fledged brunch restaurant. In the grand diner tradition, the small room is filled with regulars who know the kitchen staff and each other. But the food is no greasy truckstop fare. Come here for the Red Flannel Hash, a huge combo of potatoes, corned beef, onions, peppers, carrots, and celery, or the much-acclaimed buttermilk cornmeal pancakes, served with real maple syrup and a hunk of butter. This is also one of the only places around where you'll find biscuits and gravy that are made with genuine sausage gravy.

For unusually flavored, delicate, fluffy flapjacks, my vote goes to **Miss Millie's** for their lemon-ricotta pancakes. In the French toast category, not too many can argue with the **Liberty Cafe**'s, made with challah and topped with fresh fruit and/or pralines, and real maple syrup.

And when breakfast's gotta carry you all the way to dinner, you'll want to head to **Spaghetti Western** or **Squat & Gobble** in the Lower Haight. Spaghetti Western's portions of huevos rancheros and other ethnic egg concoctions are enough to feed a boy scout troop; Squat and Gobble makes omelets and crepes the size of carry-on bags.

## LUNCH

You can't please all of the people, all of the time. And when it comes to foodies, you're lucky if you hit it right once or twice. For the gourmand on your roster, consider some of my favorite dishes (and the locales where they're served):

**Cafe Bastille**—Everyone talks about San Francisco's European sensibility, and nowhere is this more prevalent than on Belden Place, that tiny downtown alley with all the outdoor sidewalk cafes. Cafe Bastille rules the block—a true Parisian bistro, complete with surly French waiters, art nouveau posters, and a menu of butter-, ham-, and cheese-heavy dishes. You could stick to the lowfat California-style ahi tuna salads, but my recommendation is to go native with the *Hachis Parmentier*—a traditional baked casserole of ground beef, cheese, and potatoes. Serious French comfort food.

And while we're speaking French, no one does the classic **Steak Pommes Frites** like nearby **Le Central.**

**The Fly Trap**—It's not everyone's taste, but if you like 'em, the **liver and onions** here are to die for. Named for a popular turn-of-the-century San Francisco restaurant, the Fly Trap serves up old-time SF dishes, including Celery Victor, Chicken Jerusalem, and Hangtown Fry.

**Spenger's Fish Grotto**—The sit-down restaurant is pretty good (and reasonably priced), but the scallop and shrimp sandwiches from the next-door take-out shop are the real ticket—tasty, fresh, and cheap.

**Harbor Village**—So much **dim sum,** so little time. It's not big on authentic Chinatown atmosphere, and the service can be seriously sketchy, but this bustling Embarcadero Center restaurant serves the best and tastiest assortment of dumplings in town.

**Sai's**—My favorite alternative to a double latte is **Vietnamese iced coffee** at this popular Financial District lunch spot. The coffee is made in individual brewers that sit atop your glass. Inside is a dollop of sweetened, condensed milk. When it's done dripping, you stir it up and pour it over ice. Better than a milkshake—and with a caffeine jolt that will have you running a marathon while writing the great American novel. They also make some of the best **Pho Ga** (Vietnamese chicken noodle soup) in town.

**Grace Bakery**—We could argue the merits of Acme and Uprisings and Beckmann's and Tassajara until we're blue in the face. Good bread is in the tastebuds of the beholder. But if my vote counts for anything, Grace Baking's **sourdough walnut bread** is one you might want to use as an example of what sourdough is all about. You could buy it in the store, but even better is to go to Market Hall on College Avenue in Oakland and buy it from the source. This European-style marketplace also sells fresh pasta, coffee, produce, and lots of imported gourmet goodies.

**Mo's/Avenue 9**—If you could combine the seven-ounce, juicy, barbecued-to-drippy-perfection burgers at Mo's in North Beach with the garlic fries in Gorgonzola at Avenue 9, you'd have an unbeatable combination.

**Pozole**—When you're in the mood for Mexican food, but a twelve-pound burrito from Pancho Villa's won't cut it, try a **nopalitos** (cactus) **burrito** or sauté platter from Pozole in the Castro district. The dishes here are intriguingly seasoned with things like cumin, lime-tomatillo sauce, and mango salsa, and are mostly low-cal. If the aroma from the kitchen doesn't get you salivating, the waiters—each one more hunky than the next—will (no matter what your persuasion).

**La Taqueria**—If a twelve-pound burrito is *exactly* what you had in mind, La Taqueria puts together a mean one. You could argue that La Cumbre, Pancho Villa's, Azteca, or your neighborhood taqueria does a better one, but you can't dispute that this neighborhood institution makes the best **guacamole** this side of Cesar Chavez Street. Fresh avocado, no creamy additives, seasoned with a little cilantro, lemon, and spices.

## DINNER

**Crustacean**—You can search the wharf over for Dungeness crab, but to my mind you'll find the most succulent and savory examples at this Euro/Vietnamese seafood restaurant on Russian Hill. Owned and run by the respected An Family, their **whole roasted crab** will have you licking your fingers long after they take away your plate.

**Duarte's Tavern**—Folks come from near and far to Pescadero (below San Gregorio on Highway 1) to sample the creamy, delicious, secret-recipe **artichoke** and **green chile** soups at this down-home bar and restaurant. It's dinner in a bowl.

**Grand Cafe**—The room's stunning and the atmosphere's invigorating, but when it comes to ordering, the only two words you need to know here are: **polenta soufflé.**

**LuLu**—Chefs come and go, but the **iron-griddle roasted mussels** remain: tender, smoky, and delicious—one of the reasons this trendy restaurant has survived its too-much, too-fast early-'90s celebrity.

**Ton Kiang**—After a day of sightseeing in the gale-force fog, nothing warms the bones like a steaming **clay pot stew with mustard greens** or **won ton soup** from this Richmond District institution (the cafe near Spruce, not the one at 22nd Avenue). Oh, also the **Singapore-style noodles** (you have to ask for them; they're not on the menu).

**Tommy's Joynt**—I feel about Tommy's Joynt the way I feel about the nachos at Candlestick Park—I've always harbored the fact that I love them like a guilty secret. In a town lousy with high-brow cuisine, it somehow seems crass to hanker after hofbrau food. But then I found out that Tom Petty had Tommy's delivered nightly to his hotel room when he was here for that concert series in 1997. So now I don't feel so bad. I'm partial to the **open-face**

*turkey sandwich with mashed potatoes and gravy,* but nothing preps the stomach better for a night at the Great American Music Hall (down the street) than Tommy's spicy **buffalo chili.** Yes, it's real buffalo—farm-raised just like cattle, and surprisingly lean and tender.

**Thai House**—Just like everyone in Philly is an expert on cheesesteaks, everyone in San Francisco knows the best place for Thai food. For years I swore by Thep Phanom on Fillmore; then by a small place called Mae Thip on Irving Street. But eventually each restaurant's ranking and status boiled down to how it makes certain dishes. I can't go to a Thai restaurant without sampling the **tom kar gai**—spicy-sour chicken soup with lemongrass and sometimes coconut milk. And right now, I'm completely enamored of the Tom Kar Gai at Thai House on Market Street. But when it comes to a Thai **warm mushroom "farmer's" salad** (infused with lime, cilantro, and chilies), no one can touch **Khan Toke** out in the Richmond. And as far as that old staple, **pad thai** goes, it's a toss up between **Thep Phanom** and **Manora's** on Folsom Street.

**Hunan**—The same argument holds for Chinese food. In my book, he who makes the best potstickers wins. Hunan does an outstanding job—theirs are plump and juicy, not too greasy and not too rubbery. This traditional appetizer will whet your palate for Hunan's pièces de résistance: **spicy-smoked ham and chicken** in Hunan sauce and (my favorite) **cold noodle salad with chicken and cucumbers** in a heavenly spicy peanut sauce. (Another potsticker palace is **Alice's** on Sanchez Street, where they're lightly pan-seared to a delicate crisp and are bursting with juices.)

**Red Crane**—I was really skeptical the first time I ordered these, but the **sweet and sour walnuts** at Red Crane are a taste sensation—as satisfyingly meaty as any pork product—and no bones. This neighborhood stalwart specializes in veggie dishes cleverly disguised as meat—vegetarian chicken (made with tofu), mu shu "pork," and other interesting faux carnal treats.

**Mandalay**—Equally scary was my initiation into the tea leaves salad at this Richmond district Burmese restaurant. My advice: don't tell them what's in it, just order it. After they've had a few bites of this delicious, crunchy, nutty house specialty, they won't care.

**Fringale**—I've never been disappointed with anything I've ordered at Gerald Hrigoyen's wonderful little SoMa restaurant, but the traditional French **cassoulet** has my mouth watering just thinking about it.

Khan Toke
5937 Geary Boulevard,
668-6654

Thep Phanom
400 Waller Street,
431-2526

Manora's
1600 Folsom Street,
861-6224

Hunan
924 Sansome Street,
956-7727

Alice's
1599 Sanchez Street,
282-8999

Red Crane
1115 Clement Street,
751-7226

Mandalay
4348 California Street,
386-3895

Fringale
570 4th Street,
543-0573

Slow Club
2501 Mariposa Street,
241-9390

Biscuits & Blues
401 Mason Street,
292-2583

Zuni Cafe
1658 Market Street,
552-2522

Ebisu
1283 9th Avenue, 566-1770

Roosevelt's Tamale Parlor
2817 24th Street, 550-9213

Tommaso's
1042 Kearny Street,
398-9696

Mitchell's Ice Cream
688 San Jose Avenue,
648-2300

Polly Ann Ice Cream
3142 Noriega at 38th
Avenue, 664-2472

**Slow Club**—Again, I'm sure a million of you will protest this judgement, but the **Caesar salad** at Slow Club is just about perfection in my book—made with baby leaves of Romaine lettuce and a lemony Caesar dressing with just a hint of anchovies—not too heavy on the mayo and eggs.

**Biscuits and Blues**—This down-under downtown club is a big tourist mecca, but there are several reasons why it transcends the tourist trap label. One is the weekly schedule of solid, talented blues and R&B bands; the other is the **biscuits**—flaky, tender, substantial, and totally addictive. Of course, they come as an accompaniment to the cajun/Southern menu, which is also usually darn good, though inconsistent.

**Zuni Cafe**—For nearly twenty years, chef Judy Rogers has kept foodies, tourists, and other chefs (among them Jeremiah Tower) coming back to her hip Hayes Valley restaurant for wood-oven-roasted dishes—especially the **roast chicken for two,** which Tower swears is unsurpassed.

**Ebisu**—If you're gonna do sushi, you may as well impress them with a sushi bar that puts out artistic as well as tasty hand rolls. Godzilla does an exceptional job of this, but the **Caterpillar Roll** at Ebisu is truly something to behold. Small segments of sushi stuffed with avocado and spicy tuna (and hidden pockets of wasabe) snake down the plate like the caterpillar in *Alice in Wonderland*. The seafood creature even has antenna and fish-roe eyes. The sight of it has been known to cause spontaneous applause.

**Roosevelt's Tamale Parlor**—There are definitely better places in the Mission to get **tamales,** but a lot of them aren't sit-down restaurants with a great homey Mexican kitchen kind of atmosphere. The portions are big, the price is right, and the tamales have been made from scratch, daily, since 1922.

**Tommaso's**—If you like your pizzas thick and deep and soupy with toppings, go to Zachary's in Oakland or Pizzeria Uno. But if you like them made the Italian way—thin and crispy, with an emphasis on perfect tomato sauce and uncluttered by a pile of toppings, then you should come to this North Beach institution. Tommaso's brick oven has been cranking out perfect pizzas for more than sixty years, and with any luck, they'll be around for another sixty.

# DESSERT

This could be a whole chapter in and of itself. But I'd probably have a heart attack doing the research. So here are just a few very worthy places:

**Mitchell's Ice Cream**—You can have your gelato, your frozen yogurt, your tofutti—none of it comes close to the ice cream at Mitchell's, an old-fashioned mom-and-pop shop (since 1953), located on the outskirts of the

Mission. Along with all the traditional flavors, Mitchell's makes a whole series of unusual, tropical flavors—mango, langka (a tart melon), halo halo (sweet bean), and the incredible *macapuno* (meaty coconut) and *buko* (sweet baby coconut), which should be ordered on a cone with chocolate dip. Other stand-outs are their fresh fruit ices and sorbets made with big chunks of fruit. And the best part—they're open until 11:30 p.m. on weekends.

**Polly Ann Ice Cream**—The texture isn't nearly as creamy or satisfying as Mitchell's, but Polly Ann has more flavors than you could taste in a lifetime—all handmade. If you can't decide what you want, spin the wheel and let it decide for you (just hope durian isn't one of the choices; the tropical island fruit tastes like gasoline). Another bonus—doggies (accompanied by owners) get free cones.

**Dianda's**—This Mission district Italian bakery is known the city over for its *chocolate rum cakes,* amaretto cookies, and layer cream cakes. The cannolis aren't too shabby, either.

## SOMETHING TO WASH THAT DOWN WITH

### Martinis

The **Occidental Grill,** a cigar-smoking, steak-eating, Old Boy's Club, was named for the San Francisco bar where the siphon-glass cocktail was allegedly invented by "Professor" Jerry Thomas back in the 1860s. The tale goes that the professor was asked to make something strong for a passenger embarking on the cold ferry ride across the bay to Martinez. The drink consisted of gin, bitters, vermouth, and maraschino. Later, the formula and the name of the cocktail were abbreviated to the concoction we know today. Whether or not it's true, it's a good story, and the Occidental makes the most of it, proudly displaying an illustrated portrait of the professor next to the bar and serving more martinis than you can shake a swizzle stick at.

What the **Red Room** lacks in authenticity it makes up for in volume and atmosphere. The oversized martini glasses look like they came from Pee Wee's Playhouse, and they're served by bartenders who are so cool you might feel the need for a warm coat. In deference to the bar's theme color (absolutely everything, down to the lighting and a wall of mysterious bottled elixirs, is red), you might consider ordering the martini's crimson cousin, the Cosmopolitan.

Other popular martini bars include **Maxfield's** in the Sheraton Palace Hotel, which does a $3 Martini Madness night on Thursdays;

and the **Persian Aub Zam Zam Room** (see the Yuppies tour), where you can't get anything but martinis (nor should you try).

## Margaritas

No one can have just one margarita at **Tommy's,** because they're *so damn good.* A staple in the Outer Richmond since 1965, this platter-style Mexican restaurant is famous the town over for its margaritas, made with 100 percent pure agave. Tommy's stocks an enormous array of imported tequilas, which you can sample if you join the tequila club. Needless to say, the party atmosphere prevails here, as patrons order pitcher after pitcher and proceed to get completely snockered.

## Beer

From a local brew angle, your best bets are **Gordon Biersch, San Francisco Brewing Company,** and **Thirsty Bear Brewing Company** (in that order). Gordon Biersch's märzen is a consistent winner in my book, and yuppies will find the atmosphere at the bar more than conducive to alliances of a romantic or professional kind. The SF Brewing Company makes a couple of good ales too, but the place feels distinctly like a tourist attraction (which it is). Thirsty Bear's beers are hit or miss, but their food—tapas, paella, and other Spanish specialties—is top notch.

For authentic, hearty German beers served in their appropriate two-liter glasses and boots, make a detour to **SuppenKüche** in Hayes Valley, where the young and Euro-restless say "danke" and "bitte" as they pass the Spaten.

## Wine

If you don't have time to hit the wine country, do some vertical tastings locally at **Hayes and Vine,** a cozy, chic wine bar in Hayes Valley that has none of the rarefied air that you'll find in Silverado Trail tasting rooms. Snuggle up to the bar, where they offer 35 to 40 wines by the glass on any given day. The total inventory features more than 500 wines including a number of small, hard-to-find vintages which the knowledgeable (and occasionally pierced and tattooed) staff will be only too happy to tell you about.

As Kermit likes to say, it ain't easy being green. But it's a whole lot easier here in organic-produce-no-lard-nuke-free land than in places where tofu translates as some kind of foot fungus. I mean, here, even Starbucks makes soy lattes.

# Tour 11 Green Types

Green people come in various degrees of intensity. There are the types who won't order anything with meat, but won't ask if the soup's made with chicken stock, and they might pick the meat parts out of your burrito and feel just fine about eating the rest of it. Then there are those (such as myself) who won't wear fur, but don't have a big problem with leather shoes; who support the Rainforest Action Network and the Sierra Club, but draw the line at eschewing toilet paper in favor of pine needles while backpacking. And of course, we all know someone (or someone who knows someone) who is the most extreme vegan—the vegetarian equivalent of an orthodox Jew—for whom even dishes that have once touched animal by-products are verboten. Fortunately, there are places in the Bay Area that will please the environmentally nonchalant as much as the ecologically insistent.

# MORNING

Herbivores and carnivores will find common ground and good eats Saturday mornings at the **Ferry Plaza Farmer's Market.** But you really need to get there by 10 a.m. (or earlier), otherwise the produce will all have been picked over. So drag your butt out of bed with your overly energetic house guests (who aren't bogged down by undigested pieces of beef), force some Peet's french roast down your throat, and catch a streetcar heading downtown, pointing out sights along Market Street as you go. What makes this farmer's market better than the one on Alemany or the one in the Civic Center (for tourists) is mainly location. Heaping piles of fresh-from-the-vine edibles spread out on stands along the Embarcadero, as ferryboats dance on the bay and the old clock tower beckons travelers into the port—recalling a time when this was the hub of city transportation. The contrast between green growing things and modern industry is fascinating. Inside the market, you'll find flowers, gourmet goodies from the city's best restaurants (with free samples), and heavenly organic fruit, vegetables, and herbs from Bay Area farms. Try to catch the weekly shop-with-the-chefs tour, when the likes of Brad Ogden (One Market, Lark Creek Inn) or Reed Hearon (Rose Pistola) show you how to pick produce like a pro.

Afterward, walk down the Embarcadero to **Pier 7,** an old fishing pier that was restored a few years back with vintage-style streetlamps and a wooden-plank promenade. Stroll to the end, find a comfortable bench, and watch the fishermen cast their reels into the swell as the ships roll by.

You'll have to get up even earlier to get the pick of the crop at the **Flower Market** on Sixth and Brannan. Not all visitors are willing to wake up with the sun for the perfect bouquet of American Beauties (especially if they're on vacation), but if yours are, both you and they will be rewarded with a magnificent, fragrant flower show. Though this is primarily a wholesale market for florists, many growers sell to the public.

If you haven't worked up an appetite for granola yet, trek over to the Presidio and walk the **Ecology Trail,** a short loop that takes you past coastal bluffs, forested hills, and wooded groves, where you'll observe a large variety of endangered and rare plant life.

# Breakfast

Most vegetarian cuisine seems to fall comfortably into the breakfast category—fruits, grains, wholesome muffins, tofu scrambles, etc. And though there's certainly no shortage of bacon, sausage, and corn-beef hash on diner menus, almost every good breakfast place in the city also has an assortment of vegetarian options.

**Miss Millie's** in Noe Valley wins the prize for tasty, nonstandard veggie fare. Their lemon-ricotta pancakes with blueberry sauce are to-die for, and I'm in love with their hash browns, made from roasted beets, yams, and other root vegetables instead of potatoes.

Challenging the bagel for most quickly proliferating trend in nonmeat breakfast food is the crepe. New creperies have been popping up every-where, each with more inventive fillings than the last (and many pushing crepes as dinner). **The Crepe Vine** on Irving offers all the standard stuffings—fruits, cheeses, veggies, purees—as does **Crepes on Cole.** The Mission's wonderful **Ti Couz,** which set the standard for authentic Breton crepes in this town, offers sweet and savory selections made with either buckwheat or white flour, and filled with anything from ham and cheese (for nonveggies) to mushrooms in sauce. **Savor** in Noe Valley wins the huge portions award (they don't skimp on side dishes either) and gets extra bonus points for a full selection of house-baked breads, including jalapeño and blue corn.

The granddaddy of vegetarian brunches is of course **Greens** at Fort Mason, and no visiting herbivore (or her host) should miss the experience. This groundbreaking restaurant proved that vegetarian meals don't have to consist of birdseed and tofu (and aren't necessarily low-cal). Started by the Zen Center, it still gets much of its produce from Green Gulch Farms across the bay (see below). The food is outstanding—zucchini pancakes with Gruyère, luscious portobello mushroom sandwiches, spinach and Gorgonzola salads—and the views are astounding. As the waves lap at the docks outside the picture windows, sit on one of the recycled burlwood benches and watch the sun dance off the whitecaps.

After you've digested (and it may take a few turns around the block), make your way to Building E, home of the nonprofit Oceanic Society, where you can sign up for a sea excursion to the **Farallon Islands** for the next day. If your friends are here anywhere between December and April, they might get to see a gray whale or two as the animals make their way south during their annual migration. The all-day boat tours are led by naturalists and marine mammal experts, and even if you don't see any whales, you'll get to witness the wildlife of the open ocean—pelicans, sea lions, the occasional stray windsurfer.

# Green Gulch Farms

Where else in the world can you combine organic grocery shopping with meditation, soul-searching, lunch, and an afternoon of sun-bathing, hiking, and sightseeing along one of the most pristine stretches of beach in the Bay Area?

Green Gulch Farms outside Mill Valley is first and foremost a Zen center, where you can take instruction in meditation, Buddhist philosophy, and the ritual uses of Japanese tea. One of the ways the center supports itself is by cultivating the loveliest, most delectable-looking organic produce I've ever seen—much of which is sold to San Francisco's haute cuisine restaurants. Below the meditation buildings, nestled in a wreath of tall trees, lie rows of baby lettuces and leafy vegetables, acres of herbs and edible flowers, and overflowing pots of native plants. The center welcomes lay people all week, but Sunday is the best public day. If you're open to new experiences, arrive early in the morning for the meditation program and lecture, followed by tea and lunch. After 11 a.m., there's a public produce and plant sale. Buy your dinner fixings, then take a leisurely walk through the gardens down to **Muir Beach.** After a little sun and sand, hike up the hill for an awe-inspiring overview of the California coastline. If your eco-friends are truly inspired, they can spend the night. The center's guest house—built with hand-planed and hand-pegged timber—has twelve rooms, each with its own balcony and traditional Japanese futon-style furnishings. Accommodations include meals and snacks (all vegetarian, but not vegan), which you eat with the residents. If you're not a religious type, that's okay too. No participation in any of the center's Zen life is required (having respect for those who are participating goes without saying).

If your friends happen to be here around New Year's, find out when Green Gulch is holding their **lotus lantern boat ceremony**—a Buddhist tradition that celebrates peace in the new year. Participants make little boats out of folded paper, place candles inside them, and as the sun goes down, set them afloat on the center's pond. There's also singing, poetry reading, and a tea ceremony.

While you're over on this side of the Rainbow Tunnel, you should make a detour to the **Marine Mammal Center** in Fort Cronkite near Rodeo Lagoon, where marine biologists nurse ailing and orphaned California sea lions and seals back to health. These folks are the original Bay Watch team—running to the rescue of beached whales, sea lions, dolphins, and other stranded mammals. At the facility you can see pups being bottle-fed, talk to careworkers about the whale population, and learn about the bad things in our ocean that lead to marine mammal fatalities. (This also a great place to take kids.)

## NOON

A successful outing with eco-friends should probably involve something in nature, though that doesn't necessarily mean you've got to cross a bridge to find it. The **San Francisco League of Urban Gardeners** (SLUG) oversees about fifty public gardens in San Francisco, many of which are tucked into hidden spots—on hillsides, flanking staircases, behind office buildings. Though some of the prettiest ones are difficult to find and/or get in to, they're worth the effort—if only to appreciate the ability of inner-city folk to carve out a little green sanctuary in the concrete jungle.

**Saint Mary's Urban Youth Farm,** just up from the Alemany Farmer's Market, is a demonstration garden farm that provides internships for kids from the projects. You'll find everything here that you would at a Sonoma orchard, except on a smaller scale and with a bit more freeway noise. The farm's open Saturdays from 9 a.m. to 4 p.m., and if you're one of those people who can't go near a green space without pulling a few weeds, volunteer gardeners are welcome.

Bernal Heights is a haven for urban gardens and a great up-and-coming neighborhood to spend an afternoon nosing around in. Start off with a depth charge (a shot of espresso in a big cup of regular coffee) on the sylvan patio of **Progressive Grounds,** the artsy coffeehouse on suddenly hip Cortland Avenue (for more on Cortland Avenue, see the Queer and Curious tour). Then walk west down Cortland to the **Good Prospect Community Garden,** a tidy, landscaped patch of hillside that flanks either side of a stairway with pretty flowers and tidy vines and shrubs. Sit on the steps and drink in the sun-soaked, organic, earthy smells.

Next, veer north to Eugenia Street, climb the hidden stairway, past adorable Victorians and clapboard cottages, and then catch a second set of even more hidden steps on Elsie Street, until you reach the top of Bernal Heights. On the south side of Bernal Heights Boulevard are the **Bernal Community Gardens,** a community-tended green that looks out over the southern hillside. But the real payoff is the short hike to the bald top of Bernal Hill, which affords fantastic views stretching all the way to Mount Diablo on one side and the Golden Gate on the other. (My friend Richard likes to take guests up here to watch the official "Rolling In of the Fog," since Bernal Heights stays clear of those misty fingers long after the Richmond is in pea soup.)

Other noteworthy gardens:

**Potrero Hill Community Garden**—Flanking Vermont Street (the real "crookedest street in the world") this garden affords a fabulous vista of downtown and beyond.

**Sutro Gardens**—A self-guided historical walking tour, picnic tables, sweeping views of Seal Rocks and the Pacific, and the remains of Adolph Sutro's house are some of the highlights of this picturesque green park located on that hill above the Cliff House. Walk around to the back side of the park and you'll discover a gem of a hanging garden, terraced down the hillside and filled with seasonal flowers and blooming shrubs.

**Arkansas Friendship Garden**—A group of South Africans started this garden, and the result is part tropics, part chaos. The uppermost portion is planted with banana trees, and there's a greenhouse with an entrance that's so tangled in overgrowth, it literally creates a green room.

**Dearborn Community Garden**—A prim and proper garden that sits directly behind the Pepsi-Cola bottling plant on a tiny alleyway in the Mission. Bees are also raised here.

**Ping Yuen Garden**—The only access to this remarkable garden is through the hallways of the Ping Yuen housing project, one of the oldest Chinatown projects. If you can find a way in, the contrast between beauty and blight will astound you.

**Hooker Alley Community Garden**—This side of Nob Hill is about as gray and urban as it gets, so it's thrilling to find that somewhere, somehow, vegetation has managed to thrive. The youngest gardener in this narrow strip of greenery and flowers is about sixty-eight years old.

**Michelangelo Community Garden**—A garden within a garden, located on a steep hillside above North Beach and the wharf. The flowers are tended with loving care by people who have been doing it forever (there's a waiting list of more than a year for plots). Benches offer a nice, relaxing pastoral perch.

**Garden for the Environment**—This demonstration garden keeps growing and growing and growing, now taking up about half the block between Lawton and Judah. For green thumbs thinking about moving out this way, it's a chance to see an amazing variety of plants that you thought would never grow here, blooming like there's no tomorrow. You can also pick up lots of literature about green outings and events around town.

If you hit it just right, SLUG hosts an **Open Gardens** tour in early June, when community gardens around town open their gates to the public; some of them offer free samples and treats. You can grab a list from SLUG headquarters and stroll the primrose paths at your leisure, or take a guided bus or bike tour.

Though lunch doesn't seem to be a big meal in the veggie world, often falling into the category of a nosh, you won't find a bigger and better nosh than at the **Whole Foods Market** on Franklin. This place is truly overwhelming—even for people (like us San Franciscans) who are used to great natural foods markets. Walk in from the garage and you're met with an Odwalla nourishment bar and cafe featuring elixirs, smoothies, and healthy snacks. On the way up the stairs there's a stand with a "Daily Dinner" flyer, featuring recipes and menu suggestions. And that's all before you actually enter the market. Once there, you're greeted by yards and yards of robust butter lettuces, delicate baby carrots, and golden tomatoes, all residing under photo profiles of the farmers who grew them. There are acres of bulk foods (including twenty different kinds of granola), a full bakery which makes some of the best sourdough rye bread I've ever had, a deli and take-out counter that serves better food than many restaurants (gourmet vegetarian wraps, green papaya salad, Moroccan chicken couscous, jerked sweet potatoes), a fresh, housemade pasta bar, and—if you're feeling a bit overwrought—there's even a massage station. I've never thought of a grocery store as an entertainment venue, but Whole Foods opens up whole new possibilities.

## Eco-Shopping

Shopping in the green world used to conjure images of clothes made out of tree bark, chairs made of old tires, shampoos that didn't make suds, and— of course—Birkenstocks. It certainly never smacked of high style . . . until Birkenstocks and clogs became de rigueur and aromatherapy became a household word among wealthy spa-dwellers. If Nature Boy or Girl doesn't have a haute hemp boutique where he or she comes from, spend an afternoon trying these on for size.

**World Ware** on Hayes Street proves that you don't have to be frumpy to be environmentally conscious. From cute little silhouette hemp dresses to smart organic-cotton blazers—there's nothing that even remotely resembles a burlap sack here. World Ware has an outstanding selection of natural-fiber bed linens and eco-friendly bathroom accoutrements, plus such fashionably chic items as recycled picture frames.

Everything—down to the business cards and lip balm—is made from hemp or hemp products at **Frankel Brothers Hemp Outfitters** in Noe Valley, the happy hemp store whose mission is to educate people about the wonders of this renewable industrial fiber. (Did you know that Thomas Jefferson drafted the Declaration of Independence on hemp paper?) It's mostly a clothing store, offering a wide array of hemp and hemp-blend fashions—from suits and silk-hemp blouses, to halter dresses and hats. There are even hemp-cellulose key chains—with all the strength and resilience of a plastic petroleum product, but with none of the renewable-resource raping qualities.

Pier 39 seems like the least likely place to take green types in search of souvenirs, but tucked away on the second level, between trashy trinket shops and food-on-a-stick stands are actually two great places to find gifts you can feel good about. **The City Store** is my favorite. Run in part by homeless and formerly homeless residents in cooperation with a nonprofit organization and the city of San Francisco, this is a repository for recycled San Francisco artifacts. Among the coveted items: old street and road signs such as Haight Street and (for those who remember the days before it became Cesar Chavez) Army Street, San Francisco City Limits, and the famous Forty-Nine Mile Drive; parking meters (from the days when they still took pennies); original 1922 Lombard Street bricks; police and fire department cast-offs; cable-car cable; and posters from memorable city events gone by.

A few doors away is the **National Parks Store,** which sells everything pertaining to and picturing our country's national parks. This is the store where you can get a book about the Presidio, framed graphic posters of Half Dome, or an Annapurna "a woman's place is on top" T-shirt. Sales go to support the national park system.

The plush, cushy natural-cotton robes are reason enough to go into **Green World Mercantile** on upper Polk Street, but once inside, you'll be captivated by the dried flower wreaths, crafty kitchen accessories, and home furnishings.

The old standby **Nature Company** is really not as environment-conscious as it is consumer-conscious, but it's fun shopping for the odd toy, rain stick, birdfeeder, geode, or hot springs guide.

**Zonal Gallery** believes that when old bed frames and iron gates get real rusty, they should be sent to the art gallery, not the scrap heap. The walls are covered with a fascinating array of recycled art and furnishings, as well as paintings and crafts.

## East Bay Eco-Tripping

Being the center of all things PC, it's only natural that Berkeley should also have an abundance of earth-easy places. Begin a leisurely Saturday afternoon on Fourth Street, at the confluence of earthy stream and yuppie creek. Make a mandatory stop at **Earthsake,** which features natural bedding and home furnishings, lotions and body products, and organic-cotton baby clothing by Ecosport and Earthlings. Then head across the street to **Aerial,** a wonderful store filled with architectural knick-knacks—everything from renderings to neoclassical building blocks. Nothing recycled here perhaps, but no products were tested on animals either. Across the street at **Restoration Hardware,** you can ogle turn-of-the-century-style lanterns, latches, and lightswitch plates (even though they're new, they look old). Even better, drive north on San Pablo Avenue to **Ohmega Salvage,** where you can find the real thing—crackly Italian tiles, neoclassical pediments, Greek statuary, Tiffany lamps, gilded mirrors, door knockers, skeleton keys, and tons of antique fixtures—all salvaged from the wrecking ball.

Then head over to Tenth Street for fancy garden accoutrements and clothing made with sustainable rainforest products at **Smith and Hawken.** Your friends may only know this outfit through its catalogs, and they'll be thrilled at the prospect of getting those Asiatic lily bulbs for half off (the Berkeley location features a retail shop and a discount outlet store).

By now (hopefully), you're hungry, but just because you're a veggie doesn't mean you don't crave fast food like every other red-blooded American. Some creative meatless types in Berkeley keyed into this very collegiate state of mind (hey, living in harmony with nature doesn't mean you can't recognize a good marketing concept when it smacks you in the tempeh) and opened **Smart Alec's,** an "Intelligent Fast Food" eatery on Telegraph Avenue. Order the gourmet, high-protein, cholesterol-free veggie burger; some air-baked french fries and a fruit smoothie—and feel good about yourself.

On the way home, instead of sitting in bridge traffic wasting precious fossil fuels, take the frontage road along the waterfront to just past Powell Street in Emeryville, park it, and hike out to the **mudflats.** No earthie worth his or her weight in retread Tevas will be able to resist the beauty of the mudflat sculptures—airplanes, saxophones, and abstract monuments in the tradition of Richard Serra—all crafted from recycled scrap metal, driftwood, soda cans, tires, and whatever else washed up at low tide.

# NIGHT

Even vegetarians enjoy a little nightlife. So if you're heading to the
Eleventh Street nightclub zone to catch a Merl Saunders show
benefitting the Rainforest Action Network, start your evening off at
**Hamburger Mary's.** The venerable late-night, lesbian-and-leather bar
and burger joint, is not as radical as it used to be, but it's still a great
place to give your friends a taste of the wild life San Franciscans
enjoyed in the '70s. Plus, all their burgers can be ordered made with
beef or tofu—a great compromise for hosts who can't resist the lure of
the flesh. Of course, there's nothing natural about the multiple pierc-
ings and tattoos covering many of the diners (and most of the help),
but hey—why not see how the other half lives? Oh, and the Bloody
Marys (strictly vegetarian, of course) are some of the zestiest in town.

If your destination is the Paragon, Blues, or some other Marina
district hot spot, definitely load up on the carbos at **Barney's,** which
makes the best garden burger (an oat patty mixed with zucchini, carrots, and other veggies) around. They also have a big selection of tofu
and all-beef burgers (with tons of toppings).

Over in the Castro, you can do dinner and a show at **Josie's
Cabaret and Juice Joint.** It's a gay cabaret; it's a vegetarian cafe. The
shows are campy, queer, often hilarious, and cheaper than your average
night out at the theater (see the Queer and Curious tour for more on
this); the menu served till just before showtime, usually 8 p.m., consists mostly of sandwiches, baked goods, stir-frys, and pasta. During
the shows you can also get desserts and snacks such as bagel pizzas.

## Veggies Go Uptown

Well, I've resisted saying it up to this point but... *only in San Francisco.*
I'm talking about haute vegan restaurants. Only a city such as this one
can take a cuisine that consists of legumes, tofu, and leafy greens, and
turn it into a fashionable, money-making enterprise. Your earthy
friends will be truly amazed at the quality and inventiveness of some
of these menus. Among the crop:

**Now and Zen**—Once just a bakery putting out tasty vegan pies and
cakes, this Japantown eatery has grown into a proper restaurant with
appetizers such as french onion soup and green-onion pancakes,
salads, and entrees that include Zen kabobs (tofu that approximates
meat), fillet of sole with lemon, and oversized ravioli with pine nuts,
sun-dried tomatoes, and marinara sauce. All the aforementioned
cakes and pies are available fresh from the bakery, which has since
moved into bigger digs.

**Millenium**—Beyond Greens, beyond Raw, Millennium features vegetarian cuisine for the twenty-first century—the place to take orthodox vegans for a really nice meal. The dining room is pleasantly upscale, but thankfully, even though the menu is strict, the wait-staff doesn't have a holier-than-thou attitude. Among the creative—and surprisingly flavorful—Mediterranean-inspired vegetarian dishes is a polenta torte layered with pesto and spinach, soy steak, saffron-and-corn risotto topped with squash ragout, and portobello mushrooms in cumin dressing. There's even an organic wine list.

**Herbivore**—This trendy-looking Valencia Street restaurant serves totally vegan (no dairy, no oils, no eggs) "California" cuisine—seitan sandwiches, garden burgers, vegan lasagne, Kung Pao tofu, and red curry dishes.

**Raw Living Foods**—Maybe it's a gimmick that diners will grow weary of; maybe they're on to something (frankly, I think it's the former). Raw Living Foods serves completely raw vegan food—nothing "processed, cooked, irradiated, or grown in pesticides, and including no animal products." This new "cuisine" consists of pizzas made with crust that's been baked in the sun for ten hours and topped with all sorts of veggies (from green peppers and onions to cured eggplant); sushi made from rice that has been soaked to softness rather than boiled; dehydrated falafel; pastas; and burritos filled with seasoned, marinated veggies and wrapped in purple cabbage leaf "tortillas." Liking or not liking the food is almost irrelevant. Take your green friends here for the totally San Francisco experience—guaranteed they don't have anything like this back home.

**Panhandle Pizza**—I happened on this tiny pizzeria on a research jaunt one afternoon and have been a fanatic fan ever since. From the corn meal–olive oil crusts to toppings that include fire-roasted red peppers, scallions, smoked mozzarella, artichokes, roasted garlic cloves, marinated shrimp and chicken, and the very nonveggie but awesome Aidell's andouille sausage, this place kicks pizza butt. Five of the nine house specials are vegetarian, and you can substitute soy cheese for mozzarella (or request a cheeseless).

**Red Crane**—Vegetarian Chinese food always reminds me of comedian Bobby Slayton's bit about trying to order something without pork in a Chinese restaurant, and the

**EARTH EVENTS**

If you're lucky enough to have a harmonic convergence of visiting eco-friends and **Earth Day** (the weekend of or closest to April 22), you can take your pick of fun, environmentally sound activities—from a music festival (usually held in or around Fort Mason) to the **March for the National Parks,** a wonderful fund-raising hike and tour of the Presidio led by in-the-know rangers.

**Green City Project** sponsors and cosponsors fun year-round activities, including bicycle tours of San Francisco's bayfront habitats, watershed festivals, and rooftop garden restorations (a great opportunity to see these amazing hidden green enclaves that most people don't even know exist; plus you get to do a little gardening and take in the views). For details, call their events hotline at 285-6556, or pick up a Green City Calendar at the Garden for the Environment.

The beach is always a good bet for nature lovers, but if you can combine it with **Coastal Cleanup Day** in September, you get the quintessential California surf, sun, and sand experience, and you do something good for the environment, too.

waiter keeps saying, "Ya, ya—water chestnuts, mushrooms, pork. . . ."
No worries at Red Crane. Even though it may taste like meat, it's not.
The dishes to order here are the sweet-and-sour walnuts (as meaty
and delicious as any pork version), one of the vegetarian chicken
dishes (made with tofu, and tasting amazingly like the real thing);
and the vegetarian potstickers.

## WHERE TO STAY

That **the Abigail** hotel is attached to Millennium restaurant makes it a
natural for green types, but it's also a sensible little English-style inn
with antique furnishings, cottage curtains, and twig wreaths. The only
drawbacks may be its location (in the slightly seedy Tenderloin/Civic
Center area) and the possibility that your friends may feel compro-
mised by sleeping under down (from a goose) comforters.

Despite its decidedly ungranola decor, the **Hotel Triton** hits organic
paydirt with its EcoRooms, twenty-four guest rooms equipped
with environmentally sensitive and responsible products, including
biodegradable and hypoallergenic soaps and shampoos, energy
efficient lighting, water-saving showers and toilets, recycling receptacles,
organic-cotton bed and bath linens, and a portable air-filtration unit.
The rooms are even cleaned with earth-friendly products. What
more could a tree hugger ask for?

Even in my starving student days, I always liked to think of myself as reasonable, not cheap. My husband, Pete, the penultimate Scotsman, prefers the term "thrifty." But whatever the euphemism, there's a time in almost everyone's life when their pocketbook is less padded than their resume, and the magic words are "no cover" and

# Tour 12 Cheapskates

"all-you-can-eat." Cheapskates, however, don't usually make great house guests. Chances are they spent their last dime to get to San Francisco, and now they're fully expecting to take advantage of your video store card, your toothpaste, and all those other little conveniences they're too poor to purchase, until you drive them (on your last gallon of gas) to the airport. There's a positive flip side to the cash-poor guest (and his benevolent twin, the saving-up-for-Europe host), however. It involves taking what I like to call the "Cheapskate Challenge": a leisurely, non-desperate stroll through the city, seeing how little you can spend—just for the fun of it. Anyone—even your rich friends (perhaps especially your rich friends)—can find this game entertaining. So leave your money on the dresser and let the cheap inherit the mirth.

# MORNING

A good cheapskates breakfast has a two-to-one ratio of large portions to small change. Usually that means a bacon-slinging, dishwater-coffee-pouring, barstool-at-the-counter kinda diner. Everyone's got a favorite, but I think no one's got better counter culture than **Art's Cafe** on Irving Street. A tiny place that in another day might have been referred to as a "greasy spoon," this unassuming joint offers heaping plates of eggs, hash browns, and bacon for under five bucks. Your cheapskate friends might even have money left over to feed the parking meter (then again, they're probably saving those quarters for laundry).

It's damn near impossible to find a decent down-home southern-style restaurant in San Francisco, let alone a cheap one. But the other **Art's,** a coffee shop in the Duboce Triangle, hits it on both fronts. Order the steak, pork chops, or country sausage and eggs with grits and a biscuit (between $4.50 and $6.50). If it's closer to lunchtime, get the fried-chicken plate with corn bread, collard greens, and black-eyed peas. (Dinner here is quite the bargain as well, with daily specials such as smothered chicken, chitterlings, ham hocks, and oxtails for between $7 and $8.)

Down on the waterfront, where mediocre restaurants have been known to charge $10 for an egg, you can get more bang(ers) for your buck, plus views that rival those at all the fancy schmancy places, at **Red's Java House,** the **Java House,** and the **Peer Inn.** Red's is the real thing (see the Neo-Bohemians tour)—a rickety old dive for dockworkers on a break. This is a great place to go after an all-night bender. Most of the regulars here order burgers for breakfast (sometimes accompanied by a Budweiser), so you won't feel out of place. The prices will warm the cockles of your cheapskate's heart—a full meal for less than $3. They might as well be giving it away.

If you want all that gritty, blue-collar atmosphere, but with a few other menu choices, head down the Embarcadero to the Java House on Pier 40. Another old waterfront stalwart (since 1912), the crowd—a mixture of tugboat operators, pier hands, South Beach sailboat owners, and yuppies from nearby condo complexes—come here for the three-egg omelets and pancake stacks, which you order at the counter and pick up when they yell. Prices are only about fifty cents more than at Red's, and the view of South Beach harbor and the bay is, of course, free.

For years I've wondered about that mysterious mélange of old Embarcadero waterfront dives between Pier 39 and the Ferry Building. You know the ones I'm talking about: those windowless-entrance places with the fritzed-out neon cocktail signs that never seem to have anyone going in or coming out. Some of them are actually full-on white tablecloth restaurants, but others . . . well, those are the places you go with low-budget friends who want a Bloody Mary and bacon breakfast without having to break a $20.

The Peer Inn at Pier 33 is a classic of the genre. They have a two-sided bar that's a room-size affair, with TVs all around for sports watching. The good tables are on a glassed-in patio that looks out to the old ferry docks and empty pier warehouses. Order your Bloody Mary at the bar, then head over to the grill at the far end and order your hash from the chalkboard menu. This is one of the few restaurants left in town where you can still smoke (not sure how they get around the ordinances, but probably the eating area's proximity to the bar has something to do with it).

## NOON

Sightseeing the traditional way can be expensive, but with a little ingenuity you can avoid the excess surcharges and still have the million-dollar photo ops, a little history and culture, and a gourmet lunch, too.

Hop in the old '78 Honda and head to **Treasure Island,** where the cheap fun begins with crossing the better half of the Bay Bridge and not paying the toll. Take the exit to the Treasure Island Museum, housed in one of three buildings that remain from the Golden Gate International Exposition, which was held here in 1939. The museum has been threatening to close for the last few years, but so far something or someone always comes along to save it—and more important—keep it admission-free. The small exhibit hall commemorates the exposition as well as the military history of the island, with models of the magnificent art deco pavilions and other expo memorabilia, plus uniforms, weapons, navigation instruments, and maritime artifacts. Nearby is a display about the *China Clipper,* the amphibious plane that flew the wealthy and powerful over the Pacific between 1939 and 1946.

After your cultural foray, step outside the museum onto the artificial shores, and you'll meet the San Francisco skyline eye to eye—an *ohmygod* view that you won't believe you didn't have to put a quarter into a viewfinder to see. Grab the disposable camera and shoot away.

### CITY GUIDE TOURS

So they want to learn something about the city, but they're not willing to shell out a lot of dough for one of those all-inclusive tour-with-lunch deals. No problem. **City Guides** offers some of the most informative and entertaining walking tours available anywhere—and they're absolutely free. Sponsored by the San Francisco Public Library, the neighborhood jaunts are led by a scholarly stable of history, trivia, and folklore buffs who clearly delight in what they do. There are some twenty-six tours to choose from, ranging from "Brothels, Boardinghouses, and Bawd" to Cityscapes, Roof Gardens, and Pacific Heights Mansions. You can catch one nearly every day of the week; most of them start between 10 a.m. and noon and run a couple of hours; call the main library for a schedule.

Next, spend a little time scouring the island for big movie stars; several of the hangars on this old naval base have been converted to sound studios for big Hollywood films. *Sphere* starring Sharon Stone and *Copycats* with Holly Hunter and Sigourney Weaver were both shot here, so you never know who you might run into in the commissary (have a pen ready for an autograph; it may be worth something some day). If you're lucky, they might let you stand around and watch a scene being shot. Think of it as a poor man's Universal Studios tour.

Speaking of the commissary, your friend's chintzy heart will fill with joy if you can find a way to get invited to lunch at the **Advanced Culinary Training Center,** a school on the island for big-time chefs. The center is open for lunch only (noon sharp) to students and their guests, and by prior arrangement (call ahead and ask real nicely). If you can get in, you'll be treated to an incredible three-course, gourmet meal—that rivals anything the big city restaurants have to offer—for less than $5. Salads and soups are only fifty cents; entrees just $2.50—and you get to eat this feast in a genuine former navy galley. Lunch is served Tuesdays through Fridays only.

## Quarterback, Get the Quarter Back

Clearly, no cheapskate is going to fork over $50 to a scalper for 49ers tickets, and even $30 for a college game is probably too rich for his or her blood. That's why there's **Cheapskates Hill** in Berkeley. The knoll just below the big cannon, on the hill above Memorial Stadium's north end zone, is the spot where starving students, penny pinchers, and claustrophobics watch Cal Bears football on Saturdays. Sure, they're not fifty-yard-line seats. But you won't be cursing yourself for paying all that money to sit behind the guy wearing one of those beer-caddie hardhats, either. Warning: the cannon they shoot off after each hometeam touchdown vibrates the seats 100 yards away, so unless you already have tinnitus from standing too close to the speakers at rock concerts, you might want to bring ear plugs.

## Golden Gate Park

Just hanging out in the park throwing a Frisbee is a great day out if you ask me, and it doesn't cost a thing. But if you want to see how the paying public lives (without dipping into your own wallet), you'll have to plan ahead. The **de Young Museum,** the **Asian Art Museum,** and the **Academy of Sciences** all have free admission days the first Wednesday of every month. You can also sneak in to the Academy for free during the last half hour they're open (4:30 to 5 p.m.) every day, and into the **Japanese Tea Garden** between 5:30 and 6:30 p.m. from May through September.

Most Sundays during the year, you can also sit on the benches in the Music Concourse and enjoy a concert of classical standards and rousing patriotic numbers by the **Park Band,** the oldest municipal band in the country, established in Golden Gate Park in 1882. If you haven't seen these guys before, try to imagine your high school concert band, complete with military-style uniforms and a killer arrangement of "Night on Bald Mountain"—only with actual, professional musicians. For most of the group (and definitely for the conductor, Robert Hansen, who's been with the band more than fifty years), it's a labor of love. They're paid a pittance, and each year their operating budget gets cut back. So enjoy this city institution while you can.

If you miss the summer park freebies—flower shows, Comedy Day, rollerblade competitions, soccer and tennis matches—there's always **Shakespeare in the Park** in September, the best, free high-culture extravaganza park event of the year. The San Francisco Shakespeare Festival performs the Bard's works (usually comedies) in a glen behind the Conservatory of Flowers weekends throughout the month. Bring a picnic, a lot of sunscreen, spring for a little vino (Trader Joe's has really decent Chilean wines for only $2.99), and watch as plays like *As You Like It* and *Love's Labour's Lost* are taken out of their traditional contexts and brought to the great outdoors as Indian fables and Roaring '20s romps.

## No-Cost Concerts

The granddaddy of the free concert series is the summer festival at **Stern Grove.** Most Sundays from June through August, performers who would normally charge you half a paycheck to see them do it for free in this lovely grassy amphitheater surrounded by redwood and eucalyptus trees. Performers range from the Trockadero Ballet and the Preservation Hall Jazz Band to the SF Symphony and Theatre Flamenco.

Downtown, the **San Francisco Jazz Festival** gets into the act with its annual series of free Friday lunchtime concerts in the redwood grove at the base of the **TransAmerica Pyramid.** Expect the unexpected here. Performers might be anything from traditional combos to ethnic-industrial-acid jazz groups. Chairs are provided for serious music lovers; casual jazzheads eat burritos and sprawl on the benches or grass around the little park. Afterward, take a ride to the twenty-seventh floor of the Pyramid and soak up the views of the Golden Gate Bridge, Coit Tower, and Alcatraz. The observation area near the tiny triangular top of this San Francisco icon is open to the public on weekdays and is absolutely free.

Throughout the summer, radio station **KFOG** hosts an irregular series of free rock and pop concerts in Justin Herman Plaza at the Embarcadero Center. Sometimes they're promoting new bands (Gin Blossoms and Tim

Finn were two offerings in years past); sometimes it's a listener appreciation thing (like their annual Sky Concert with fireworks in July). Occasionally you can also hit big time—such as when U2 played for free because they were making a documentary. However you slice it, there are no ticket lines, no service charge, and no $4 beers (lighters optional).

# NIGHT

San Francisco may very well be the one town where there *is* a free lunch, or at the very least, a free happy hour. And I'm not just talking chicken wings and chips and salsa. The day the Fairmont's **Tonga Room** shuts down I think I'll have to go into seclusion for a week-long period of mourning. For pure tiki-tacky ambience, there is nothing else in the city that comes close. And it's almost impossible to beat (in volume and price) their enormous, all-you-can-eat happy hour, with its luau-style buffet ($5 from 5 to 7 p.m.). But the food is merely the flame on the rum drink. At the Tonga you can chow down on chow mein, sip something enormous and blue through a gigantic straw, and bask in the glow of tiki torches and Pirates of the Caribbean cargo nets while listening to a band play "Caribbean Queen" on an island in a swimming pool. Then there's the cocktail menu, which features an amazing array of fruity, umbrella-laden, comes-in-a-coconut-with-smoke-billowing-out-the-sides drinks—all boasting names like the "Scorpion" ("one too many may sting"), and the oddly compelling "Bora Bora Horror!" And then, just when you think it can't get any better, the thunder claps, the lightning flashes, and you're in the midst of a poolside monsoon. Can you stand it? It's like *Blue Hawaii* meets the Muppets.

If you're willing to eat a little early, you can have an entire Mexican dinner for free at the ever-popular **Cadillac Bar,** where someone is always singing "Happy Birthday" (in Spanish) and they serve tequila poppers by the truckload. The boisterous bar and restaurant (the noise can sometimes get deafening) offers a full, no-charge buffet of nachos, tacos, chimichangas, fajitas, quesadillas, and the like weekdays from 4 to 7 p.m. And you also get $1 off margaritas and beer for a buck. *Bueno!*

A better deal still is all-you-can-eat oyster night at the **El Rio.** Hard to imagine that in a town where six oysters can run you upwards of $10, this Mission district bar and club (which proudly boasts the motto "Your Dive" above its doorway) gives them away *free* every week during Friday happy hour from 5 to 7 p.m. Slurp down as many Chesapeakes or Blue Points on-the-half-shell as you can stomach, chase them with a very reasonably priced beer, and pat your pocketbook contentedly as you think to yourself: "The world is *my* oyster (you get your own shellfish)."

If you happen to miss Friday oyster night (though I can't imagine why you would), the El Rio has other bargains that you won't want to pass up. On Mondays, they have $1 well drinks and Pabst Blue Ribbon; on Wednesdays, it's $2 margaritas all night long. The latter should be savored amongst the palm trees and tiki torches on the tropical backyard patio.

## Eat, Drink, and Be Thrifty

Despite the ever-increasing invasion of restaurants like Rose Pistola, which threaten to turn North Beach into a big-budget zone, there are still several places that offer the traditional five-course family-style dinners for somewhere between $12 and $22. At first you might not think this a bargain. But consider that you get soup, salad, pasta, an entree (sometimes two entrees), and dessert for that price. Then those pocketbooks are starting to feel pretty hefty, huh? Among the remaining family-style restaurants are the **Basque Hotel and Restaurant, Des Alpes, Gold Spike, New Pisa, La Felce,** and my favorite, **Capp's Corner**—where you eat next to the bar, and you're served dinner by the all-knowing Betty in the coke-bottle glasses, who's been there since the dawn of time.

The cost-conscious consumer will almost always include one pizza dinner on the itinerary. But that doesn't have to mean eating out of the box in front of the TV. Take them to the Monday night all-you-can-eat pizza feed at **Goat Hill Pizza** on picturesque Potrero Hill. For $8, you get to inhale from the unlimited salad bar and choose from a dozen different varieties of hot-from-the-oven pizzas as they're carted around from table to table. The views of downtown are just extra cheese on the pie.

If you don't want to gorge yourself, but you also don't want to eat at Burger King, other inexpensive options include:

**Gira Polli**—Every day before 6:30 p.m., this popular North Beach eatery offers the most mouth-watering, perfectly roasted whole chickens for just $6.95, $10 with potatoes and vegetables.

**Pasta Pomodoro**—This minichain of fresh, healthy, quick-service (as opposed to fast food) pasta restaurants is a good deal no matter what time of day. Favorite dishes such as gnocchi with Gorgonzola and tomatoes, or pasta with mussels, calamari, and scallops are generally priced between $4.50 and $6.50.

**We Be Sushi**—Sushi is not cheap man's food, but We Be, with locations all around the city, makes it almost reasonable. Prices per roll are about half what you'd pay elsewhere, though they're not always so impeccably fresh. Assorted sushi combos run (at last check) about $8. Be sure to read the menu for the rejected alternative names to We Be Sushi (they tried to name the restaurant "McSushi," but a certain fast food chain said "I don't think so"); my favorite: Sushi and the Banshees.

**California Culinary Academy**—A great place for people who want to experience the California cuisine scene but don't want to take out a second mortgage to do it. The academy has trained some of the best chefs in town. But before they can graduate to Zare or Postrio, they have to put in their hours creating culinary masterpieces for school credit. Diners at the academy reap the benefits of their theses. Dinners at the Careme Room are pricey, but Monday through Thursday nights at the Academy Grill, you can get a buffet of appetizers, grilled and roasted meats, and dessert for about $9.95.

**Beer/Wine/Sake**—You don't need to be cheap to enjoy a tour of the **Anchor Brewing Co.** (see the Parents tour), but even people willing to shell out a few bucks for beer will be thrilled that the tasting at the end is free (and ample).

Wine tasting in recent years has gotten increasingly spendy, with Napa wineries charging on average $3 for three to four tastings (but hey—you get to keep that lovely wine glass). Most Sonoma wineries are still free, though several now limit the number of wines you can taste. The friendly folks at **Benziger Family Winery** in Glen Ellen offer close to a dozen wines for free tasting, and you get a bonus freebie in the form of a tram tour of the vineyards, plus there's an interesting exhibit showing how wine is made.

If your goal is to drink a lot for free and you don't much care about the requisite history and science lesson, then **Takara Sake Factory** in Berkeley is for you. In their Japanese-style tasting room, you can belly up to the bar and taste cup upon cup of Sho Chiku Bai rice wine or plum wine, until upright is no longer your natural position. Of course, they'll expect you to maybe buy a bottle or two after all this hospitality, but heck, you'll be too soused to care.

## What Price Culture?

The ultimate victory in a cheapskate challenge is when you can live large and spend small, partaking in those things normally reserved for the leisure class but paying workingman's prices.

For art lovers there's **First Thursdays,** a great way to view museum-quality art at chi-chi downtown galleries, without paying admission, and also enjoy an evening of free wine and hors d'oeuvres. The first Thursday of every month, galleries that are part of the San Francisco Art Dealers Association hold open houses from 5:30 to 7:30 p.m. to promote their current shows. Mosey your way up Geary or Post Streets where many of the galleries are housed (there are groups of galleries at 251 Post and 49 Geary), stopping in at the ones that are offering good bite-size edibles (mostly cheese these days, sorry) and full glasses of chardonnay. Remember to stand in front of one painting at each place, ponder your wine glass contemplatively, and say something about the work's resonant emotional complexity.

I mention it in the Culture Vultures tour, but penny pinchers will probably appreciate this tip even more. The **Opera** and **Symphony** both offer cheap seats, and if you happen to luck out, they might just be really great seats. For the opera, try the box office first thing in the morning on the day of the performance for either standing-room only tickets ($8) or returned/donated tickets (charges vary). A select number of student rush tickets (about half price) go on sale two hours before the curtain. If you want to hear some of the stars of the opera, past and present, do famous arias, you'll have to get your cash-poor friends to show up in September for the annual free **Opera in the Park** event. Pavarotti and Sills have sung here, as have Thomas Hampson and Frederica von Stade.

The symphony offers seats behind the stage for $10, but you'll need to queue up two hours prior to show time and have cash on hand (two ticket limit). Or, if you don't mind a couple of stops and starts, you can also attend open rehearsals on select mornings for $15; the price includes doughnuts and coffee, and an informative talk by the music director.

For other theater, dance, and music offerings, hit the **Tix Bay Area** kiosk in Union Square on the day of the show, and you might be able to snag half-off tickets.

For film buffs bemoaning the ever-rising cost of movies, the city still has a couple of bargains. The **Balboa Theater** in the Outer Richmond offers great double features, usually early second-runs of major movies just after they've left the big venues—for $6 (that's $3 a movie if you're calculating). Get there early, grab a slice of pizza from across the street or a carton of super-cheap Vietnamese food from next door (they let you bring it in), and you can have dinner and a movie for under $10.

Up at UCSF on Parnassus Heights, you can see popular second-run flicks before they go to video (everything from *Jerry Maguire* to *Space Jam* in '97) for $3.50, at the **Cole Hall Cinema.** Showings are mostly Thursday and Friday nights from September through May, with the occasional bargain-priced ($2) Sunday matinee.

## WHERE TO STAY

Chances are if they're really cheap, they'll be crashing on your sofa or your floor. Next best alternative is the **Fort Mason Youth Hostel,** where for just $16 a night, you get a room on a stretch of the city's most coveted piece of oceanfront real estate. This is truly the Ritz of youth hostels: the rooms are clean and relatively spacious; the kitchen is pristine, with clear-door refrigerators that house individual cubby holes; it's centrally located right between the Marina district and Fisherman's Wharf; and you get panoramic ocean views from here till next Tuesday. They also offer free movies, free walking tours, an espresso stand, and other amenities. It's so plush, it'll have you thinking twice about your $1,200 one-bedroom apartment with the view of the brick wall.

A beautiful, historic, Italianate Victorian hotel near Fisherman's Wharf for less than $60 a night? Impossible you say? Then you haven't checked out the **San Remo Hotel,** one of the best—if not *the* best—lodging bargain in the city. The hotel was built in 1906 by banker A. P. Giannini to help house earthquake refugees, and has been recently restored to its turn-of-the-century glory. Inside, stained-glass skylights, brass fixtures, and hanging plants give the place a greenhouse feel. Rooms are small, tasteful, clean, and spare, decorated with simple antiques such as pine armoires and iron beds. Neighbors do have to share bathrooms, but they're kept immaculately clean, and feature nice touches such as claw-foot tubs and pull-chain toilets. Downstairs there's a cocktail lounge and piano bar, where you can get hot appetizers in the evening, and continental breakfast in the morning.

Shopaholics come in all shapes and sizes, and they feed their addiction for all kinds of reasons. For some, it's the bargain mentality. They've plowed through every thrift store and outlet within a forty-mile radius of their home, and now they've come here looking for fresh meat. For others, it's the prospect of bringing back something that

# Tour 13 Shopaholics

is uniquely San Francisco, something they can't find where they live. And for still others, shopping is simply their favorite form of entertainment, with a vacation in San Francisco merely being a conduit for pursuing their preferred pastime at their leisure, rather than on their lunch hour. Whatever their motives, it's your job as host to indulge their cravings—that is, as long as they're paying with their own credit card.

## THE OUTLETS

For a while there in the '80s, factory outlets were cropping up South of Market faster than trendy restaurants. And some of them were actually good deals. I mean, the **Gunne Sax** outlet alone provided me and thousands of other girls with the prom dress of their dreams—at a price that made moms sigh with relief. But along with the Gunne Saxes, the CP Shades, the Esprits, and the Mill Valley Cottons, came your shoddily made fake designer clothes; your manufacturers that no one's ever heard of; and your discount stores that offered very little in the way of real bargains. Then, riding the wave of this outlet mania came the gargantuan off-price outlet malls, many of which claimed to offer deep discounts on designer merchandise, but really just offered lower-end lines by the same label, at very average prices.

All this whining is my way of saying that just because there's a slash through the $700 price tag on that Donna Karan dress, it doesn't automatically mean that you're getting a deal. Here are some places worth noting:

**Isda and Company**—This attractive little boutique on South Park is the wholesale outlet for local designer Isda Funari's classy, modern career and casual wear. The inventory includes samples, overruns, seconds, and returns from department stores—and everything is sold at wholesale prices (no markup). Peruse the sales racks for even bigger bargains: a recent clearance area offered sample vests (size eight only) that would sell for at least $60 at Macy's, for 40 percent off $30.

**City Lights**—The place to go for hefty, all-cotton leggings, exercise wear, sweaters, and dresses. This label is sold in lots of department and retail stores at steep prices, and while the nicer clothing (i.e., dresses and skirts) can be a bit spendy, there are always the irregular racks, and the $5 and $10 bargain bins for shorts, T-shirts, and the odd cotton cardigan.

**Jeanne Marc Downs**—Jeanne Marc designs are not everyone's taste. The fabrics tend toward bold, bright colors with busy, Asian-inspired patterns. But if you like the look, then this outlet store is worth your while. Discounts on past-season dresses, pantsuits, jackets, and skirts can be as much as 70 percent off retail.

**North Face Outlet**—Considering the cost of things like Gortex jackets at the full-price store, the prices at the outlet look pretty good. Still, not everything here is cheap. The outlet sells a slightly lower-end line of merchandise, which is distinguished by a black "O" in the stitching of the North Face label. But if you can wait until a sale, you can save yourself some serious bucks on outdoor gear—everything from fleece jackets and snowboard pants to tents, hiking boots, and sleeping bags.

**Napa Premium Outlets**—If you're taking your shopaholic friend to the wine country, you absolutely can't pass up this outlet center. Unlike the ones in Vacaville, this is not your typical London Fog/ Bass/Levi's strip mall. In Napa, you'll find off-price outlets for labels you really like, including J. Crew, BCBG, Carole Little, Ann Taylor, Timberland, Liz Claiborne, Calvin Klein, Jones New York, TSE Cashmere, and Tommy Hilfiger. Discounts average from 25 to 65 percent; look for irregulars and overruns, and additional reductions on clearance racks. I once walked away from the J. Crew outlet with three new outfits for under $100. Score!

**St. Helena Factory Outlets**—You'll find this swank shopping center farther north on Highway 29, just past the Beringer Winery. It offers only a few outlets, but if you like Coach, Donna Karan, or Joan and David, you'll want to make a detour through here. To my mind, the Donna Karan outlet is a huge rip-off. Most of it looks like it comes from a knockoff line that's inferior to her lower-priced DKNY collection. And it's still incredibly expensive. The Joan and David outlet, however, can be quite the deal. The shoes are usually past season, and sizes can be few and far between, but it's a whole lot cheaper than at Macy's. The Coach store also offers some good bargains. I picked up a gorgeous suede Coach handbag, originally priced close to $300, for under $100.

Last, even though they no doubt have record stores in their hometowns, you and/or your friends might be enticed by the prices at the **Tower Records Outlet,** the little-known SoMa outlet store that's the San Francisco clearinghouse for the Tower Records empire. The shop sells discontinued stock, leftovers, and cut-outs of CDs, cassettes, laser discs, videos, and books. Prices are rock bottom on both new and used items; just don't expect to find the latest releases.

## SECONDHAND CLOTHES AND OTHER WORLDLY GOODS

There are people who live for the preowned (aka used or secondhand). My friend Paul is one of them. He is also the nattiest dresser I know, with closets full of '50s bowling shirts and burnt-orange golf cardigans, '60s leather blazers that are all the rage now, zoot suits, and tons of '70s Quiana and psychedelic Austin Powers polyester shirts. He is the only person I know who could wear an authentic, circa 1977 rhinestone necklace that says "Foxy," and have people stopping him in the streets to tell him how cool he is. Why I'm telling you this, I don't know. But I do know that if your visiting friends are serious vintage and thrift store hounds, sending them to American Rag probably isn't gonna cut it.

For serious bargains on high-end stuff, peruse the chi-chi secondhand stores on **Upper Fillmore,** where the well-heeled residents of Pacific Heights toss the designer suits and dresses they've grown tired of. Profits from the **Next-to-New** shop go to benefit the Junior League—so you know what social strata the donations are coming from (though some of the items may be a bit too bridge-club stuffy for younger tastes). **Crossroads Trading Company** has a large inventory of stylish and trendy women's name-brand clothes, plus a lot of quality vintage stuff from the '30s and '40s. **Victorian House** is the place to pick up Brioni suits, double-breasted cashmere trench coats from Barney's, and the other stuff Mayor Brown has discarded—for a song.

Nearby on Sacramento Street is **Good Byes,** which sells men's and women's new and preowned top-quality clothing and shoes. I once saw a practically brand-new women's Armani tuxedo for $200. In the women's shoe section, there are brands such as Ferragamo and Bally, and good deals can also be found on men's sportcoats and ties.

Like the Salvation Army, Goodwill stores are generally only for the dedicated bargain hunter who doesn't mind rifling through racks of junk to find an overlooked gem. Make an exception for the **Goodwill Boutique** tucked away on West Portal Avenue, midway between Stonestown and the Sunset district. This is the clearinghouse for all the upscale clothing items culled from all the local Goodwill stores. I've found nice, if slightly outdated, designer dresses, blazers, and suits, plus lots of tops, skirts, and pants from places like the Gap, the Limited, and Banana Republic. And prices are dirt cheap (i.e., a Jones New York dress for $15).

Speaking of **the Gap,** the stores on **Market and Dolores** and **Polk and California Streets** are the ones where they send all the other stores' leftovers and end-of-season stuff, and where you'll find the biggest selection of closeout sale items.

So maybe they didn't come here looking for a set of 1920s cookie cutters, or a classic, stainless-steel blender, but once inside **Cookin',** it's amazing what your guests will find they absolutely can't live without. The small store sells vintage and refurbished gourmet cookware and kitchen gear—everything from hand-crank meat grinders to cake molds.

If you didn't have time to get up to the Napa Valley, but your friends would still like to sample (and buy) a little fruit of the vine, take them to the **Wine Club** on Harrison Street. Don't let the windowless warehouse exterior or the word "club" scare you away. You don't need to be a member, and the insides are quite hospitable and inviting. Belly up to the tasting bar and try some of the wines recommended by the staff of friendly experts. It's really almost better than being at a winery, because here you get to taste a variety of labels and vintages. Plus, the prices are half what you'd pay at a winery.

## ONLY IN SAN FRANCISCO

Souvenir hunting is an essential part of the whole tourist ritual, and really shouldn't be overlooked if you want to create a positive shopping experience for your purchase-happy friends (even though they clearly suffer from some kind of obsessive-compulsive disorder). A few suggestions:

**Mark Reuben Galleries**—This gallery (with locations in the SF Shopping Centre and Sausalito) has a huge inventory of old San Francisco photos, including classics like that shot of the half-built Golden Gate Bridge, the Sutro Baths, Joe DiMaggio when he played for the San Francisco Seals in the Pacific Coast League, and the aftermath of the 1906 earthquake.

**Golden Gate Bridge Shop**—Most of the stuff at this toll plaza shop is ticky-tacky crap. But the one thing they do sell that's worth making a shopping stop for are authentic pieces of cable and rivets from the Golden Gate Bridge. If your pals are looking for something even more substantial, perhaps an original Lombard Street brick from the **City Store** in Pier 39 would do (see the Green Types tour for more info about this shop).

**Marshall's**—Weirdly enough, this national discount clothing store out in Metro Center in Colma has a small housewares department. And believe it or not, in that housewares department you can often find good, hand-painted Italian ceramics—plates, vases, bowls, salt-and-pepper shakers, mugs, and more. But instead of paying $100 a plate, you pay $19.99. *Va bene!* Unfortunately, the stock varies wildly from month to month, and there are times when you may come up dry. But it's worth trying your luck. Just make sure to look on the back for the "Made in Italy" stamp.

**Biordi**—Unlike Marshall's, you won't find many bargains here, but you are guaranteed a full selection of beautiful, handmade Italian pottery. All the famous artisans and designs are represented, in pieces as small as cardholder trays, and as a large as outdoor planters.

**Exploratorium Store**—The science geek in you will go into sensory overload at this great museum shop, which carries everything from kaleidoscopes and kinetic energy balls to glow-in-the-dark maps of the night sky, science experiment kits, and M. C. Escher clocks.

**Uncle Mame**—Big Boy dolls, *Partridge Family* lunch boxes, *Charlie's Angels* action figures, eyeball-shaped black-and-white TVs from the '60s, and Betty Page T-shirts are just a few of the kitschy pop culture items at this kooky Castro district store.

**La Tienda**—This is the retail shop for the Mexican Museum, and a great place to go Christmas shopping. The place is filled with hand-made Mexican crafts, folk art, tin ornaments, tree of life dioramas, Day of the Dead shrines, coconut masks, and other delights.

**Maison d'Etre**—Where else but in South Park are you going to pick up the odd peeling-paint park bench, that slightly rusted bed frame, old watering cans, handmade lamps, and patinated garden ornaments?

**Panetti's**—There have been years where I did all my holiday gift shopping at this store. My best friend got the earrings shaped like tiny chairs and the refrigerator magnet poetry; my sister-in-law got the enormous silver spoon mug rack; my other sister-in-law got the hand-enameled cat pin; my mom got the frog garden torch; and my mother-in-law got the handcrafted ceramic teapot.

**Flax**—It bills itself as an art supply store, but it's so much more than that. I've spent hours looking at the handpainted clocks, boxes, and Russian eggs, the art chairs, the rubber briefcases shaped like cats and Scottie dogs, and the 3-D jigsaw puzzles.

**Gamescape**—Located in the Western Addition, this little shop sells every kind of game imaginable, but their specialty is nonstandard games—the kind you won't find at places like Toys R Us. Look particularly for imported items, party games, strategy and role-playing games (including five varieties of Go), and unusual word games.

## San Francisco Clothing Designers

**Metier**—A chic downtown shop that carries a large selection of local and international designers, including Lat Naylor and Chaiken and Capone.

**Ambiance**—Soft, drapey baby-doll dresses and long, smooth silhouettes in solid colors with embossed patterns are the signature look of owner/designer Gloria Garrett. Women swear by this Haight Street store, which also sells vintage clothing, including (in 1997) wonderful, Chinese-style short evening jackets.

**Diana Slavin**—Located on tiny Claude Lane, this boutique features the designs of its namesake, who creates smart, slimming, but not-too-flashy skirts, jackets, pants, and dresses that you can wear to work or out on the town. Lots of black.

**Margaret O'Leary**—Also on Claude Lane is the retail outlet for the Irish-born O'Leary, who comes from a long line of knitters and weavers. Her popular hand-loomed sweaters, cardigans, opera coats, tunics, and twin sets in chenille, wool, and cotton are carried in some of the finest stores in the country, but this is the only free-standing store devoted exclusively to O'Leary's designs.

**RistaRose**—Young, hip designers Ivana Ristic and Lynn Rosenzweig are the team behind this cool couture shop on Grant Avenue, which creates modern evening wear with a New York edginess that borders on the Gothic. They also make some of the prettiest, most original wedding gowns around.

**Knitz and Leather**—Up the street, the owners of this tiny boutique make exquisite chenille sweaters and leather jackets—all by hand. The selection is small, and the prices pretty high, but after you try one of those jackets on, you won't want to go back to that mass-produced stuff.

## WHERE TO STAY

Although just about every hotel located in the vicinity of Union Square could be considered a shoppers' hotel, only one really positions itself as such: **the Maxwell.** A recent addition to the Chip Conley/Joie de Vivre chain of boutique hotels, the Maxwell has unique services designed specifically for shoppers, among them: high-tech foot spas for post-pavement-pounding pampering; a unique, personal guide to Union Square retailers; and a shopping newsletter highlighting best buys and interesting items. They also offer great shop/stay packages (as do a number of Union Square hotels), including the "Urban Shopper" deal, in which you get a room, continental breakfast for two, parking, a muni pass for two, an in-room foot massage, and a guide to local flea markets and second-hand shops.

Anyone who lives here knows that just going from your office to your car can be more exercise than most people get in a week. We live in a giant, natural gymnasium, where getting from Point A to Point B inevitably involves navigating up and down those steep hills. Most people, rather than replace their clutch every few months, opt to

# Tour 14 Fitness Freaks and Heavy Sweaters

hoof it, bike it, skate it, or public transport it (which can entail a bizarre sort of standing, balancing, stretching yoga exercise of its own). So with all these inadvertent workouts, a lot of us feel like we don't really need to do a whole lot more—that is, until Mr./Ms. Fitness Freak shows up at your door with weights in hand, sweating and panting from having just jogged in from the airport. And there you are at 11 a.m., still in your robe and slippers, pint of Ben and Jerry's in hand, and the queasy look of the unmotivated on your face. Best strategy: suck in the gut, strap on the old Nikes, and show them what those seven hills are really made of.

# MORNING-NOON

There are more places to hike in San Francisco than you can shake one of those fancy walking sticks at—and they're not all in Golden Gate Park. After your breakfast of champions (heavy sweaters don't do fattening, lethargy-inducing brunchy-brunchy, remember?), pack up a couple of Clif Bars and go climb the city.

If you can set aside your religious beliefs (or, perhaps, embrace them), the hike up **Mount Davidson** is truly inspirational, and a good aerobic workout. The trail to the summit is best reached off of Portola Drive (take Teresita to the intersection of Myra Way and Sherwood Court). From here, there's a wide path that leads up the mountain. At 938 feet, this is the highest peak in San Francisco, and though others offer more flashy bay and ocean views, when you get to the top of Mount Davidson, you really feel like you've climbed right through the marine layer to the top of the world. Though you may have mixed feelings about the 100-foot concrete cross that pierces this wooded mountaintop, you should definitely walk to the base of it and look straight up. The sheer bulk and size of the thing is quite awesome and humbling—it's easy to see why putting crosses on mountaintops has been common practice for conversion-happy padres over the centuries.

I have to admit I'm a bit partial to **Glen Park Canyon,** since I live nearby, but honestly this is one of those rare places where you feel like you're in the country, in the middle of the city. Glen Canyon was the spark that set off the local environmental movement back in the '70s, when developers threatened to pave over the green hills, free-flowing creek, and craggy buttes. As recently as 1997, park preservationists won a fight to keep cars out of the canyon.

Start off your trek with a leisurely stroll across the grassy fields, past the softball diamonds, to the clubhouse. Just behind the building you can pick up the path that leads through the canyon. Follow the bouncing-ball-chasing dogs down the dirt trail until you reach the bridge, under which a rare natural creek trickles during the winter, spring, and sometimes even through the summer months. It's a picturesque little habitat that residents have lovingly restored with native plants. From here you can hike your way up the sides of the canyon, scaling the various rock formations for different overviews of the terrain. Any one of these vista points makes a great sun-and-snack stop.

For serious weekend warriors or aspiring decathletes, **Lake Merced** has it all. Start by jogging, rollerblading, or biking around the lake (approximately five miles). Next, rent a rowboat for a strenuous sculling exercise amid the shorebirds (watch out for stray tee shots and fly fishermen). Afterwards, maybe take in nine holes of golf at Harding Park, or a little windsurfing (all-equipment-included beginners lessons are offered). Now you're ready for a big grilled-chicken sandwich, a lite beer, and some ESPN at the **Boat House,** where you may be entertained by the likes of Carol (36 DD) Doda and her Lucky Stiffs, or a down-home blues band.

Out of the city, my favorite places to hike with tourists are the **Palomarin Trail** to the waterfall on the beach at **Point Reyes,** a singularly spectacular combination of surf and turf with a freshwater swimming lake thrown in for good measure (about five and a half miles); the ever-popular **Tennessee Valley** trail to the beach, which is a short jaunt (if you don't take any strenuous detours) that leads to a sweet little beach/cove with panoramic views of the Pacific; and the **Point Bonita Lighthouse** trail, a stunning (if brief) path that takes you along steep ocean cliffs to a working lighthouse, which sits on a point on the edge of the earth. The Park Service regularly schedules evening and full-moon walks out to the lighthouse (a photographer's dream come true), but reservations are required; call 331-1540.

## Feel the Burn

No law says sightseeing can't be part of a training regimen. So, rather than run the bleachers at Kezar, do a thigh-burner up and down the city's **secret stairways,** where hidden San Francisco reveals itself in hillside cottages overgrown with rambling roses and ivy, magical keyhole views, and neoclassical sculpture. The granddaddy of stairway walks is of course the **Filbert Street Steps** (see the Virgins tour) which, with fitness fiends, should be done from the bottom of Sansome Street, up.

In the Upper Market area are the wonderful **Vulcan Stairs,** located at the end of Ord Street, off Seventeenth Street. This tiny byway invariably produces a chronic case of address envy among both residents and tourists. Tucked along the steps are sweet little cottages with overgrown flower gardens and cobblestone terraces that should, by all rights, be up in Sonoma or along some sleepy country lane. The serenity of this spot may even cause your endorphin-loving friend to take a breather. Not a problem; he can finish his set on the staircase located just a few blocks higher, on the equally pretty **Upper Terrace Street.**

The stairs that begin at the bottom of **Pacheco Street** or the top of **Mendosa** (depending on which end you start at) win the award for longest set and are a guaranteed calorie burner. They're also a great sightseeing jaunt, located in the district of Forest Hill, one of the least-known ritzy neighborhoods in the city. Forest Hill is almost like a separate village (consider that up until about ten years ago, the residents paved their own streets). The stairs are actually divided into three sets: from the top, the first one starts at Mendosa and goes down to Santa Rita; from here you jog around the bend and catch the next set at Ninth Avenue and Castenada; and the third tier goes from Castenada to Magellan on Pacheco. On your descent, you'll get a residential-architectural eyeful—modern Tudors, next to Maybeckian shingle-styles, next to modern neoclassical mansions, abutting Mother Goose houses. From the bottom, if your knees are still intact, head down to West Portal Avenue for some nonfat frozen yogurt at **Double Rainbow** or **Shaw's** (now there's a blast from the past), or a shot of liquid energy at **Peet's.**

The majestic **Lyon Street Steps,** located at the western end of Broadway, rival Filbert Street for spectacular panoramic vistas. From the top you gaze down upon the Palace of Fine Arts, the Marina, and the bay all the way to Alcatraz. For maximum *ooh* and *aah* effect, start at the bottom, run to the top, and don't turn around till you get there (the flower boxes, planters, and statuary along the way should keep you occupied).

## Pedal Power

So, okay, motorists and the mayor aren't so crazy about this event, but how better to give your out-of-town exercise hound a Tour d'EssEff than by riding in **Critical Mass,** held the last Friday of every month beginning at 5:30 p.m. in Justin Herman Plaza. The organizers' motto—"promoting pedaling, not petroleum"—is really just the tip of the iceberg. Critical Mass is about free-spiritedness and grassroots activism—two of the fundamental principles that San Francisco was founded on. From stockbrokers to bike messengers to the guy who has a dog that stands behind him on his bike seat with its paws on his shoulders—there's no better way to experience the diversity of this wacky town. It's also a great way to see the city and get a little exercise while you're at it. Routes are made known on the day of the ride, so just go with the flow and see where you end up.

As far as biking in the city goes—why mess with tradition? I'm not a huge biker, but I have tried to steer my two-wheeler down Valencia Street in traffic, and frankly, it ain't no fun. Anyway, out-of-towners want to see something besides asphalt and cars while they sweat up those hills. To my mind, the two best routes for your money are still **Golden Gate Park to Ocean Beach,** and along the **Great Highway** bike path till it ends. If you want to extend that trek, stay on the Great Highway past Fort Funston, until it curves around and drops you off at Lake Merced, where you can continue for another five miles before heading home.

The most scenic trip is, of course, the ride across the **Golden Gate Bridge,** which you can begin in the Presidio, on the Golden Gate Promenade in the Marina, in Fisherman's Wharf, or in the bridge's south parking lot if you're feeling wimpy. My choice is usually Fisherman's Wharf, because it allows you the option of taking the ferry back. After you make your way carefully across the bridge's west side (make sure to warn novices about scary speeding bikers; a shove in the wrong direction can launch you into oncoming traffic), head down the road past Fort Baker into Sausalito. Tootle along Bridgeway to the end of town (stopping for snapshots and souvenirs along the way), and hook up with the jogging/bicycling path that skirts the Mill Valley waterfront. Follow the trail to the Tiburon/East Blithedale overpass and take the bike path all the way to Tiburon. Park your bike, and enjoy a well-earned seafood salad and cold beverage at **Sam's.** After you've knocked back a few, you'll be glad that all you have to do is walk your bike onto the ferry and let the sag wagon take you home. (If your friends are renting bikes and attempting to explore on their own, steer them to **Blazing Saddles,** which rents bikes equipped with a map holder and a computer navigation system that tells you your mileage, what the best routes are, and what to see along the way).

## Mountain Biking on Mount Tamalpais

Marin County is generally acknowledged as the cradle of mountain biking civilization, and most serious mountain bikers already know about the most popular trails, and probably the obscure ones, too. But if you're only spurred to occasional action by a visit from your fanatical biking friends, you might want to have the following route up your arsenal.

Bike trails crisscross the mountain (often to the chagrin of hikers), and many of them lead to **Old Railroad Grade.** You can pick up the grade at any number of spots, depending on how far you want to go. If you're feeling ambitious, start in Mill Valley off West Blithedale Avenue. If not, drive up Summit Avenue and park at the end (about halfway up the mountain). The grade is a steady climb (not too steep) that follows the old Mount Tam railway tracks. About a mile and a half from the summit of the East Peak is **West Point Inn,** a rustic log cabin built in 1904 that's accessible only to hikers and bikers. Take a break here for a pancake breakfast (available weekend mornings throughout the summer) or a PowerBar and a fresh lemonade, before making your way to the top and a rewarding view of the Marin coastline all the way to the Pacific. Once you've reached the peak, there's a snack bar with more substantial items such as hot dogs and bagels and cream cheese. (If you're lucky they'll have frozen fruit bars—ask for them; they're not on the menu.)

Option two is to make a weekend out of it and stay the night at the West Point Inn. If fitness-dude/dudette happens to be here in June, get up in the morning and hike down the Bootjack Trail to the **Mountain Theater,** where they present old Broadway musicals such as *South Pacific* and *Guys and Dolls* on weekends. Finish it off with a cold one on the deck overlooking the world at the **Mountain Home Inn.**

## Beyond the San Francisco City Limits

South of the city, you can't beat **Crystal Springs Reservoir** for a pleasant, picturesque little jaunt on foot or on two wheels. The biking/jogging path starts at the gate just off the Highway 92 West exit (going toward Half Moon Bay). Though you might have to dodge joggers, the nice, flat path takes you along the reservoir through a lovely wooded area, and up to the dam where you can hook up with the trail that goes over Skyline Boulevard.

The granddaddy of all-inclusive combo recreational/sightseeing areas near town is probably **Angel Island,** where you can mountain bike, hike, or sea kayak while soaking up some truly amazing views of the city on the sheltered beachhead. The best part for out-of-towners is that you don't have to bring anything with you except your stamina. There's a bicycle and sea kayak rental shop on the island (kayakers can paddle on their own, or take a guided tour with Sea Trek) and a snack bar. Catch the Angel Island Ferry from Tiburon, and don't miss the last boat back to the mainland, or you'll be camping out (if it's any compensation, the campsites are pretty nice).

## Wine Country

Touring wineries on bicycles is a guilt-free way to indulge, because whatever calories you gain drinking and noshing, you lose biking to the next stop. My suggestion is to steer clear of Highway 29, the Silverado Trail, and basically the Napa Valley entirely. There's nothing that'll kill your buzz quicker than the sight of a Lincoln Town Car weaving its way at full tilt down the road you're pedaling on. Instead, head to the less-trafficked, more pastoral confines of Sonoma County, specifically the nice, flat, wide **Dry Creek Valley.** Park the car in Healdsburg, so later you can come back and hang out in the park, explore the shops, or eat dinner at one of the charming restaurants around the old town square. Dry Creek Road starts at Healdsburg Avenue and you can pretty much stay on it until you get tired or too drunk. Turn off at Lambert Bridge Road to West Dry Creek Road to make a loop of approximately fourteen miles. On the way, you'll run into about six wineries, including the outstanding **Pezzi King** and **Kendall-Jackson.**

Another nice, easy course is through the **Sonoma town center,** a pretty self-explanatory route—just follow the signs to the nearby wineries (Gundlach-Bundschu, Ravenswood, Sebastiani, and Buena Vista are all nearby). Of course, if you're up here already, and you're a health nut, you can't really stay anywhere but the **Sonoma Mission Inn,** where you can massage, Jacuzzi, aromatherapy, and lounge your aching muscles by a natural hot spring pool while dining on lowfat spa cuisine.

## More Recreating

Sure, you can stand on the shore and gaze out at the bay like a normal person, or you can jump in and see the surf up close and personal with the weathered veterans of the **Dolphin Club.** It may not be the cleanest water around, but guaranteed, ploughing through the waves with Alcatraz on one side and the Ghirardelli clock tower on the other is an experience you and your triathlete friends will never forget. Dolphin Club members swim nearly every day (look for the orange swim caps bobbing in the waves); make inquiries at the clubhouse/locker room at the foot of Aquatic Park.

**Golf** may not give you abs of steel, but it is a nice way to spend a sunny afternoon. And at least here in the Bay Area, walking the course can double as a sightseeing excursion, particularly at **Lincoln Park.** Tell your friends to bring their cameras for the photo ops at the thirteenth and seventeenth holes, and afterwards, head to the **Pacific Cafe,** at Geary and Thirty-Fourth Avenue, for a healthy dinner of fresh local fish cooked every which way you can think of. If there's a line (and there often is), the management will provide glasses of complimentary white wine while you wait.

**Rollerblading** is the mountain biking of the '90s, and if you can do it right (without holding on to railings or small children), it's darn good exercise, too. My rollerblading friends recommend the **Marina Green and Promenade** and **Golden Gate Park** for best blading terrain (advanced skaters will want to try the obstacle course located next to the Conservatory of Flowers off JFK Drive in the park). You can rent blades at **Skates on Haight** or **Skate Pro Sports** on Thirty-Fifth Avenue and Irving. If you feel like combining exercise with a little socializing, join the party thrown every Friday night by the **Midnight Rollers**—an impromptu group that meets at around 8 p.m. at Justin Herman Plaza, and skates 12.5 miles around the city (skate at your own pace).

## Rock Climbing

There are hundreds of places where people do this for real, but if you don't have time for Class 5 training on real rock, and you still have a hankering to rappel down a steep wall, **Mission Cliffs** is a great way to spend a strenuous afternoon. This indoor rock-climbing gym looks like some kind of set for

Cirque du Soleil: dozens of people hang on ropes at various levels, clinging to the sides of a fifty-foot wall which is covered with colorful loops, toe holds, and niches. Some are practicing for an ascent on El Capitan; others are just doing it for grins. Drop-in beginner classes are offered daily; they provide instruction and all the equipment. The gym's location, at Nineteenth and Harrison, is not exactly common tourist stomping grounds, but you're not far from **La Cumbre** and **La Taqueria,** two of the Mission district's best burrito joints (hey—athletes need to carbo load).

## NIGHT

*Newsflash:* Dancing counts as exercise (the accompanying twelve-ounce curls are pushing the envelope). For the maximum sweatfest, head to **DNA Lounge** on their '70s and '80s deejay dance party nights (usually Fridays and Saturdays), or try the young and ethnically inclined **Sound Factory** for more a industrial, techno bump and grind. If you want to shake your maracas, there's nothing like **Cesar's Latin Palace** on Fridays for salsa dancing; get there early for free lessons.

## WHERE TO STAY

Many of the larger downtown hotels have good fitness centers on the premises, including the **Ritz-Carlton,** the **St. Francis,** and the **Nikko** (the Nikko actually has a full-fledged gym with a swimming pool, which you can use for free if you sign up for certain hotel packages. If you're on the bare-bones program, there's a $6 day-use fee).

If you're staying at the **Grand Hyatt,** the **Sheraton Palace,** the **Beresford,** the **Diva,** the **Donatello,** the **Juliana,** the **Cartwright,** the **Hilton,** or a few other downtown hotels, you can work out at any of the **Pinnacle Fitness Centers** for $10 a day; call Pinnacle to see if your hotel qualifies (it's $15 per day without a hotel connection).

The best reciprocal deals in town are at the **Harbor Court Hotel** and the **Hotel Griffon,** both adorable little boutique properties located on the south waterfront, both of which offer complimentary guest use of the next-door **Embarcadero YMCA**—a beautiful facility, with all the latest machines and equipment, plus a regulation swimming pool, a Jacuzzi, steam, and sauna. After working out their issues on the Stairmaster (issues like, why they have to stay in a hotel when you have a perfectly good sofa), your visitors can sip Calistoga at a sidewalk table at **Harry Denton's,** or have a lovely, low-cal meal at **Roti.**

**Nob Hill Lambourne** is the place to put up your fitness-obsessed executive. Each room comes equipped with a stationary bike, a treadmill, or a rowing machine; and if he or she is feeling really reclusive (or is recovering from a face-lift), they can also have a private yoga lesson in their room. More social types might want to use the nearby Fairmont Hotel's facilities for $15. Rooms at the Lambourne also feature feather mattresses and aromatherapy products; and the hotel offers massages, facials, and manicures on demand.

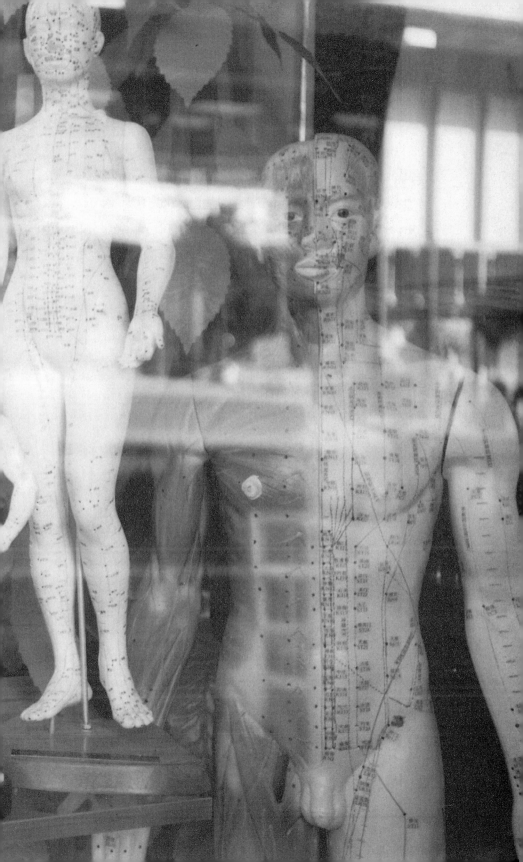

Back in the '80s, when conspicuous consumption was at an all-time high, someone came up with the cute label "yuppie" to describe the high-living, free-spending lifestyle of the nation's young urban (and upwardly mobile) professionals. It was a moniker that was reviled by many and acknowledged by few. Yuppie was followed

# Tour 15 Yuppies

in short order by dinks (double income, no kids), and sadly, in the post-Reagan years, by puppies (poor urban professionals). These days, with middle management jobs on the rise and credit card interest rates on the wane, there's a renewed sense of upscale optimism.

San Francisco is certainly no stranger to the nouveau riche or the plain old filthy rich for that matter. Ever since the gold rush made mansion owners out of former tent dwellers, we've had places that cater to those who want to indulge in—and can afford—the finer things. Let's face it, practically everyone who lives here is a yuppie—how else could someone afford to live in a city where the average house costs more than the president's annual salary? So when your upwardly mobile friends come to town, slip the maître d' a $20 and embrace the yuppie label in all its monogram-wearing, cell phone–toting glory.

# MORNING

If you are a genuine, card-carrying yuppie, there are three areas of town where you can comfortably brunch and take your morning constitutional (which might consist of rollerblading, sailing, golfing, or taking a brisk walk to the newsstand to pick up the *Wall Street Journal*). Those areas are Cow Hollow, the Marina, and Pacific Heights.

In Pacific Heights, the day begins at either **Pauli's Cafe** or **Ella's.** If you live in the neighborhood, I'm not telling you anything you don't already know. If you don't live here, but aspire to, then this is a great way to make your introductions. Pauli's on upper Fillmore is the place for piles of potatoes, eggs Benedict and Florentine, and Grand Marnier French toast. The lines can get long in the late morning, so stop first at Peet's Coffee for a double cap, and amuse yourself by window-shopping at superchic boutiques like Jim-Elle, Cielo, Gimme Shoes, and L'Uomo. Ella's is technically in Presidio Heights, where the real Old Money resides, but that never stopped the young and ambitious from overstepping their bounds. Besides, this the ultimate in gourmet brunches, and worth the invariable Sunday morning lines. Everything here is made from scratch, even the bread for the French toast. Not only is the orange juice fresh-squeezed, it's squeezed from blood oranges. The coffeecake and sticky buns are to die for, and my friend Rob swears there are no better buttermilk pancakes in town.

On Union Street, in addition to the traditional and truly excellent brunch at **Doidges Kitchen** (one of the only brunch spots that takes reservations; order the French toast or eggs Benedict), the youthful denizens of Cow Hollow and the Nut (as in Chestnut Street) crave the turkey-bacon and avocado omelets and fresh fruit pancakes at **Home Plate** on Lombard. If you have a young lawyer/realtor/stockbroker friend looking to meet someone of his or her ilk, this is the breakfast spot for you. Sign up on the outside chalkboard and don't let the parade pass you by. Afterwards, work off the calories by joining the conga line of spandex shorts as they blade down the boardwalk in front of **Marina Green,** leaving phone numbers in their wake.

## The Yachting Set

Sure, you could take a ferryboat tour around the bay like the regular folk, or you could charter a yacht and cruise in style like Ari Onassis on holiday. **Pacific Marine Yachts** features a small fleet of luxury yachts just for the occasion, equipped with salons, bars, galleys, and dance floors—one even has a private state room with a Jacuzzi. If your friends are more into the America's Cup lifestyle, charter the

***Adventure Cat,*** a fifty-five-foot catamaran that looks like a sailboat but feels like a luxury liner. Unfortunately you might have to share the boat with others, but you can keep up appearances for the people-watching from the shore by gesturing demonstratively and pretending to give orders to the crew. Then, when you're far enough away, prop up your feet, sip champagne, and let the hired hands do all the work.

## NOON

There's nothing like a little shopping spree to stimulate the economy. So grab your favorite platinum card–holder, and follow the gold brick road down to Union Square. Start at the top of Post and Powell Streets with **Saks Fifth Avenue.** Hit the Donna Karan collection; don't miss the sale racks—especially the shoes. Guys should head down the street to the **Saks Men's Store** for a little Dolce and Gabbana therapy. Next, a little Elsa Peretti teardrop pendant, some Paloma Picasso earrings, and maybe a silver baby spoon at **Tiffany and Co.** No lawyer working his or her way up to partnerhood will want to bypass **Bullock and Jones,** a haberdashery with a 140-year history of purveying expensive suits to the nouveau riche (they were one of the first fine clothiers to the gold rush millionaires). They've got all the labels you want to show off: Brioni, Zegna, and for women, the city's only Salvatore Ferragamo boutique. From here, a requisite trip to the Italian designer boutiques **Armani, Versace,** and **Gucci;** and the stores where shoes are referred to as "footwear": **Bally** and **Cole-Haan.** The country club set and former preppies who have graduated to yuppiedom will need to pick up a button-down shirt and something in paisley or plaid from **Polo;** the accompanying saddle and harness can be had at **Hermès.**

Even if they're still waiting for the trust fund to kick in before buying that rolling ring at **Cartier,** there's no harm in trying it on. And since you're already in the neighborhood, why not stop in to admire the intricate gold links encrusted with jewels at **Bulgari** next door?

Men looking to get sponsored at the club, or trying to get in good with the old man, will need to drop a couple of hundred on Dominican cigars, clips, and humidor boxes at **Alfred Dunhill.**

And though they might have come here with enough luggage to fill a small moving van, every stylish affluent type still needs something with the trademark "LV" from legendary luggage makers **Louis Vuitton.**

Wrap things up on Maiden Lane with a signature **Chanel** handbag; one of those perfect, skinny $300 turtlenecks from **Jil Sander;** and—of course—a dip into **Neiman Marcus** for a truffle at the Petroussin boutique and something in chartreuse from the couture section.

After all that power shopping, join the Ladies Who Lunch at charming **Cafe Akimbo** above Maiden Lane. For years, this site was occupied by the Mayfair Tearoom—the dainty lunch spot for blue-blood (and blue-haired) high society women. The crowd hasn't changed that much, but the food has improved dramatically. Akimbo's light-fare menu consists of things like mixed greens with chili-spiked prawns in roasted garlic dressing; poached calamari in miso-mustard dressing; linguini with Chinese roast duck, shiitake mushrooms, and snow peas; and vichyssoise—perfect nibbles for the diet-conscious shopper. Request a window seat so that you can eavesdrop on all the comings and goings and air-kissing below.

If a fashionably late lunch accompanied by a cocktail or two is more what you had in mind, go to **Rumpus.** Though nothing will ever be able to replace Trader Vic's, Rumpus's hidden location—at the end of a narrow alley called Tillman Place—has that same sort of secret handshake aura. The restaurant serves American food with an Anglo slant: lamb shanks, New York steak with potatoes and cabbage, veal chops, onion tarts. Definitely try something from their unusual and exemplary wine list; this is the only place in town where you'll find a large and well-chosen selection of rosés (and we're not talking Lancer's).

# NIGHT

Contrary to popular belief, the North American yuppie does not exist on cell phones, corner offices, and BMWs alone. The yuppie diet also includes nightlife, sometimes in ample portions. In San Francisco, where so many young people with newly minted college degrees suddenly find themselves aloft on exorbitant pay structures, there is no shortage of places in which they can congregate with like-minded folk. When the yuppie wallet spilleth over, these are the bars that sop up the mess.

**Johnny Love's** is pretty much ex-fraternity/sorority mecca, a one-stop shop for all your drinking, dancing, dress-up, drop-name needs. Presided over by owner/bartender/charmer Johnny "Love" Metheny, the original San Francisco location (it has since been augmented by a suburban branch in Walnut Creek) built its reputation on wild nights, when Johnny takes to the top of the bar with a gaggle of his favorite gals (often stewardesses) and shakes his groove thing. It's a bit of a show—as is everything Johnny does—but it's basically good clean fun, if you're not prone to claustrophobia or adverse to rubbing up against slightly inebriated young advertising execs. If you're going Thursday through Saturday nights after 9 p.m., be prepared to wait at the gate.

**Harry Denton's** waterfront bar and restaurant is a great place to let your hair down in an atmosphere of quasi-restrained, upscale respectability. Genial host Harry creates an aura of perennial festivity with plush decor, classy dressing, and a pop or jazz combo in the corner next to the grand piano. Champagne is the thing to drink here, followed in short order by cascades of effervescent laughter (if you're female) or ironic long looks across the bar (if you're male). For those into a more voyeuristic experience, the best strategy is a position at one of the sidewalk tables, where you can enjoy a cocktail as you watch the steady stream of stretch limos unloading their eligible cargo.

A step up from Harry's waterfront location is his **Starlight Room,** a penthouse suite where swank gents slip greenbacks to the door guy, and glamorous gals get away with wearing dresses so revealing you'd think they were auditioning for *Beverly Hills 90210.* Sip grown-up cocktails and do the white-man's overbite as you dance to Motown favorites while the city puts on a light show below.

The **Up and Down Club** is a place where yuppies who fancy themselves this side of Bohemian will feel comfortable. A stiff cover charge ensures that underground acid-jazz heads won't be milling around the bar while you're trying to order your Bombay Sapphire martini. Another layer of upscale respectability comes in the form of supermodel Christy Turlington, who is one of the owners. The downstairs is generally filled with beautiful people trying to look unglamorous while supping on dainty appetizers and listening to up-and-coming jazz acts. Upstairs is for shaking your groove thing to deejay sounds of the '70s and '80s. In the past, the club has been instrumental in promoting real talents like Alphabet Soup and Josh Jones, so at least those $6 cocktails are supporting a righteous artistic cause.

It's in the decidedly "down market" Haight-Ashbury, but the exclusivity of the **Persian Aub Zam Zam Room** and its singular offering (the gin martini) make this a must for aspiring country club members. If you can figure out the hours, which are completely random, and pass muster with owner Bruno, you will be served a truly divine martini. If he doesn't find you acceptable, Bruno will tell you that his establishment is closed, or that the bar down the street might be more accommodating. Best strategy is to put on your best Eddie Haskell manners, don't ask for a beer list or make off-color jokes, and suck up like hell.

# The Triangle

The isosceles configuration of bars on Filbert and Pierce Streets is not nearly the meat market it was when the Dartmouth Social Club occupied the northeast corner, but it's still pretty darn beefy. These days, you can look for choice cuts at the bar at **City Tavern,** where smartly dressed young ladies sip martinis and slurp oysters, and presentable young men suck down Red Tail Ales and contemplate steaks.

Across the street is the **Balboa Cafe,** which was the city's hottest pick-up joint back in the late '70s/early '80s. Nowadays the encounters are more meaningful, and the menu is greatly expanded—though the thick, juicy burger on a long french roll is still your best bet.

Perhaps nowhere else in town fills the six-figure bill better than nearby **Plump Jack Cafe,** owned by the city's penultimate yuppies—boy-supervisor Gavin Newsom and his trust-fund pal Bill Getty, who opened the restaurant as an offshoot of their next-door wine shop. The menu is haute California cuisine at its hautest, but the blue-blood crowd of movers, shakers, wheelers, and dealers flock here almost more for the fabulously exclusive (but surprisingly well priced) wine list. Amateur oenophiles—and what yuppie isn't—will want to test out their recently cultivated palates by ordering a different wine with each course (perhaps the ever-popular Silver Oak cab or a Matanzas Creek merlot?). Then watch the sommelier for nods of approval.

Beyond the triangle are several other dining spots where you can brush shoulders with the well-connected, among them:

**Rubicon**—A chance encounter with celebrity owners Robin Williams, Robert de Niro, or Francis Ford Coppola is reason enough to come here, but you'll stay for the food, which—despite the departure of chef Traci des Jardins—remains top notch (and top dollar).

**Bix**—Bring your finest Cubans (money speaks louder than Fidel Castro) and sidle up to the bar with the big boys at this super-cool, back-alley supper club, located in what was once a gold assayer's office. The place exudes just the right amount of two-olive ambience, from the handsome gent at the grand piano to the glittering crowd of double-breasted suits and three-strand pearls.

**Pier 23**—On weekend nights, this place oozes young ad agency execs and smartly dressed sales types who drink beers, munch on calamari, and try not to talk shop. The best action is on the back deck, where you can take a breather for some stellar bay views and a little heatlamp action.

## More Yuppie Bars

**One Market**—The bar area here is the yup's yup hang out. These are the people who aspire to, or soon will, leave yuppiedom altogether and get on with the business of simply being extremely rich.

**Blues**—A yuppie bar cleverly disguised as a blues joint. Take a look at the band. Even the harmonica player drives a BMW.

**Blue Light Cafe**—Here the yuppies cling to their recent days as college students. The alma mater sweatshirt is king, but instead of going to class during the week, everyone here goes to work—mostly to sell commercial real estate. Oddly enough, the place was started about ten years ago by musician Boz Scaggs, who envisioned it more as a funky New Orleans addition to button-down Union Street. And for a time, it was really low-key. Then suddenly it was discovered by the young, single, and monied crowd, and these days there's a line down the street to get in on Saturday nights.

**Paragon**—Indeed, the paragon of the yuppie bar. The only people more beautiful and well-dressed than the women here are the men. Everyone's pocket is well-lined, and the clientele never met a trend it didn't like.

**Union Street Ale House**—More East Coast private college graduates and microbrewed beers than you can shake a stick at. Keep your eye out (and your head down) for chugging contests.

## WHERE TO STAY

Where does a Fortune 500 young exec sleep? Anywhere he or she wants. But probably the **Ritz Carlton** will be acceptable. This hotel knows how a new vice president likes to be treated. Plush terry robes (with that ever-important Ritz insignia), marble bathrooms, a private car at your disposal, and deferential and totally discreet service at all hours. Plus, if you've ever stayed here before—no matter how long ago—they will automatically deliver your eggs, coffee, and shirts just the way you first said you'd like them.

Hotelier Chip Conley has come up with a lot of clever ideas over the years, but in my estimation, none can top **Castanoa,** a camping "resort" designed for those who want to commune with nature but don't want to get dirty. Scheduled to open in the summer of 1998, the 400-acre ranch is located on a pristine stretch of coastline six miles south of Pescadero and just a mile from Año Nuevo State Park. Conley describes it as a weekend nature retreat for the Jeep Cherokee/Range Rover, Trek mountain bike, North Face daypack, Patagonia jacket crowd—a place where you can have the wilderness and all the creature comforts, too. After you've spent the afternoon hiking, mountain biking, berry picking, birdwatching, windsurfing, or sea kayaking, return to your campsite and relax inside your safari tent, equipped with real beds and comforters, blankets, and floor rugs designed by Shabby Chic and Ralph Lauren. Then instead of Oscar Meyer weenies on the grill, run up to the store for some premarinated chicken fillets or Aidell's chicken-apple sausages, and bring them back to your campsite BBQ. If sea kayaking has made you a little sore between the shoulder blades, Cascade Ranch offers complete spa services—massage, hot tub, and sauna. And if you really don't want to rough it, there are more upscale cabins for rent, as well as a rustic (but luxurious) inn.

I freely admit to having a bad case of '60s envy. I grew up in the Inner Sunset, not fifteen minutes from the Haight-Ashbury, and yet as far as my consciousness was concerned, the psychedelic revolution could have taken place in Poughkeepsie. I have two memories of the '60s. One is of a costume party my parents went to dressed up

# Tour 16 Current and Former Hippies

as beatniks. My mom wore a plastic miniskirt; my dad a beret and goatee. I thought they were hippies. I bragged to all my friends. I was laughed out of first grade.

The other is of our next-door-neighbor's daughter, who grew her hair wild, got pregnant before she was married, and refused to wear her dental bridge to fill the gaps where she had had two eye teeth pulled. I was terribly impressed.

To this day, I have clung to the tragically romantic notion that because of some cosmically bad timing, I missed out on the greatest party the world has ever known. I've held to this belief despite the testimony of actual hippies that the '60s were not nearly as much fun as they were cracked up to be.

It is clear that I'm not alone in my nostalgia. A couple of years ago, I was walking past a restaurant that was hosting a group of Japanese businessmen. In what appeared to be a very formal exchange of gifts, the American hosts presented the Japanese visitors with an array of neon, tie-dyed T-shirts, to which the Japanese responded with squeals of unmitigated delight, putting them on directly over their suits.

Even though the patchouli cloud of love, drugs, free sex, Beatle boots, and the Grateful Dead has long since dissipated, there are still a number of places you and your has-been or wannabe guests can go to rekindle the '60s spirit.

## MORNING–NOON

All trips back to the '60s eventually lead to San Francisco's former free love foyer, the Haight-Ashbury district, which long ago buried its ashes in a formal Death of the Hippie ceremony in Buena Vista Park. Still, the neighborhood holds symbolic appeal for those wishing to visit the sacred sites, so grab your favorite throwback and follow your inner-flower-child to ground zero, the **corner of Haight and Ashbury Streets.** As you stand at the famous crossroads, reminisce about a time when LSD was legal. Next walk up two blocks to **710 Ashbury Street,** the stately Victorian that once housed the standard-bearers of the San Francisco Sound, the Grateful Dead. Since the death of ringleader Jerry Garcia, the house has taken on even more of a temple-like aura. Fresh flowers commonly appear on the steps; wandering waifs stare up at the windows with mournful, worshipful eyes, muttering bits and pieces of Grateful Dead song lyrics. But as corny as it sounds, the house is a piece of hippie history and worth a stop.

For breakfast, there are any number of granola-head hotspots, but the best food can be found at **Squat and Gobble** (huge omelets, scrambles, crepes, and home-fries), the **Pork Store Cafe** (enormous piles of pancakes, grits, and eggs over-easy), and **All You Knead** (muffins, scones, and other baked goods). Sandwiches, salads, and a spirit of tolerance and acceptance are on the menu at the aptly named **People's Cafe,** where outside the carnival continues to provide diners with hours of far-out fun.

Afterwards, stop in at **Daljeet's** clothing store and pick up a little leather number and some Beatle boots. This is the former home of the I/Thou Coffee Shop, the nerve center of the Haight, opened by a professor from SF State University. The I/Thou hosted everything from poetry readings to meetings between the hippies and the local "straight" community. Downstairs was also, at one time, the studio of Grateful Dead poster artist Mouse.

Next, take a stroll through **the Panhandle,** site of many of the Summer of Love concerts starring bands such as the Charlatans, Big Brother and the Holding Company, and even Jimi Hendrix. Pay your respects at **112 Lyon Street,** the one-time residence of Country Joe McDonald and the late legendary rock singer Janis Joplin.

At the west end of the Panhandle, in Sharon Meadow, is infamous **Hippie Hill,** a grassy knoll (located, appropriately, right next to the children's playground) that proves the old adage that things change, but they stay the same. Once the hippies' central gathering spot, the place still resonates with groovy vibes. Grab a veggie burrito (with black beans) from **Zona Rosa** or a scoop of Cherry Garcia ice cream from **Ben and Jerry's,** sit on top of the hill, and watch the happening unfold—conga drummers doing their tribal thing; modern-day flower children twirling and dancing to the rhythm; little kids doing barrel rolls down the hill; dogs chasing frisbees—it's like a perpetual Human Be-In.

If that gets you in the mood, make sure to stop by the **Polo Fields,** site of the real Human Be-In, when San Francisco hippies and Berkeley radicals—from Allen Ginsberg to Timothy Leary—united for a mass consciousness-sharing in January 1967. The pilgrimage to the field began at dawn, and by midafternoon, tens of thousands of people had gathered to listen to music, readings, speakers, chanters, and prayers. Much to the police department's surprise, by nightfall the field had been left exactly as it was found—without a speck of trash.

There's really been nothing as all-encompassing since the Be-In (though I suspect Jerry Garcia's and Bill Graham's memorials came pretty close), but concerts at the Polo Fields and Sharon Meadow are still a great way to spend a free-to-be Saturday afternoon with your favorite throwback. Usually on the circuit are **Reggae Fest** in October at Sharon Meadow, **Footstock** (the Bay to Breakers post-mortem) at the Polo Fields in May, and various blues and alternative rock blow-outs in the summer months.

Ironically, the coffeehouse that most exemplifies the lost ideals of the Love Generation is not even in the Haight. **Sacred Grounds** on Hayes and Cole is an ersatz community center for genuine hippies and earthies. The coffeehouse features impromptu jam sessions, poetry readings, literature to aid your spiritual awakening, homemade soups and salads, and really good strong coffee. Coincidentally, it's also located a block from the site where the Blue Unicorn—the first official hippie hangout—once stood.

The biggest acid flashback of the year happens during the first weekend of June at the **Haight Street Fair.** If you squint real hard and ignore the Gap store and some of other latter-day trappings of commercialism that have sprung up in the neighborhood, it might as well be 1967. The streets are awash in a kaleidoscope of tie-dye; street musicians sing protest songs; long-haired girls wear daisies behind their ears, there's dancing in the streets, tofu burgers on the grill, and a feeling that people are once again making love, not war. This is a good time to pick up a set of love beads and other trappings of the aura. If your born-again Baby Boomers aren't here during the fair, send them to the following shops:

**Positively Haight Street**—For tie-dye anything, Guatemalan pullovers, granny dresses, psychedelic posters, beads, and a very bright, upbeat attitude. The place still embodies the best intentions of that summer long ago.

**Psychedelic Shop**—This reincarcation of the original Haight store is a mecca for rock posters, Grateful Dead memorabilia and obscure recordings, buttons, tie-dye T-shirts, Hackey Sacks, pipes, papers, and various and sundry psychedelia.

**Golden Triangle** or **Pipe Dreams**—The '90s equivalents of the '60s headshop, where you can find every kind of smoking paraphernalia and accessory ever made (all for tobacco, of course)—from handmade ceramic bongs to hookahs.

**Haight Ashbury T-Shirts**—The selection is enormous and includes my favorite T-shirt slogan: "Haight-Ashbury: When the Going Gets Weird, the Weird Turn Pro."

**Distractions**—For starters, they've got candle votives, patchouli oil, incense, and lava lamps. Head to the back of the store and you hit the throwback pièce de résistance—black-light posters (and black lights) just like the ones you used to have on your ceiling.

**Great Expectations**—The place to pick up Timothy Leary's memoir; to get *Ringo Levio*, the autobiography of head Digger Emmet Grogan; or to buy your own copy of *The Haight-Ashbury: A History* by Charles Perry. Also a great source for Deadhead and Haight T-shirts.

**ArtRock**—One minute in this gallery and you'll kick yourself for throwing away those old '6os concert posters, 'cause now they're worth some serious bucks. The good news is that these days you have a legitimate job and can buy back your wild youth. The Mission Street gallery carries an enormous collection of original and reissued '6os rock posters and handbills, including classics by Stanley Mouse, Victor Moscoso, and Wes Wilson. They also carry original Jerry Garcia lithographs, album cover art, and an extensive selection of new poster art. If you're a fan of neon-graphic artist Frank Kozik, this is the place for you. If your friends don't see the poster they're looking for, or can't make up their minds, ArtRock does a huge mail-order business with fully illustrated catalogs of their complete inventory.

# NIGHT

They say you can never go back. But what do they know? To relive that altered-state experience, with or without the help of illegal substances, go to the Pink Floyd show at **Laserium.** While colorful laser lights dance in swirling patterns overhead and "Dark Side of the Moon" reverberates in your ears, let your mind loose to wander back (or travel for the first time) to one of Bill Graham's infamous Trips Festivals. This is also a great place for ex-hippies to bond with their teenage children (especially considering the average age at Laserium shows is about seventeen).

The **Red Vic** movie house is one of the few places left in the Haight that still seems to uphold the one-for-all, all-for-one spirit of the community. An independent cooperative that shows art, foreign, cult, and downright unusual films, the movie choices seem to be based more on the quirky tastes of the owners than held together by some sort of cinematic theme-glue (in a typical week you might encounter *Harold and Maude*, Dr. Suess shorts, and *Last Tango in Paris*). The theater itself is really more of a glorified living room, furnished with hand-me-down sofas and loveseats, which you share with a friendly assortment of neighborhood types. Be sure to sample some of the atypical movie snacks, including fresh juices, raisin-carrot muffins, and popcorn served with an optional topping of brewer's yeast (kinda like butter, only different).

Down the street, **Kan Zaman** is a throwback Middle Eastern restaurant where you can pretend you're George Harrison visiting the maharishi as you sit on large floor pillows smoking honey-apple tobacco through an enormous hookah while the Fat Chance belly dancers hypnotize you with their hips. Assume the lotus position, nosh on hummus, kebabs, tabouli, and other tasty fare, and give peace a chance.

At the core of the hippie experience was the music, and even though Jerry and Janis and Jimi are all gone, San Francisco hasn't let the music—or that freewheeling feeling—fade away. For erstwhile flower children, a trip to (or at) the **Fillmore Auditorium** is a must. Get there early, head upstairs to the cafe, and spend an hour perusing the phenomenal psychedelic poster collection, culled from the archives of Bill Graham Presents. Here, perfectly preserved in all their letter-squashing, neon-drenched splendor, are the most famous artworks of the era—all advertisements for concerts at the Fillmore. Among the gems are the original Grateful Dead skull-and-roses poster, the white dove/peace sign Jefferson Airplane poster, and colorful bills announcing shows for performers ranging from Otis Redding to Pink Floyd and Led Zeppelin. While the opening band plays, prowl the hallways and corridors looking at the photos of the musical greats who have graced this stage over the years. It's like being in the rock and roll hall of fame. After the show, grab a free apple from the box at the top of the stairs (a tradition started by Bill Graham back in 1965), and on your way out, pick up a free poster commemorating the performance—it'll probably be worth something someday.

If you haven't quite had your fill of jam sessions for one night, cross the street and have a nightcap at the **Boom Boom Room**—a hard-working blues bar owned in part by Mr. Lucky himself, John Lee Hooker. Before the Boom Boom, there was Jack's, and before that other blues clubs, dating all the way back to 1932. The room is loud—often so loud you have to use sign language with your tablemate—but the bands can be darn good.

If nothing at the Fillmore or the Boom Boom Room sounds appealing, try the **Maritime Hall** on Harrison Street, where Chet Helms, head hippie for the concert promotion company called Family Dog in the '60s, now produces retro-alternative shows. Here you can freely revel in revivals with the likes of Hot Tuna, Taj Mahal, Merl Saunders, and David Grisman, while tripping out to the amoeboid-like images being projected on the walls. Family Dog's original hangout was the **Avalon Ballroom** on Sutter Street and Van Ness Avenue, now the Regency II movie theater. The Avalon hosted some of the most best bands of the era, among them the Lovin' Spoonful, Jefferson Airplane, the Blues Project, the Grateful Dead, and Big Brother and the Holding Company (Janis Joplin, in fact, made her debut with Big Brother here). Even though recliner seats now cover what was the Avalon's dance floor, you can approximate the psychedelic experience by sitting in the back and watching the light play off the old columns as the latest Disney cartoon extravaganza flashes across the screen.

Still jonesing for the Dead? Join the throng of twenty-something Deadheads who are still managing to "have a great show" every Monday night at **Nickie's BBQ** on lower Haight, where tapehead Dan plays the best of his live recordings of Jerry and the Boys. It's a hand-twirling, head bobbing, tie-dye saturated jam session worthy of a parking lot outside the Oakland Coliseum.

For a great granola-and-guitar night, head over to Berkeley's **Freight and Salvage,** a concert venue for old folkies and new singer-songwriters. Offerings on the mostly acoustic music menu include everything from bluegrass and klezmer music to Mare Winningham, Peter Rowan, and the Modern Mandolin Quartet.

## WHERE TO STAY

The **Red Victorian Bed and Breakfast** is a great place for those who remember the Summer of Love and those who wish they could. A delirious conglomeration of inn, peace center, gallery of meditative arts, and flower-child dreamhouse, the Red Vic B&B was in fact a hippie crashpad in its heyday, and that spirit seems to have lingered here while the rest of the Haight turned to more acquisitive concerns. The lobby doubles as a gallery for owner Sami Sunchild's "visual poetry"—canvases embroidered with psychedelic lettering that offer inspirational messages such as "Yes to Life" and "Be Somebody Magnificent. You Can Do It." Upstairs there are eighteen rooms, each decorated in a different theme. Guest favorites include the flashback Flower Child Room, the Peacock Suite (which verily overflows with peacock feathers and patterns), and the room boasting the Aquarium Bathroom.

Pam Brennan lives in and runs the very respectable but definitely hippie B&B known as **Herb'n Inn.** Pam's husband Bruce leads "flower power" tours of the Haight on Tuesdays and Saturdays. Inside the four-room inn is a small but steadily growing museum of '60s psychedelia.

For flower children who grew up, moved off the commune, and became successful despite their best intentions, there's **Spencer House**— a lavishly restored 1887 Queen Anne Victorian on Haight and Baker Streets. This elegant, luxurious inn—a stone's throw from the heart of the Haight-Ashbury—had its heyday as a hippie hangout, too (at one point, it even doubled as a porn moviehouse). It was restored in the mid-'80s to its former grandeur (the owners live in a completely renovated penthouse on the top floor). Rooms are richly appointed with feather beds, duvets, settees, antique furnishings, Victorian fixtures, and fine linens and draperies. A full breakfast is served at a long, formal dining table on the main floor.

This tour is by no means the final word on gay and lesbian hangouts and activities in the Bay Area. There are other books and periodicals that, collectively, cover the scene in full, among them: *Betty and Pansy's Severe Queer Review*, *The Gay Guide*, *Odyssey Magazine*, and *San Francisco Bay Times*. But, as a straight person with gay friends, living

# Tour 17 Queer and Curious

in a gay mecca, I have often been faced with the problem of trying to come up with places that are fun for both persuasions—places that are gay- or lesbian-oriented, where straight people won't feel out of place, or places that are fairly mainstream, but simultaneously gay friendly. After all, your friends presumably came here to see you, not just to galavant off by themselves every night to the clubs.

## MORNING

Call it what you will, but **Cafe Flore**—aka Cafe Hairdo, Cafe Whore, Cafe Bore—is still the place to be on weekend mornings, but you'll have to get there at opening time to get a seat on the outdoor patio—especially in warm weather. This Castro institution is usually 90 percent homo at any given time of day, but heteros won't feel uncomfortable. There's too much activity, chatter, coffee banter, breakfast, people-watching, and eye contact going on for it to be an issue. The main thing for foreigners is that Cafe Flore is fun, the food and the coffee are good (though a tad overpriced), and you really get a feel for the pulse of the gay scene—at least this side of Twin Peaks.

For women, **Red Dora's Bearded Lady Dyke Cafe** on Fourteenth and Valencia (see the Avant-Garde Aunts tour), **Cafe Commons** on Mission Street (see the Neo-Bohemians tour), and **Just for You** on Potrero Hill are a nice introduction to the San Francisco lesbian scene. Red Dora's is an unassuming cafe and sometimes performance space where everyone's welcome. The lesbian-owned Cafe Commons is simply a wonderful place to while away a morning over coffee, bagels, homemade vegetarian soups, and the *New York Times*. Hit the back deck if the weather's agreeable. Just for You is a low-key lesbian diner—just a couple of tables and a small counter—where you can get eggs over easy with bacon and homestyle potatoes, three different kinds of huevos rancheros, and scrambles with homemade bread.

One of the most fascinating, social, and educational gay-oriented outings (no pun intended) I've come across is Trevor Hailey's **Cruisin' the Castro Tour,** which meets most mornings at the corner of Castro and Market at 10 a.m. The irrepressible Trevor is a retired army nurse, who came to San Francisco and the Castro district in 1972, just as the gay revolution was coming to full flower. On her tour you'll learn all about gay history in the district and the city; about the Lavender Cowboys, an all-male square-dance group of the gold rush–era; about the rise and violent death of Supervisor Harvey Milk, including a visit to the site of his old camera shop; about the pre-Castro gay ghettos such as North Beach and Polk Street; about the Castro Cathedral (aka the Castro Theatre); and about the Sisters of Perpetual Indulgence. Midway through the tour there's a stop for brunch at **Caffe Luna Piena,** a cozy, little indoor/outdoor restaurant that serves a nice mix of vegetarian and nonvegetarian breakfast fare. I was pleasantly surprised to learn from Trevor that a big percentage of the people who take her tour are not gay: the day I was there, the group consisted of a gay man from Germany doing research; a couple of French tourists (straight); and four middle-aged moms from Montana on a wild all-gals weekend. And they all seemed to thoroughly enjoy themselves.

One Castro stop that's not on the tour but is worth checking out is **Hello Gorgeous!,** a place that's part store, part museum, and part lifelong personal tribute to Barbra Streisand. Owner Ken Joachim is clearly *verklempt* about Babs: he hocked his home in the wine country to finance this venture. The small gallery is filled with renderings and paintings of Funny Girl, as well as collectibles, posters, videos, CDs, and other memorabilia that chronicle her thirty-five-plus-year career. My favorite touch is the makeover station, where you can fulfill your wildest Linda Richman fantasies (talk amongst yourselves) by trying on wigs and nails like buttah, just like Barbra wore in some of her most famous movie roles.

Just up the street, you can stock up on gay/lesbian literature at
**A Different Light,** one of the few bookshops in the country that dedicates
the majority of its space to gay and lesbian authors and subjects.

## NOON

The **Marina Green** is one of those odd confluences—a mecca for straight
yuppies and gay men alike, both of whom compete for volleyball space and
the best washboard stomachs, on the grass just west of the yacht harbor.
The recreation field, with its fabulous Golden Gate views, affords one the
opportunity of cruising (lots of brief briefs and shirtless sunbathers) and
sightseeing at the same time.

Of course, if you really want to see some skin, you should head over to
**Baker Beach,** famous the town over for its nude status (see the Extroverts
tour). Send your gay friends to the far north end; naked heteros should veer
slightly south.

If they like the lounge-in-the-sun lifestyle and prefer the company of
women, take them to **Osento** for a little hot tub/cold pool R&R. This women-
only (mostly lesbian) spa and massage facility, located in an old Victorian on
Valencia Street, has a great relaxed attitude that will make straight women
feel instantly at ease. (For more details, see the Avant-Garde Aunts tour.)

## In the Market

You've gotta buy groceries anyway, so why not have a little fun? The
**Diamond Heights Safeway,** located in what is referred to these days as the
"Swish Alps," is to clean-cut gay men what the Marina Safeway was to
hetero swingles in the early '80s. Direct your shopping cart to the produce
aisles and see what's ripe.

On Market Street just below Castro, the **Harvest Ranch Market** is a
great gourmet deli and natural foods cafe, featuring a huge assortment of
ready-to-go items including an extensive salad bar with all kinds of fancy
offerings, as well as sushi, fresh focaccia and sandwiches, homemade
soups, and veggie burritos. It's a great place to stock up for a picnic with
the help of a handsome grocer; or you could plunk yourself down on one
of the benches out front and let the Castro scene unfold.

## Remembrance Sites

The **AIDS Memorial Grove** is without a doubt the most serene and special
spot in Golden Gate Park. And it's not just a place to take your gay friends.
It is a place to take your straight friends, parents, grandparents, and teenage
nephews. Centered around a small grove of redwoods, volunteers and city
park workers have fashioned a quiet, reflective, peaceful glen filled with

singing birds and hundreds of forget-me-nots. A small creek lined with round stones runs through it, and all around are small stone benches where you can sit and contemplate. A circular platform at the head of the grove has the names of the major donors carved into it— Vietnam Memorial–style. In the center, people have placed flowers, tokens, and remembrances. Surprisingly, the grove is not a sad place, but a place of healing.

In Grace Cathedral, just to the right of the entrance, is the **AIDS Memorial Chapel** and the Keith Haring altarpiece, a beautiful triptych in gold, that is alive with the playful dancing figures that were Haring's hallmark. This stunning work of modern art (Haring's last work before he died of AIDS) offers a wonderful message of hope, as well as a quiet place to reflect, for those whose lives have been touched by the disease.

And in a small storefront on Market Street near Castro, you'll find the birthplace of **The Names Project,** perhaps the single most-recognized symbol of AIDS grieving and remembrance in the world. At the headquarters, you can watch as panels are finished and cata-loged; see photos of the full display of the quilt on the Capitol Mall; watch a video about the making of the quilt and what the project has come to symbolize; or just spend a few minutes gazing at the panels that adorn the walls—a poignant and purposeful reminder that AIDS victims are first and foremost people, not just statistics.

## Celebrate Good Times

The **Gay, Lesbian, and Transgender Pride Parade** every June is not just a party for gays, lesbians, and transgenders. It's a celebration of diversity; it's street theater; it's Fluorescent Wig Day; it's What-the-Hey Day; it's a day when life is indeed a cabaret—and anyone who shares this spirit should feel right at home. The parade is traditionally led off by the notorious Dykes on Bikes, San Francisco's very own gender-bending Wild Bunch; they're followed by everything from con-tingents of drag queens and gay cops to the ever-popular Lesbian/Gay Freedom Day Marching Band. From the sidelines, the crowds cheer in rainbows of support and good humor. Best strategy is to grab a beer, find a pair of shoulders to sit on, and let it all hang out.

The **Castro Street Fair** in October is like a small version of the parade, except you get to shop for nifty arts and crafts, snack on gourmet goodies, and stay in one place. And of course there's always Halloween (see the Extroverts tour), which has gotten so big, they've sent the rubberneckers to Civic Center. The best and most elaborate costumes are still in the Castro on Halloween Eve proper (not the weekend preceding or following).

For something a little more on the dark side, the **Folsom Street Fair** in October may be more to your liking. This festival of leather, chains, piercing, bare buns and breasts, and general S&M kinkiness is definitely NOT for everyone. But if you and your friends are feeling open-minded (or curious), it's certainly an interesting—if not unusual—way to see underground gay life in San Francisco.

# NIGHT

**Bernal Heights** and **Hayes Valley** are San Francisco's newest lesbian/gay-oriented neighborhoods—though neither are predominantly same sex, making them a nice compromise for mixed-group socializing. Hot spots in Bernal Heights include the dyke bar **Wild Side West,** the oldest women's bar in the city—having recently celebrated its thirtieth anniversary. When I lived in Bernal Heights I used to come here to play pool, and it took me several visits before I realized it was a lesbian hangout—though all the signs were certainly there (the naked women artwork on the walls and the toilets that double as chairs and planters—one painted with hungry-looking teeth—should have been a dead giveaway). That's because above all this is a homey, friendly, neighborhood bar where you can have a beer, chit chat with strangers, and play pinball or pool.

Just up the street from Wild Side West, the **Liberty Cafe** is one of the best New American restaurants in town, catering to a mix of neighborhood regulars and cross-town foodies. And across the street, the lesbian-owned **Bernal Books** offers a great selection of literature for and about women.

Hayes Valley is inhabited by a fairly well-heeled and culturally astute crowd of hip straights and gays. The see-and-be-seen, ripped-and-cut guys like to work out at **Muscle Systems** on Hayes Street, a men-only gym which features a Jacuzzi and sauna, along with the requisite exercise equipment (the day-use fee was $8 at last check). Afterwards, fortify yourselves with a couple of glasses of cabernet at the **Hayes and Vine** wine bar, a pleasantly androgynous (and cozy) establishment that offers a great selection of small and unusual vintages from near and far.

Over on Gough Street, underneath the Albion House Inn, is **Charpes Grille,** a warm, friendly gathering place for middle-aged tourists and gay couples, that serves above average continental cuisine, and offers entertainment in the form of jazz singing at a piano bar.

## Stepping Out

The **Metronome Ballroom** on Potrero Hill is a mainstream dance hall where most nights you can take lessons in swing, fox trot, tango, salsa, or two-step; and then later, you can practice what you learned at a dance party. It's primarily hetero, but everyone is made to feel welcome. If you swing the other way, try hitting this hot spot on same-sex night, usually scheduled for two evenings each month.

If your friends are here around Christmas and they want to shake their groove thing and get in the holiday spirit at the same time, take them to the **Dance-Along Nutcracker,** which is rapidly becoming a San Francisco holiday tradition. Performed by the Lesbian/Gay Freedom Band and the San Francisco Cheer, this wacky version of the ballet classic involves a bunch of guys dressed in tutus performing various parts of the *Nutcracker* and getting the audience to dance along with them in the aisles. Lots of audience members (children and adults) dress up in tutus, too. It's wonderful silliness for kids of all ages.

If that's not sweaty enough for you, head directly to **The Stud**— once a strictly gay dance club, now a place where leather and lace, straights and gays mix it up to '70s music, hip hop, and techno-funk.

More serious gay performance art can be found at **Theatre Rhinoceros** in the Mission, where you might encounter anything from Cuban performance artist Carmelita Tropicana to serious dramas to light-hearted romps (a recent offering on the main stage promised a comedy about "sex, drugs, and drag queen denial"). If your friends are visiting in late November or early December, definitely take them to the Rhino's **annual reading of Truman Capote's *Christmas Story.***

If the theater is your destination, make a night of it by starting off with dinner at **Mecca**, a smart, neoindustrial restaurant/supper club on upper Market Street that attracts a cool, gender-bending crowd and sports an excellent Mediterranean menu. It's quite the scene on weekends; you'll need to make reservations about a week in advance.

If you didn't have time for supper, there's always **Sparky's,** the late-night wonder diner on Church Street. This is one of the few places in town where you can actually get decent food at three in the morning—that is, if you stick to the burgers, omelets, and pizzas. I can't vouch for the fancy food items.

## Club Compromise

It's taken a long time, but San Francisco has finally arrived at a place where parents and their outgoing gay children can bond in an atmosphere of mutual fun and show tune appreciation. **Martuni's** is also the kind of place to take visiting New Yorkers who have aspirations of playing the Algonquin Room. An upscale, mainstream gay bar of the smoky-mirrors-and-marble-column variety, Martuni's features open-mic cabaret singing nightly. As you sit and sip cocktails, "amateur" singers (some of these guys and gals seem like they're warming up their chops for professional careers) get up and perform standards and show tunes to piano accompaniment. There's something for everyone: aspiring lounge acts can work on their audience appeal; the folks can sing along to Gershwin, Rodgers and Hammerstein, and Sinatra; and you can suck down a few martinis while you secretly admire the chanteuse in the corner.

When you want to see campy drag cabaret or queer-oriented comedy, just click your heels together three times and remember there's no place like **Josie's Cabaret and Juice Joint.** This cafe/performance club is the perfect spot to go with your high school friends who turned out to be gay (or in my case, to go see your high school friend, who turned out to be gay, do drag) in a friendly, nonconfrontational and nonalcoholic, vegetarian atmosphere. On any given night you might see the likes of Musty Chiffon, the psychedelic cabaret star; the Kinsey Sicks, America's favorite dragapella beauty shop quartet; Vanity Case, the wig-happy songstress; the Two-Bit Tango, a Dyke Detective Story; or Lypsinka, the famous lip-syncing diva. It's mostly good, moderately clean fun, and hey—if my mom can handle it, so can you.

If you want to see drag the way it was done in the old days, back when female impersonators were popular with the middle-aged and middle America crowd, then **Finocchio's** is the club for you. For more than fifty years, the men-who-dress-like-women have been donning glam wigs, fluttering false eyelashes, cinching their corsets, and offering up a bawdy vaudeville-style revue of torch songs and tasteless jokes. It's seriously campy and touristy—but that's what makes it all the more fun.

There are no drag queens at **Bimbo's 365,** unless you have suspicions about Dolphina, the busty "optical illusion" mermaid in the fish bowl, who occasionally appears behind the bar, but it's still one of the most fabulous, plush nightclubs in town. The lounge hasn't changed much since it opened in the 1940s, and there's something about all that red velvet and red vinyl, the Final Net and curlers in the bathroom, and the cocktail cabinets filled with miniature liquor bottles, that gives the place a decidedly campy edge. At any moment you might expect to see Ricky Ricardo or

Louis Prima bursting through the curtain leading a conga line. Come here for a Copacabana-style dance party.

At long last, years after the demise of Maud's and Amelia's, a new lesbian bar has finally surfaced. The **Lexington Club** off Valencia Street, say my associates, is rife with lipstick lesbians, and it's in one of the currently grooviest areas in town—two incentives to drop by for a cocktail, no matter what your persuasion.

The **El Rio** (see the Cheapskates tour to find out about their Friday night happy hour) is a down-home bar and performance venue that welcomes a happily integrated crowd most nights. The tropical Caribbean/tiki garden out back is reason enough to hang out here on salsa-dancing Sunday afternoons—particularly if you're a girl who likes girls. If you aren't, there's always shuffleboard.

**Mary's Backside** is the bar behind the bar at Hamburger Mary's, and a good place to escape the noise of the former (though I personally kinda like the hustle and bustle). Whereas the restaurant has pretty much gone mainstream, Mary's Backside Bar still maintains more of a dyke stance.

## WHERE TO STAY

As you may imagine, all the hotels in this town are pretty gay-friendly. And if your friends are here to hang with you, and not to prowl the corridors in the wee hours, than the hotel choice should be based more on convenience of location. But if they want to get specific, there are also a number of good gay and lesbian lodging options in the city.

Five rooms are available at **24 Henry Guesthouse,** which is a beautiful, 122-year-old Victorian home that promotes itself as a gay inn. The house also features communal sitting rooms, a library, and a full buffet-style breakfast.

The pedestrian-looking **Beck's Motor Lodge** is a Travel Lodge–style motel conveniently located in the heart of the Castro. It's the kind of place you'd put up relatives who were coming to visit you for the first time since you came out. Betty and Pansy (of *Severe Queer Review* fame) warn that there may be a lot of late-night activity here.

Located on Fourteenth Street and Church, the country-style, twelve-room **Willows Inn** caters mostly to men, and features furnishings made out of bent-willow branches. Other nice touches include continental breakfast served in your room, kimonos, and decanted port on your bedstand. One drawback: shared bathrooms (though there are washbasins in each room).

**Bock's Bed and Breakfast** is a comfortable spot for women located in a safe and sane part of town (on Willard Street right near the UC Med Center). There are three spacious suites; one with a private deck and view. From here, you can walk to Cole Valley, the Haight, or up the hill to Mount Sutro.

They came, they saw, they snapped their fingers. For better or worse, the beatniks' mystique lingers on in cafes and dark alleyways, in bookstores and jazz clubs, along sleek, cool underground corridors and, of course—on the road. A lot of people say that the '90s are just the '60s turned upside down. But in San Francisco,

# Tour 18 Neo-Bohemians

I think they're more like the '50s turned sideways, without all the avocado green refrigerators. Consider the modern-day Bohemian's accoutrements: cigarettes, experimental jazz, pouty lipstick, poetry, coffee, and a tendency toward unemployment. Yes, I have seen the face of twenty-something San Francisco and it is wearing a beret and a goatee.

But despite the neobeatniks' occasionally annoying hipper-than-thou idiosyncrasies, they may very well be the best kind of visitors. Why? Because for many of them, hanging out in cafes and coffeehouses (sometimes several during the course of a day) is considered an actual event. No doubt you see the inner beauty of this scenario: while indulging in one of your favorite activities, you get to feel like you're showing your friends the sights.

# MORNING-NOONISH

## North Beach

The key is to pick coffeehouses with character (and characters) that perhaps offer something beyond the standard indie-filmmaking-gen-X-bike-messenger banter. In the old beatnik quarter of North Beach, there's an embarrassment of cafe riches, but not too many have—*how you say?*—the right "vibe." On boho Grant Avenue, eschew the obvious lures—Caffè Trieste, Savoy Tivoli—in favor of the **Italian/French Baking Company,** a small storefront with a big bakery in back that offers a half-dozen kinds of biscotti and bread sticks, as well as some heavenly specialty treats such as eccles cakes (don't ask, just try 'em). Grab an espresso and a hazelnut biscotti, perch on a stool, and gaze out with appropriate insouciance at the tantalizing North Beach street scene.

Another good stop is **Mario's Bohemian Cigar Store,** which, despite its ground-zero location (on the corner of Columbus and Union) and its popularity, still feels authentic. A narrow corridor (about wide enough for a person to stand with one arm extended dangling a long cigarette holder) divides the tables from the bar. They have coffee, but you might want to opt for a pale ale instead. And absolutely don't leave before trying one of Mario's eggplant focaccia sandwiches. Afterward, head down the street to **Lyle Tuttle's Tattoo Parlor and Museum** where the now-retired Lyle displays an interesting collection of early tattoo equipment and designs. Tuttle's a legend in the biz, having inked everyone from Janis Joplin to Cher. Hard to believe we've come so far in this peculiar realm that looking at old flash (popular tattoo images) of hula girls and sailors would make one nostalgic. But there you are.

If you're seriously thinking about adding a couple of chain-links to that permanently penned fence around your ankle, there's a bigger stable of skin artists working up the street at **Tattoo City** (owner Ed Hardy also specializes in tattoo makeovers for those, like Johnny Depp, who need to turn "Winona Forever" into "Kiss Me Kate").

Though it's a cliché by now, I would be remiss if I talked about North Beach and beatniks and didn't mention **City Lights Booksellers, Vesuvio,** or **Specs'.** City Lights, of course, is where Beat bard/publisher/artist Lawrence Ferlinghetti has kept the candle dripping over the chianti bottle for more than forty years, and where you can find nearly everything ever written by and about Kerouac, Corso, McClure, Ginsberg, et al. The poetry section is outstanding, as you might imagine—and not just filled with tributes to '50s counterculture.

Ferlinghetti and his Little Publishing House That Could have continued to champion emerging voices in contemporary poetry, and the bookshop is a whirlwind education for anyone even remotely curious about San Francisco's predilection towards waywardness and unconventional thinking.

Once you've found the obscure literary journal of your fancy, take it into Vesuvio, the famous bar and literary hangout that was once the favorite watering hole of Jack Kerouac. (Even blasé Bohemians will enjoy the oft-told tale of the night Kerouac was supposed to head down to Big Sur for an historic meeting with writer Henry Miller, but instead ended up at Vesuvio on an all-night bender. The twain never did meet.) Vesuvio's interior looks like what might have happened if Queen Victoria had hired the Mad Hatter as her decorator. And though the crowd these days consists mostly of "squares," you can still feel the Beat in the bar stools. (Kerouac fans might also want to make a side trip to 29 Russell Street on Russian Hill, where the Beat icon lived while writing *On the Road*.)

Across the street, the cast of characters at Specs', on tiny Adler Place, is a bit less predictable and therefore all the more tantalizing. Once a beatnik hangout managed by Henri Lenoir, the same guy who owned Vesuvio, the bar has maintained a healthy sense of irreverence over the years. Ponder the deeper meaning of the shrunken head collection, have your handwriting analyzed, or attempt to explain the ramifications of the hanging whale penis bone to a group of Spanish sailors on shore leave. If you hang out here long enough, there's a good chance you'll have a close encounter with an actual poet, novelist, or someone who knows someone who's working on a screenplay. Definitely spend a few minutes with the baskets of postcards at the bar, written by tourists from around the world.

A few blocks and a million ideological light years away from Specs, on the border of Fisherman's Wharf, is **Cafe Francisco,** which, considering its precarious locale, is one of the last places you'd expect to find any self-respecting hipster. But somehow this quiet cafe manages to skirt the wharf scourge. Hardwood floors, old wood-back booths for two, and a collective of crusty, Charles Bukowski–esque salts who hang out at the sidewalk tables lend an air of ingenuousness to the place.

## Lower Haight

Divisadero is the dividing line between the old Haight (or what's left of it) and the new Haight, which resides—philosophically—somewhere around the intersection of New Bohemia and Gen X Slackerville. Middle ground can be found at the **Horse Shoe Coffeehouse**—the kind of place where the beatniks might have met the hippies halfway. It's a great spot to scope out the next big thing—tattoos, piercing, Camel no filters—but probably not ideal for resolving the problems of the world (hard to hear yourself think over the music). Coffee's strong and cheap, though. And if you're hungry, you should be across the street at **Kate's Kitchen** anyway, chowing down on either Flannel Hash (a heaping plate of eggs, corn-beef chunks, potatoes, bell peppers, and cheese), or the French Toast Orgy—thick-sliced and battered bread piled to overflowing with granola, fruit, and syrup.

## SoMa

South of Market used to be more of a weekday cafe place, but with old warehouses converting to loft residences faster than they can put out new versions of Windows, coffeehouses down here are starting to get that good, lived-in feel. **South Park Cafe,** a small, sunny French cafe located on the bucolic oval between Second and Third and Bryant and Brannan, is a great place to go with neo-Bohemians who 1) are computer nerds or 2) did the whole ex-patriate stint in Prague. The place oozes Euro-hip—from the picture windows that open out onto the sidewalk to the reading racks of international newspapers. Most important, they serve their cafe au lait in big bowls. *Bien sur.* Serious on-line junkies or FOSOJ (Friends of Serious On-line Junkies) should consider **Coffee Net, CyberWorld Cafe,** or **Internet Caffe Alfredo** for some midmorning philosophical cyber-angst. Unfortunately, being a computer nerd has become painfully mainstream these days, but still, there are those really far out Web sites, and of course the chat rooms.

Down Bryant Street on the South Embarcadero is **Red's Java House,** the place to take your grunge refugee friends so they can bond with the regular crowd of longshoremen and tugboat operators. The coffee actually stinks, but so what. This is 100 percent, genuine, no-pretense atmosphere. For under $3 you get to sit in a shack on the edge of the bay, smoking cigarettes, eating a burger, drinking a Budweiser, and imagining San Francisco's old working waterfront—back before the peach-and-teal set moved in. Now *that's* sightseeing.

## Cole Valley

**Jammin' Java** on Waller and Cole, while offering refuge from the sometimes scary Haight Street sidewalk scene, is still stimulating enough to ensure that your caffeine buzz doesn't go to waste. There's great people-watching from the sidewalk tables or through their big storefront windows. They also score points for their Common Mispronunciations guide, which offers helpful hints on the correct way to say terms such as latte (la-tay) and coffee (cwa-fee).

## The Mission

In the Mission, where New Bohemia has settled in for the decade, you might need to do a progressive cafe crawl, beginning at **Cafe Que Tal** on Guerrero—for a low-key, read-the-morning-paper, get-your-bearings experience. Later, for more serious cafe dwelling (as opposed to cafe squatting), you should progress to **Muddy Waters** or (my personal favorite) **Cafe La Bohème,** where habitués have elevated the act of lingering to an art form. Sure, it's about coffee, but it's also about chess, temping, left-wing politics, burning out, art, and life in the slow lane. This is the spot to hit if you want your friends to get a sense of how fringe (if not sometimes frayed) San Francisco lives. In the afternoon, when you hit that three o'clock snooze button, head to **Cafe Commons** in the Outer Mission for a truly great double mocha and some hearty and healthy nonliquid sustenance (even Bohemians can't survive on coffee alone). This cozy lesbian-owned neighborhood spot is a peaceful oasis, where you can sit and chat or read, and have a bit to eat inside or on the enclosed deck out back. It's the kind of cafe Bobby McFerrin frequents, if that says anything.

**DAYTRIP ALTERNATIVE**

If you can rouse the cafe rats from their chairs (maybe bribe them with a few buzz beans), hop in the old Karmann Ghia and head down to **Big Sur** and the **Henry Miller Library.** Any hipster worth his or her salt had a *Tropic of Cancer* period in college, and will probably jump at the chance to make a pilgrimage to Miller's home turf on this beautiful, untamed stretch of coastline. The library and small museum contain such artifacts as Miller's typewriter and his artwork.

## Potrero Hill

**Farley's** is perhaps the city's ultimate cafe. Highlights include a magazine rack that offers a wealth of intriguingly bizarre reading, including (at last peruse) *Bunny Hop: Soft Porn for Tomorrow's Hipsters* (containing the riveting article "What's the Worst Thing You've Ever Done to Your Pet?"), *UFO magazine,* and the always-popular *Too Much Coffee, Man* comic books. I also love the "no lowfat milk" policy and the quasifamous Farley's T-shirts, imprinted with the molecular structure of caffeine and mottos such as "Death Before Decaf." This should have been the place filmmaker Mike Moore referred to in *Roger and Me* when he said, "San Francisco is a city where everyone has a job, but no one seems to be working."

## Richmond District

The **Blue Danube** is a traditional favorite, and it's close to lots of other places that could substitute for a coffeehouse, such as the **Plough and Stars** pub. With its long, wooden tables, perfect-temperature Guinness (which looks a lot like coffee), and authentic Irish angst (accompanied by live Irish music), retro beatnik types should have no trouble making the transition. While you're down here, you must drag anyone who's ever thought about wearing a beret to **Green Apple Books** for a spin through the fiction annex, where you might pick up a dog-eared copy of *Love in the Time of Cholera.*

## Sunset District

In the Inner Sunset, nothing's really been the same since the Owl and the Monkey closed, but **Jammin' Java** on Ninth and Judah has a great indoor/outdoor setup, with a deck enclosed by flower boxes and big dormer windows that open to the street.

Farther into the avenues, someone finally broke the Outer Sunset culture-death barrier and opened a cool coffeehouse. The decidedly low budget **Java Beach** at Land's End attracts a groovy little mix of surfers, beachies, and cheap-rent hipsters who while away the hours playing board games, reading, and drinking french roast. On a clear day, you can sit and watch the breakers and bikers from sidewalk benches as you contemplate the minutia of life. For a true San Francisco beatnik experience, take your bad poetry to the beach and burn it in a ritual bonfire. Then head back to the cafe for a little existential banter about what it all means (Java Beach is open every day until 11 p.m.).

Oh, and in case you're wondering—by definition, Bohemian and Marina district are two mutually exclusive terms. Nuff said.

## See the Light

After you've had enough caffeine and you're feeling the need to cleanse and purge, head down to the **Church of Saint John Coltrane,** one of the best ways I've ever found to spend a slacker Sunday. Services at this African Orthodox Church begin around noon, but you needn't be African nor orthodox to get enlightened. All you need is a beat and a fondness for the music of patron saint and jazz genius John Coltrane (which, in Neo-Bohemia, is like asking if you like strong coffee). Once you step through the doors, you'll find yourself swept up in a cacophony of saxophones and hallelujahs. The small storefront revival hall features a modest candlelit altar and about a dozen wooden pews. All around the room are enormous, colorful, Russian icon–style paintings (by the church's Rev. Mark Dukes) featuring Coltrane embodying Jesus, Buddha, Mary, and other deities. A drummer, bassist, guitar player, and several saxophonists take up about half the hall. As the service gets under way, more saxophones come crawling out of the woodwork, and a full-throated chorus of gospel singers fill up the front. The bishop, resplendent in fuschia robes, alternates between the congas and the soprano sax. Pretty soon everyone's stomping their feet and clapping their hands, and the room's rocking in a full-on jazz jam. Should you feel inspired, the congregation is invited to join in the band—you can bring your own instrument (several people do), or you can borrow a tambourine or sleigh bells. By the time you leave, you'll be wondering if it's pure coincidence that John Coltrane and Jesus Christ have the same initials.

# NIGHT

As evening falls and the conversation shifts from intense coffee chatter to
more languorous, squinty-eyed discussion, latter-day Bohemians head to
**Cafe du Nord**—a place so hip, one visit is the equivalent of two or three just
about everywhere else. Just like the Cellar in the beatnik days of yore, this
bar/club lures the hepcats down, down, down—to a subterranean former
speakeasy, where you'd expect some guy named Jocko to ask you for a password
through an eye-level slot in the door. Du Nord is like a museum of cool:
retro lounge lizards in Quiana shirts pose against a magnificent forty-foot
mahogany bar (an original from the club's Roaring Twenties days); cigarettes
dangle off the full lips of modern-day flappers—their long black fingernails
tapping out rhythms on high ball glasses. In the back room, pool sharks
nod expectantly to the edgy groove of an acid jazz combo. Du Nord has been
almost prescient in its ability to foresee the next hot thing—from bachelor
pad music to swing dancing to spoken word nights (their latest contribution
is a monthly happening called "Wordfuck"—for erotic readings and poetry).
It's easy to see how coming here can turn into an all-night outing, especially
if you decide to eat (the food's not half bad), and peak people-watching
hours don't begin until after 9 p.m. (One drawback: there's often a line,
and waiting in line isn't really part of the whole boho oeuvre.)

The resurgence of poetry readings and spoken word events around
town is one of the biggest tip-offs that the Beat is back in San Francisco.
The trend (as all trends) tends to ebb and flow from month to month, but in
addition to Cafe du Nord and various and sundry coffeehouses, you can
almost always count on Sundays at the **Paradise Lounge** for your fix of
adjective-laden angst. With its maze of microenvironments (multilevel bars,
as many as three bands playing at the same time, a big back pool room), the
Paradise qualifies as a great boho hangout even without poetry readings.
Prep yourself by watching Mike Meyers's hilarious tribute to beatnik
coffeehouse culture in the movie *So I Married an Axe Murderer.* Then head
to the upstairs lounge Sunday evenings, when authors read from their latest
releases, aspiring poets recite verse, and Gen X literati get down.

Rarely do you find a place where Bohemians can be fastidious and cool
at the same time, which is why **Brainwash** is such an anomaly. A groovy
cafe and bar that offers an eclectic mix of live music acts, beer, and by-the-
hour on-line services, it is also a laundromat. Tucked in back are dozens of
high-tech, computerized washers and dryers, where you can air (or dampen)
your dirty little secrets. A numbered light board in the cafe gives you the
blink and nod when your load is done. If this set up doesn't pose enough of
a dilemma for your antiestablishment-type guests, try the bathrooms, which
are segregated for "readers" and "writers." Definitely sit midroom, so you
can overhear some truly bizarre conversations, which veer wildly from

German philosophy (a result of Brainwash's proximity to the Global Youth Hostel) to multimedia techno talk.

Chances are **Infusion,** which is currently the "it" spot for young, South of Market neo-Bohemians (it's located right in the middle of Multimedia Gulch), may eventually go the way of Cava 555, its once-all-the-rage champagne-flowing predecessor in this location. But in the meantime, this restaurant and bar is way, *way*. In case you haven't been keeping up on this latest trend in cocktails (where have you been?), an infusion is vodka that has been soaking in a decanter with any one of a variety of fruits and vegetables until it takes on the flavor of said fruit or vegetable. The restaurant stocks a good dozen of them behind the bar. Some of these concoctions are quite tasty (watermelon, strawberry, jalapeño, lemon); some—at least to my way of drinking—are a bit strange (fig, cucumber, vanilla bean, coffee bean). But after two or three, you'll be waxing rhapsodic (or waxing the floor with your butt), even if the vodka tastes like eggplant, so order the most appealing flavor first. The crowd here is thick with hep, entrepreneurial types. Around nine o'clock, a small combo starts up in a tiny loft overlooking the dining room, making the din sometimes overwhelming, but nonetheless enjoyable. The best part about Infusion is that the food is good—and it's served until 1 a.m. on weekends.

Good, traditional theater is fine and well, but experimental, occasionally bad theater is what Bohemians live for. **Somar Theater** is rarely bad, but occasionally you do hit something that's just completely out there. Like many nontraditional performance spaces, the theater is attached to a gallery, which offers exhibits by local artists, including the annual Open Studios exhibit every October. How could any non-conformist not be thrilled with plays that cover such diverse topics as transsexual superheroes and cereal killers?

You'd think that any place that bills itself as a "Bohemian Cafe" would be precisely the opposite. But in fact, **Frankie's Bohemian Cafe** in Pacific Flats (the no-man's land between Pacific Heights and the Western Addition) is pretty cool. High points include good beers on tap, a youngish and pleasantly unmotivated crowd, and a groovy menu of big, healthy dishes, including a yummy Czechoslovakian one called a Brambory: a giant zucchini-and-potato pancake topped with everything from BBQ shrimp to guacamole, sour cream, and cheese. A couple of doors down is the **Divisadero Ale House,** a popular, smoky little watering hole where you can play Liar's Dice with dotless dice—a wonderfully existential predicament.

## Valencia Street

If you're short on time, you might want to do the "add water and stir" tour of Beat San Francisco along **Valencia Street**—a one-stop boulevard for all your nightly boho needs. Park (carefully) around Sixteenth Street and work your way down the promenade, beginning with a drink at either the **Albion** (for the great bathroom graffiti), **Jack's** (more tap beers than you can think of), **Liquid** (the hipster bar du jour), or **Doctor Bombay's** (for a less-crowded cocktail and a smoke). Then catch a Beat noir flick at the fabulous **Roxie Cinema** (showings at recent fests have included *The Life of Allen Ginsberg, Burroughs: The Movie,* and the all-time classic, *Bucket of Blood*). Next, peruse the bookshelves for a copy of *On the Road* or *On Civil Disobedience* at **Dog-Eared Books** or **Modern Times;** then head over to **Aquarius Records** or **Radio Valencia** to bring yourself up to date on the retro lounge music scene. In addition to cutting-edge music of the recorded variety and a tempting cafe menu of soups, sandwiches, and such, Radio Valencia also features live performers (mostly experimental jazz and bluegrass) Friday through Sunday. Local acid jazz favorites the Broun Fellinis and Mingus Amungus play regularly down the street at the **Elbo Room,** a formerly undergroundish bar/club that's in danger of toppling over into mainstream status (at last check, the bridge-and-tunnel crowds hadn't discovered it yet). Running on empty? Valencia restaurants offer some of the most diverse dining in the city. You can join the tapas revolution (or as I like to call it, Spanish dim sum) at **Picaro, Esperpento,** or **Timo's. Ti Couz** is the spot for savory and sweet crepes (for dessert, try the one with Nutella inside). If your tastes swing east, there's **Amira** and **Arabian Nights** for pan-Arabian cuisine, **Saigon Saigon** and **The Slanted Door** for Vietnamese food, **Firecracker** for Chinese, **Rasoi** for Indian, great-old standby **We Be Sushi** for cheap sushi, and **Val 21** for hybrid California-Asian. For good, cheap Mexican food, hit **La Cumbre** or **Pancho Villa's** (their burritos are the size of small babies). The Mexican food at **La Rondalla** isn't stellar, but you go here more for the entertainment value anyway. Sip a cheap margarita and admire the year-round Christmas decor, while mariachis serenade you with "Guantanamera." Finally, finish off the evening sitting cross-legged on the floor drinking a Turkish coffee at **Cafe Istanbul.**

### OTHER PLACES

**Storyville**—Genuine, nonhomogenized jazz for serious hipsters in the never-trendy lower Panhandle.

**Red Room**—The all-red, all-the-time decor (lighting too); a smoky, slo-mo, David Lynch ambience; and martinis the size of gasoline funnels lend enough quirky atmosphere to this bar to keep it from entering the yuppie zone.

**Club Deluxe**—The scenesters in this place have actually regressed a decade, back to the '40s, complete with party dresses and swing dancing, but the Deluxe manages to keep its cool. Young rebels will revel in the retro groove, even once they realize they've actually become their parents.

# WHERE TO STAY

**Hotel Bohème** is the perfect hotel for latent Bohemians, emerging artists, or movie stars, like Frances "Fargo" McDormand, who you almost recognize. Step inside, walk up the narrow staircase, and know what it's like to be listening to Allen Ginsberg read "Howl" from the room above the club (Ginsberg, in fact, had been a guest here, as have McDormand and husband/director Joel Coen). Some rooms look straight out over Columbus Avenue, others look through an Old World maze of laundry lines and fire escapes. Press your face to the glass of one room and you even get a great view of Coit Tower. The rooms are small and creatively appointed with charming touches like mosquito-netting canopies. The hallways are decorated with marvelous Beat-era photographs by Jerry Stoll, who captures late-1950s North Beach in all its smoky, full-lipped, jazz cat, back-alley glory. To keep guests abreast of the nightlife on the street below, the staff maintains a culture chalkboard, which posts offerings such as Irish music at O'Reilly's pub and hours for opera singing at Caffè Trieste. Be sure to say hello to Gaya, the resident poet, who doubles as night manager and concierge, and who does regular readings around the neighborhood. Like, *crazy* daddy-o.

**Hotel Rex** is one of the latest offerings from Chip Conley, who's taken the town by storm with his theme-oriented, budget-minded, funky-chic hotels. The Rex has a Bohemian slant, geared toward artists, filmmakers, and writers. It hosts regular salon gatherings, readings, and book signings, which are made all the more tantalizing by the possibility of participation or interruption by a celebrity artist–type, in town for a film fest or a lecture at the Herbst.

You can't swing a dead cat in this town without hitting someone who's got "issues." In San Francisco, we eschew the cause célèbre in favor of the cause du jour. And we vehemently defend our viewpoints for at least a week—until we find another cause that suits our needs even better. In addition to all the usual popular causes—

# Tour 19 The Politically Correct

redwood trees, whales, clean water—people here rally behind incredibly specific, personal issues, such as the enforcement of pooper-scooper laws, the right to go naked in public, the folly of introducing nonnative plants to the environment, the boycotting of Snapple because of a rumored connection to right-wing extremists groups. In this neck of the woods, being PC (politically correct) is not just a passing fancy, it's a lifestyle choice. For tourists, the good part about our being so protest happy is that for every thing that's deemed to be PI (politically incorrect), there's probably some fraction group that's got an argument supporting the opposite viewpoint (and if there isn't, you can usually ad lib something pretty convincing—so long as you back it up with a petition).

# MORNING

Coffee, that seemingly universally loved morning beverage, actually has the potential to be quite controversial here in PCville. And because it's my book, I'm taking this opportunity to use it as a platform to vent my views on the subject. First off, Starbucks. The folks who own Starbucks are the imperialist pigs/Stepford Wives of the coffee world. They come in here like CIA mercenaries, scope out an already successful mom-and-pop coffeehouse, offer a nearby landlord three times the rent, and open up next door or across the street. Then they take nice, free-thinking urban youth and brainwash them into mindless droids who can only talk in Starbucks Speak. Hand the cashier droid your travel mug and ask for a lowfat double latte, and a cult-like smile appears on his face as he calls out "double, tall, blended personal latte" to the coffee-making droid who repeats the order in a little sing-song exchange. It's downright chilling. I'll confess I've been lured in by their clever marketing gimmicks—the gift packs tied with green ribbon, the pretty painted mugs, the fancy Frappuccino drinks, the Kenny G CDs (well, um, maybe not those), not to mention the fact that there's one conveniently located in the building where I work, but *come on*—the beans aren't even roasted here! They're from Seattle, fergodsake. If you're so crazy about Seattle, why not just move there? Maybe that'll be cloudy enough for ya. (Okay, in Starbucks' defense, they do support a number of PC causes, and they've started to employ the mentally disabled. But still . . .)

So, where should you go? First choice would have to be **Martha & Brothers Coffee Company,** a small, local operation owned by an extended family of Nicaraguan immigrants. The beans are roasted fresh daily at a San Francisco roastery, the politics are left-leaning and Third World–sympathizing, and they employ recent emigrés and the elderly. Plus, any place where the "World News" section of the *Chronicle* is more in demand than the front page or the "Datebook" has got to be high on the PC scale.

Afterwards, if you're at the Twenty-Fourth Street location, walk down to **Global Exchange,** a "fair trade center" that sells crafts, clothing, and furnishings made in developing countries. The shop buys directly from small producers in Third World nations, often paying in advance, to help impoverished artisans become economically viable. The eclectic selection includes Guatemalan embroidered shirts and baby clothes, Peruvian and Kenyan jewelry and small crafts, Mexican masks and folk art, dolls and figurines from Zambia, and all manner of handwoven things.

If you're not on Twenty-Fourth Street and are still in search of nonoffensive coffee, take your pick between **Peet's,** the Italian roast kings, who began in Berkeley many moons ago and taught Starbucks everything it knows (and that's no idle boast; the former partners parted ways, one to continue Peet's, the other to found Starbucks and try to take over the world). **Spinelli** is another local operation; or there are any number of small-time, single-owner, neighborhood beaneries that serve locally roasted coffees and support the little(r) guy.

## NOON

What's so PC about **Mission Dolores** you may well ask? I mean, isn't it really just an egregious example of colonialism at its in-your-face worst? Yes and no. The PC credo also states that unless we learn from our past mistakes we are destined to repeat them. And nowhere in San Francisco is this theory more relevant than at the Mission Dolores cemetery, where some 5,000 Costanoan Indians lay buried—victims of white man's diseases and cultural intolerance. Formally named Misión San Francisco de Asis, the establishment of this Catholic outpost (the third of twenty-one California missions) predates the Declaration of Independence by five days. The actual church was completed in 1791 (it's the oldest building in San Francisco—so a visit here earns PC bonus points under the "respecting your elders" clause) and still boasts its original four-foot-thick adobe walls and redwood-log support beams. From an architectural standpoint, the adobe mission is truly magnificent. Inside the chapel, a dozen or so rows of humble pews lead up to a handpainted, decorative wooden altar replete with religious figures, which was crafted in Mexico in 1796. Original Ohlone Indian designs adorn the ceiling. And in the floor, markers indicate the burial sites of several early San Francisco pioneers, including William Leidesdorff, the nineteenth-century African-American businessman who built the first City Hall (which goes to show you that San Francisco heard the call of racial tolerance long before it caught on elsewhere). The basilica next door, built in 1918, is not nearly as charming as the mission, but contains some lovely stained-glass windows. The real treat here is the cemetery and garden in back, where PC types (and film buffs—this, of course, being one of the major locales in Alfred Hitchcock's *Vertigo*) will no doubt wish to pay homage. The picturesque, serene garden, a fragrant mix of roses, redwood trees, salvia, and native plants, features mostly the gravestones of post–gold rush Irish immigrants and Mexican settlers. The city and the church have recently commissioned a memorial to the Costanoans that will stand at the back, where most of them are presumed to lie buried.

### GLIDE MEMORIAL CHURCH

If your friends are convinced that religious zeal is the exclusive domain of right-wing conservatives, they need a dose of **Glide Memorial.** The Tenderloin district church is presided over by the good and powerful Reverend Cecil Williams, who preaches a mean Sunday morning service —it will raise your social consciousness almost as much as it elevates your spirits. As you sway, sweat, and lift your hands to the joyous harmonies of the gospel chorus, look around you: every walk of life is represented here. Prostitutes stand next to homeless Vietnam vets stand next to Marina district yuppies stand next to Maya Angelou. If there was a PC hall of fame, this place would be in it.

# Coit Tower

This is your chance to do some actual, traditional sightseeing without falling off the PC bandwagon. Ostensibly you're taking your friends here to see the PWAP (Public Works of Art Project) murals, not the showstopping views, but since you're up here anyway, what's the harm? The murals, which circumnavigate the tower's lobby walls, were created by twenty-six local artists in 1934 under Roosevelt's New Deal reform program. On the surface, they seem to be nothing more than a depiction of Bay Area life at the height of the Depression, with panels illustrating the Financial District, libraries, California industry, agriculture, and so forth. But look a little closer and you'll see why at the time they were considered so subversive that civic leaders voted to close the lobby to the public. On the magazine rack, amid issues of *Esquire*, there's a copy of the socialist newspaper, the *Daily Worker*. In the library, a man reaches for Marx's *Das Kapital*. And other newspapers sport headlines referring to the destruction of controversial artwork, the 1934 dockworkers strike, and labor issues. Afterward, go ahead and take the elevator to the observation deck. After all, the tower was the gift of Lillie Hitchcock Coit, a turn-of-the-century women's libber who preferred chasing firetrucks and swilling bourbon to marriage and maternity.

# Seasonally PC

In the summer, the city hosts tons of benefit performances, fund-raiser events, and good-cause concerts—a great time to expose your friends to the time-honored San Francisco tradition of guilt-free entertainment. High on the PC charts is the **San Francisco Mime Troupe,** which has been performing its nonsilent brand of left-wing musical-political satire in Bay Area parks for more than thirty-five years. (It was a benefit for the Mime Troupe, which had been jailed on obscenity charges after a performance back in 1967, that launched Bill Graham's career as a concert promoter.) The troupe has stayed true to its credo, slaying capitalist America's sacred cows and lampooning the foibles of modern society, from Watergate and corporate downsizing to the tobacco industry and the religious right. Performances take place nearly every weekend throughout the summer, and are always free (donations gladly accepted).

Every October, rocker Neil Young gets a cavalcade of emerging and legendary musical talent to do an all-acoustic gig at his **Bridge School Benefit** at Shoreline Amphitheatre. Though it's certainly not a universal cause like the whales or the rainforests (the Peninsula school, where his son is a student, works with severely handicapped, nonspeaking children), you can still go and feel good about yourself.

**Peet's**
3419 California Street, 221-8506;
2257 Market Street, 626-6416;
54 West Portal Avenue, 731-0375;
and other locations throughout the city

**Spinelli**
3966 24th Street, 550-7416;
2455 Fillmore Street, 929-8808;
712 Irving Street, 731-9757

**Glide Memorial Church**
330 Ellis Street, 771-6300

**Mission Dolores**
3321 16th Street, 621-8203

**Coit Tower**
1 Telegraph Hill, 362-0808

**The San Francisco Mime Troupe**
855 Treat Street, 285-1717

**Bridge School Benefit**
Shoreline Amphitheatre, Mountain View
510-762-BASS

The overriding reason to attend is the chance to see the biggest names in the business—Elton John, Pearl Jam, Elvis Costello, Simon and Garfunkel, Tom Petty, Van Halen, Bruce Springsteen—play spontaneous unplugged duets with Neil and each other.

I know it's a long shot, but if your PC friends just happen to be here on April Fool's Day, take them to the annual **Saint Stupid's Day Parade,** and join the antiestablishment as they skip down Montgomery Street thumbing their collective noses at corporate America and doing what San Franciscans do best—acting like happy lunatics. Bring an extra pair of socks for the ritual "sock exchange" on the steps of the Pacific Stock Exchange.

**COMMONWEALTH CLUB OF CALIFORNIA**

Left-wing or right-wing, everyone gets equal time at the Commonwealth Club luncheons, where the people who are making the headlines and the decisions speak to an influential crowd of political and professional muckety-mucks. From Madeline Albright to Colin Powell, it's like watching *Nightline* without Ted Koppel.

# PC Shopping and Snacking

Though shopping in the luxury boutiques around Union Square is basically a PC no-no, there's nothing terribly PI about the square itself, site of many a pro-Union rally during the Civil War. If you'd like to put your money where your conscience is, try the **Hospitality House Store** in nearby Crocker Galleria, which sells wonderful paintings, pottery, greeting cards, and crafts created by mostly homeless people in the Hospitality House studio in the Tenderloin. The studio has helped launch the careers of artists such as Larry Clark, whose images have graced the cover of *Time* Magazine, and Jane Winkelman, who made it big with an Absolut Vodka ad. The quality of the art is remarkably good; the subject matter often incredibly moving; and the prices are unbelievably reasonable. Sixty percent of the revenue from sales goes to the artists, the other 40 percent to the studio.

For luggage you can live with, head to **Used Rubber USA** in the Lower Haight. Briefcases, handbags, and backpacks made from recycled innertubes, jewelry and clothing fasteners made from truck tires, and clocks made out of old hub caps are just a sampling of the stylish and ingenious products at this unique store. Sadly, it doesn't even begin to make a dent in the landfills around the country, where old tires (which never, ever degrade) cover as much acreage as a big city.

In November and December, go holiday shopping at the **Helpers Homes Bazaar** in Ghirardelli Square, which sells cute crafts, ornaments, and stuffed animals made by disabled adults as part of an organization that houses and works with them. Their miniature furry mice swathed in gowns made by famous designers such as Ralph Lauren and Diane Von Furstenberg are a perennial hit, and make a great gift. Afterwards, while you're in the spirit, head down to **Saint Anthony's Dining Room** and get a slice of humble pie serving holiday meals to the hungry and homeless. The venerable soup kitchen always needs volunteers. Later, treat yourself to some fantastic home-baked bread, pastries, or a hearty organic breakfast at **Brother Juniper's Bread Box,** a wholesome restaurant where the bounty all goes to Raphael House, a nearby homeless shelter. Or indulge yourself in a pint of **Ben and Jerry's** ice cream, while moseying around Haight Street or North Beach. With 1 percent of the profits going to worthy causes such as Amnesty International and Greenpeace, it's perfectly PC to indulge.

## PC in Pacific Heights

It's hard to be PC in Pacific Heights. Amid all the ultraexpensive designer boutiques, the restaurants where a $10 oyster on a plate constitutes a meal, and the shops that sell diamond doggie tiaras, it's hard to know where to turn to patronize places that aren't on the banned list. But they're there. Fillmore Street, for instance, boasts a large number of charitable thrift and secondhand stores, where you can often find the cast-off contents from the city's most exclusive closets. The sartorially splendid Mayor Willie Brown periodically deposits his hardly worn Brioni suits at **Victorian House,** where you can pick them up for a fraction of what he paid for them. **Repeat Performance,** a thrift store for the San Francisco Symphony, is the place to look for preowned evening gowns (hey—it's a step up from buying them new, and it benefits a good cause).

At the top of Pierce Street is **Alta Plaza Park,** a place where dogs of all walks, trots, and stations in life freely intermingle—and poop is scooped indiscriminately. It also affords outstanding views of downtown. Plop yourself down on a warm, grassy spot and watch pedigreed poodles frolic with mangy mutts, while their owners look on from a safe distance. If you get bored with that, take a surreptitious tour around romance novelist Danielle Steel's ridiculously enormous mansion (the former Spreckels Mansion), located a few blocks east on Washington and Octavia. The sprawling block-long extravagance, with its glass-enclosed swimming pool and servants quarters, violates just about every principle in the PC handbook—a sobering reminder of the wastefulness and excesses in our society.

## People's Republic of Berkeley

Aside from being the PC capital of the Western world, Berkeley is simply a great place to hang out. To be environmentally as well as politically in line (and to avoid sitting in the all-too-common Bay Bridge traffic), take BART to downtown Berkeley and walk up through campus.

Begin with a tour of the major sites of '60s political protest:

**Sproul Plaza**—Birthplace of the Free Speech Movement and site of many a Civil Rights and Vietnam War protest. Park yourself on the steps and imagine student-activist Mario Savio giving his famous "the machine will not work" speech. Then march up toward Sather Gate and pick up political literature at the various recruiting and information dissemination tables. If you're lucky, you'll find some kind of protest that you can either join with, or exercise your right to vehemently disagree with. Even better, pick your own pet peeve, make a couple of signs, and start a movement.

**People's Park**—From park to political rally site to parking lot to bum campground to volleyball court and back to park again: People's Park proves the adage that what goes around eventually comes around.

**Chez Panisse**—You can get away with dinner at Chez Panisse, because after all, it is the birthplace of California cuisine and one of the first restaurants to insist on using locally grown, organic produce, which led the way for sustainable organic farming in the Bay Area.

**Brennan's**—Located in the industrial district down near the waterfront, Brennan's has been serving no-nonsense meals to hard-working men and women since 1878. None of this highfalutin kweezeen that's all over nearby Fourth Street, Brennan's is strictly meat and potatoes fare for blue-collar folk, old timers, and starving students. Best bets are the brisket, turkey with mashed potatoes, or huge french dip sandwiches. Oh, and make sure to order one of their famous Irish coffees at the bar and mingle a while with the regulars. They'll have you climbing off that bourgeois pedestal in no time.

# NIGHT

A socially conscious night on the town doesn't have to mean you're collecting for UNICEF while all the other kids are trick-or-treating. San Franciscans, after all, wrote the book on guilt-free indulgence. (The nouveau beatniks and the hippies practically killed themselves having fun in the name of bucking convention.)

**Enrico's** is the perfect example. In the late '50s and early '60s, when former owner Enrico Banducci ran this outdoor cafe/nightclub, his sidewalk seating and hipster attitude provided a forum (and fodder) for many a beatnik rant. And his willingness to take a chance on unknown entertainers helped launch the careers of performers like Barbra Streisand, Woody Allen, and Bill Cosby. After the strip clubs took over Broadway, Enrico's hit the skids, but like a phoenix rising from the asses (er, ashes), the restaurant has come back big time in the '90s. These days, it's like the main float in the Broadway parade, co-existing happily with strippers, jazz lovers, tourists, and beatniks in the spirit of cooperation and harmony. There's good jazz most nights of the week, and the food is right up there with the best of the houses of California cuisine. For the socially conscientious, the sound of strip-joint barkers mingling with your organic baby lettuces should only enhance the experience.

It's probably easier to pick a PC dining establishment by ruling out places that you *can't* eat, rather than identifying the places you can. In other words, forget any restaurant that serves traditionally raised veal, gill-netted tuna, or game animals; forget fast food joints like Burger King that tear down rainforests for cattle-grazing land; and skip seafood such as jumbo shrimp, sailfish, and turtles, that are either overfished or endangered. Also nix French restaurants (nuclear testing); Israeli or Palestinian eateries (depending on your political alignment); places that use white paper napkins (bleaching process pollutes streams; paper destroys trees); styrofoam cups (piling up in landfills); or any place without handicapped access. And that's before you've considered all the *hidden* evils: restaurants that give substandard wages or don't offer health benefits; places that don't hire illegal immigrants or do hire illegal immigrants, etc. etc. etc. Pretty soon you'll be reduced to finding a vegan restaurant that's run by battered women and elderly environmentalists, where all the food is cooked via solar-heated panels and served on plates made by struggling Guatemalan artisans (hey, I think I may be on to something). A person could starve.

The alternative is to do as the PC natives do and say *the hell with it.* Use your best judgement, avoid the French food (did I mention they also eat horse meat?), and never forget that your body is your temple or other house of nondenominational worship.

## A Walk on the Waterfront
The south Embarcadero waterfront has a lot to offer the liberally inclined. Starting out in the early evening at the far south end by the Fourth Street Bridge, take a stroll down through old China Basin where a small, blue-collar houseboat community has managed to hold its ground against the ever-more-insistent encroachment of big city developments (the new ballpark, scheduled to open in 1999, might finally mean the swan song for this idyllic community, however). The inlet here is the last remaining strand of Mission Creek, which was once part of the much larger Mission Bay, long since filled in to make way for warehouses and dry docks. In the peaceful little channel underneath the freeway, you can still see seabirds nesting and occasional

sea lions bobbing near the docks; the small green strand along the shoreline is the restoration project of the houseboaters, who used their own funds to spruce it up.

After the houseboats, walk along the waterfront, past the old Sailing Ship Restaurant and Red's Java House (another relic of the old waterfront, where longshoremen still congregate in the wee morning hours over cheap grub and even cheaper coffee), to the portion of the Embarcadero called **Herb Caen Way.** The city's most famous columnist, beloved by laborers and loft-dwellers alike, championed the underdog and celebrated the assortment of happy misfits that make their home in San Francisco. At Brannan Street you'll hit **Delancey Street** restaurant, the classy American bistro built and run by the Delancey Street Foundation, the organization that helps drug addicts, ex-cons, and other down-and-outers get back on their feet. The restaurant is manned by members of the program, with the help of consulting chefs, which may explain the multiethnic menu. No doubt in deference to founder Mimi Silber, there's almost always some kind of matzo ball soup/latkes/knish available; other selections run the gamut from pot roast and gumbo to salmon mousse. If it's warm enough, sit on the glassed-in patio and gaze out at the lights of the Bay Bridge reflected in the water.

**A QUICK HIT LIST OF PLACES WHERE YOU CAN SHOW YOUR SUPPORT**

*Cause:* Old-growth redwood forests
*Destination:* Muir Woods in Marin or Avenue of the Giants in Humboldt County.

*Cause:* Whales and other endangered marine mammals
*Destination:* Point Reyes or Monterey, where you can watch the gray whale migration; Año Nuevo State Park near Pescadero, where you can tour the sea elephant breeding grounds; the Marine Mammal Center in Sausalito, where they rehabilitate injured dolphins and sea lions.

*Cause:* Global warming
*Destination:* Pier 39 or Paramount's Great America, where you can ride the nonfossil-fuel burning bumper cars; Critical Mass, the monthly anarchistic bike ride through the streets of downtown San Francisco (begins at Justin Herman Plaza).

There are the culture sparrows—small-town folk for whom San Francisco is indeed the Big City, who come here looking to peck at the kind of big city culture they can't get at the state fair. On the positive side, these sorts of guests can inspire you to finally getting around to seeing that Fabergé egg exhibit; on the negative side,

# Tour 20 Culture Vultures

as host, it may mean having to see *Phantom of the Opera* for the fourth time.

Then there are the culture vultures—those voracious, guidebook-toting trivia buffs whose appetite for the arts is insatiable. They come here to peck meat off the city's cultural bones until not even a scrap of street theater is left. For them, no museum is too small; no piece of historical minutia too obscure; no dance group too interpretive. The benefits are obvious: you'll finally go to the places you often thought about visiting back when you first moved here. Places that sounded lofty and intellectually intriguing and definitely black turtle-neck. On the dark side, you may find yourself in an audience of six, watching some extremely bad theater, with no hope of making an inconspicuous exit. Either way, it's an "experience."

# MORNING-NOON

Being culturally conscious doesn't just mean staying awake during the third act, it means taking a big spoon and dipping it into San Francisco's bubbling ethnic melting pot. Start Saturday off with a whirlwind education in the deep-rooted tradition of Mexican muralism on a **Precita Eyes Mural Arts Center** tour of the Mission district. The neighborhood is a hotbed of public murals (more than sixty in an eight-block area), most of which tell the history of the Chicano and Latin community. The tour is led by artists who work with the center, and who know all the stories behind the murals and the people who did them (pay special attention when you get to Balmy Alley, where practically every garage, doorway, and cement wall is covered with art).

Next head down to Fort Mason, where you can expand your world view across three continents at the **Mexican Museum, Museo Italo Americano,** and the **African-American Historical and Cultural Society.** The small Mexican Museum (scheduled to move to bigger digs in the Yerba Buena area in 1999) presents rotating exhibits of Mexican, Mexican-American, Latin, and Chicano art, from pre-Hispanic to modern day. Holdings include some important pieces by the father of Mexican muralism, Diego Rivera, as well as Rodolfo Morales and Frida Kahlo.

The Museo Italo Americano doesn't have a huge space or a vast collection, but like the Italian contingent in North Beach, a little devotion goes a long way. Your *paisano* friends from New York will admire the tenacity of this small society, which has dedicated itself to preserving Italian culture in this western outpost. The shows consist mostly of contemporary Italian and Italian-American painting, etchings, and photography, as well as of works that foster appreciation of modern Italian culture and art.

The African-American Historical and Cultural Society is more of a resource center and research facility for those interested in the history of African-Americans on the West Coast, but the exhibitions (often mounted in the nearby Bayfront Gallery) can be truly exceptional.

## Additional Alternative Museums

Of course you'll want to make a pilgrimage to the triple crown of local museums—the de Young, the Legion of Honor, and the Asian Art Museum—but once you've done that, try something a little more obscure.

**Wells Fargo History Museum**—Actual gold nuggets found in the streams up north in the 1850s and a genuine Concord stagecoach are

**Nitty Gritty.**

**Precita Eyes Mural Arts Center**
348 Precita Avenue,
285-2287

**Fort Mason**
Buchanan Street and Marina
Boulevard, 979-3010

**Mexican Museum**
Building D, Fort Mason,
441-0404

**Museo Italo Americano**
Laguna Street and Marina
Boulevard, 673-2200

**African-American Historical and Cultural Society**
Building C, Fort Mason,
441-0640

**Wells Fargo History Museum**
420 Montgomery Street,
396-2619

the main attractions here, a fun little slice of western pioneering history in the middle of the Financial District.

**Pacific Heritage Museum**—Located on the site of the old U.S. Subtreasury and the city's first mint, you can still see the original coin vaults from strategically placed windows. The museum features Thai decorative and ceremonial objects, costumes, ancient Chinese pottery, calligraphy, and old photographs that trace San Francisco's ties to the Pacific Rim.

**North Beach Museum**—Located on the upper level of the Eureka Bank, the small museum has memorabilia and photographs of North Beach, Chinatown, and Fisherman's Wharf in the old days.

**Presidio Army Museum**—Inside, you'll be riveted by the dioramas of the city circa 1906, the 1915 Panama-Pacific Exposition, and the Spanish Presidio. Out back, don't miss the board-and-batten refugee cottages, exactly like the ones they put up in Golden Gate Park and the Presidio after the earthquake (many of which were carted off to other parts of the city, fixed up, and are now selling for a couple hundred thousand dollars).

**Ansel Adams Center**—Anyone who's a fan of the naturalist photographer, or anyone who's never seen Yosemite through Adams's eyes, or anyone who's interested in what's happening on the cutting edge of contemporary photography owes himself or herself a visit to the center, run by the Friends of Photography, a conglomerate whose founders included Adams, Brett Weston, and Beaumont Newhall.

**Main Library**—The library hosts some terrific exhibits about the life and times of San Francisco, ranging from an historic look at Angel Island to fond remembrances of the wacky and wonderful denizens who gave the city its character. Lots of other interesting memorabilia—souvenir programs from the opening of the Golden Gate Bridge, postcards from the Pan-Pacific Expo—can be found inside the glass cases of the San Francisco History Room.

## THE ART MART

There are dozens of galleries in this town, some of which sell serious art to collectors and people who know, others of which sell shlock to people who don't know. I don't pretend to be an arbiter of either, but I know what I like. Here is a brief rundown of places probably worth a second look.

**Vorpal Gallery**—This expansive space near the Opera House features masterworks by Goya, Dürer, Homer, Picasso, and Delacroix. But Vorpal's claim to fame is having introduced the American public to Dutch artist M. C. Escher in the '60s. They still have one of the most extensive collections of his work in the world. You'll find that there's a lot more to the guy than what you see in those optical illusion jigsaw puzzles.

**Campbell-Thiebaud Gallery**—Owned in part by artist Wayne Thiebaud's son Paul, this is a prime spot to view and purchase work by the Bay Area artist, whose works grace the halls of many a museum of modern art. Included in the mix are several of Thiebaud's San Francisco street scenes and his famous cakes and pies.

**Art Exchange**—If your friends are interested in purchasing art, but their last names aren't Trump or Getty, take them to Art Exchange. This gallery sells original, quality cast-offs from museums and private collections, at very reasonable (if not occasionally remarkable) prices. Media includes sculpture, painting, prints, and works on paper. The racks and bins can be like a bargain basement sale at the Met.

**Thomas Reynolds Fine Art**—If your guests are looking for art as souvenir, ignore your first instinct to go to Fisherman's Wharf and steer them instead to Thomas Reynolds, located in the chic Upper Fillmore district. Reynolds, a former magazine editor, carries a lot of San Francisco cityscapes by emerging, talented local artists who haven't yet developed an urge to drop one of their names.

## SoMa goes SoHo

The opening of the Museum of Modern Art and the Center for the Arts sparked a gallery boom South of Market that shows no signs of slowing down. On a whirlwind tour, your first stop should be **Crown Point Press,** a working atelier specializing in etchings and woodblock prints that has collaborated over the years with such artists as Richard Diebenkorn, Christopher Brown, and John Cage. Hardwood floors and skylights create a warm, welcoming atmosphere that's almost like being inside someone's incredibly tastefully decorated flat. Afterwards, stop in next door for an early dinner (or late lunch) at **Hawthorne Lane.** Culture snobs (and foodies) will appreciate the fact that the chefs here were previously the stars of Postrio, but unlike Postrio, you don't have to wait two weeks to get in. Even if the reservations are booked up, several tables near the bar are always reserved for walk-ins. And the walls are covered with prints from Crown Point Press.

Several small, cutting-edge galleries have begun populating the dingy alleyways around SFMOMA and the Academy of Art College, offering some interesting alternatives to the usual oil-on-canvas diet you're fed downtown. **SF Camerawork** on Natoma Street deals in photography and has featured works by artists that include Talking Heads founder David

Byrne. **Minna Street Gallery** is one of those new breeds of art galleries (like 330 Ritch Street) that doubles as a performance and events space. Eclectic shows have included the Clubfoot Orchestra accompanying an animation show; an exhibit of anti-Barbies, including the now quasifamous Trailer Trash Barbie; and a happy hour (with food and beverages) featuring electronic music.

**Aurobora Press** is a fine-art printing press dedicated to monoprints and monotypes as well as a small body of work that's produced on-site.

Obviously, if you're a culture vulture cruising South of Market, the **Museum of Modern Art** is your prime destination. But even for voracious art appetites, the whole museum in one day can be a bit much. If you're watching your intake, definitely make room for the permanent collection of paintings, which includes a couple of important Matisses, Robert Indiana's famous *Love*, and an eclectic selection of works by Salvador Dali, Diego Rivera, and Robert Arneson, among others. The multimedia installations are always intriguing (if not occasionally perturbing), and the fifth floor is worth going to just so you can walk across the see-through metal bridge under that amazing cylindrical skylight. The one thing that you absolutely shouldn't miss is the MOMA store, which is second-only perhaps to the Met's shop. The modern-art jewelry alone will keep you in Christmas presents for years; and the bookshelves offer a great selection of quirky little volumes by local artists, which will occupy your friends for hours.

To complete the cultural mind melt, finish off the day with dinner at one of those fusion cuisine restaurants that we've become so famous for. The **Moa Room** near the Mission district offers "borderless" cuisine—a happy and successful integration of flavors from the Americas, the Pacific Rim, southern Europe, and northern Africa. The menu reads like a United Nations catering committee: tuna tartare with cucumber salad and wasabi vinaigrette, wild mushroom tamales, saffron eggplant gratin with sweet potato chips and swiss chard. Most of the fruits, vegetables, and herbs used here are grown on the owners' organic farm near Calistoga.

Over in Pacific Heights, **Oritalia** has shown that despite the cultural tensions between the denizens of North Beach and Chinatown, Asian and Italian sensibilities can indeed coexist in peace and harmony. Try the portobello mushrooms in plum sauce or mu shu calamari with whole wheat pancakes, or get a bunch of small plates and celebrate the fact that one man's capellini is another man's soba.

# NIGHT

Nothing whets the civilized appetite more than a night at the symphony, ballet, or opera. Lucky thing for your visiting arts animals that we have world-class entries in all three categories.

Getting tickets to the **San Francisco Opera** can be a challenge even if your name is Getty, but if you make a little work of it, you can often find extra seats the night of the performance. A small number of student rush tickets go on sale at the box office two hours before show-time and, occasionally, season-ticket holders who can't make it for one reason or another donate their tickets so that some lucky soul (maybe you) gets primo seats spitting distance from the soprano. If your pals are just overwhelmed by the grandeur of Wagner and don't care where they sit, there's also a limited number of standing-room-only spots available behind the orchestra section for $8, but you'll have to get to the box office by 10:30 a.m. the day of the performance. After intermission, if there are open seats, the ushers will usually let you sit down.

**Symphony** tickets are a little easier to procure on short notice. Even if the performance is officially sold out, you can cue up for $10 center terrace tickets two hours prior to curtain time (two tickets per person, cash only, and not during choral performances). In some ways, although the sound may not be as pristine as in the boxes, it's a more thrilling experience for visitors. The seats are located on the stage, directly to the side of and behind the orchestra, so that you can practically read the brass section's scores. Plus, the reverse view looking out to the audience allows you to experience the full architectural splendor of Davies Hall.

For a real behind-the-scenes look at the historic War Memorial Opera House, join the **guided tour** offered hourly on Mondays from 10 a.m. to 2 p.m. You get to go backstage among the props and sets and learn about the history of the building and some of the landmark performances held here (it was, for instance, the site of the first American performance of the *Nutcracker* ballet). Tours explaining the architectural and acoustic highlights of Davies Symphony Hall are offered Saturdays with advance reservations (both tours were $3 at last check).

You can work up a powerful hunger listening to Liszt, and Mentos at intermission won't do much to assuage it. Just around the corner from the symphony hall, on a funky, industrial sidestreet in a nouveau metal-corrugated building, is chic little **Vicolo** pizza. Sit and discuss Handel's harmonics over a cornmeal thin-crust pizza topped with goat cheese and artichoke hearts.

For something a little more substantial and cozy, try **Stelline** or **Caffe Delle Stelle,** both extremely popular with the symphony/opera crowd. Be forewarned: if you dine beforehand, you might end up sacrificing the first act in order to linger over a steaming plate of polenta with pesto and Gorgonzola, roasted potatoes with spicy garlic aioli, or ossobuco.

While you're down here, why not walk around and show off the rest of the Civic Center? The **Veterans' Building and Herbst Theatre,** next to the Opera House, was the site of the signing of the United Nations charter in 1945.

Across the way, **City Hall,** with its soaring French Renaissance copper dome and stately granite columns (it rises some sixteen feet higher than the nation's capitol) is like the sun around which all other civic buildings rotate. Located at the city's very center, it's viewable for miles from the west side of town. Even more impressive than the exterior is City Hall's enormous interior rotunda, which sits at the base of a grand stairway down which you can picture French kings descending towing thirty-foot trains.

If you're dealing with serious performance art aficionados who are either obsessed with Isadora Duncan, in search of a lost musical score, or dying to see the San Francisco Ballet perform *Romeo and Juliet* even though it's not in this season's repertoire, head to the **Performing Arts Library and Museum,** a block up on Grove Street. The small gallery shows rotating exhibits on performing arts—from puppetry to opera to vaudeville—mostly as they relate to San Francisco. A short video shows clips of various productions. In back is an extensive library with just about every book on the arts ever written, plus archives on conductors, choreographers, theatrical and dance companies, and artists. You can even listen to old recordings of rare musical scores.

If they still can't find what they're looking for, head to Hayes Street and **Richard Hilkert Booksellers,** where they might rub shoulders with the likes of symphony conductor Michael Tilson Thomas while sifting through the stacks for a book on costumes or interiors of the world's great opera houses. The sophisticated and natty Hilkert has amassed a comprehensive collection of volumes on interior design and the arts, which are wedged into every nook and cranny and piled all the way to the ceiling. If your field of intellectual interest is even narrower and more obscure, take heart. There's a bookstore in San Francisco that's got you covered. Among them are

**The Limelight**—A one-stop shop for aspiring filmmakers and screenwriters, with books on film technique, TV production, method acting, and—the best part—a large selection of recent-release and classic unbound (and occasionally yet-unpublished) screenplays.

**Drama Books**—This largely undiscovered shop expands on the Limelight theme with a broad spectrum of books about stage and screen—everything from biographies on theater legends to manuals on costume and stage design.

**Government Printing Office Bookstore**—You won't believe some of the stuff the government publishes. It's enough to turn us all into conspiracy theorists.

**Socialist Action Bookstore**—Catch up on the latest plot to overthrow the government or oppress workers at this bookshop-cum-lecture room. Among the selection are works by Leon Trotsky and Malcolm X, biographies of Che Guevara, and books on the history of labor strikes.

**Vedanta Society Bookstore**—Half the reason to go here is for the building—best described as Queen Victoria meets the rajah. The small store inside sells books about eastern religion and Indian philosophy.

**SF Mystery Bookstore**—The place to hit before the plane ride home. This neighborhood treasure specializes in mysteries, suspense novels, hard-boiled detective fiction, and true-crime drama.

**A Different Light**—One of the few bookstores in the country devoted to gay and lesbian literature.

**William Stout Architectural Books**—From neoclassic to postmodern, this shop carries just about every volume on architecture you'd ever want to shake a slide rule at, as well as offering a healthy helping of books on art, graphics, and design.

**Good Vibrations**—As the ad says, this is "a clean, well-lighted place" for sex toys and erotica, how-to and self-help manuals, photography, and lots of books about Doing It.

**City Lights**—The birthplace of the Beat. Under the all-watchful eye of poet/publisher Lawrence Ferlinghetti, City Lights continues to promote and provide great poetry by the bards of the Beat generation and their progeny.

**California Historical Society**—The best collection in town of books on, about, and written by San Francisco and San Franciscans—from tales of western pioneers to Ambrose Bierce, Mark Twain, Joan Didion, and the architectural history of Russian Hill. A must for local history hounds and tourists.

**Marcus Books**—African and African-American literature.

**Book Bay at Fort Mason**—This is where the city's public libraries send their cast-offs. Great prices—especially on big sale weekends.

**Automobilia**—Books and videos on antique, vintage, and just plain cool cars.

**Modern Times Bookstore**—Left-leaning, socialist, and feminist works.

**Bound Together Book Collective**—Anarchist literature.

# The Theatah

The San Francisco theater scene is a curious animal—a mixed bag of brilliant, experimental works on their way to bigger and better things and flea-bitten road company productions on their last tour leg. The mainstream culture vulture might be satisfied with a night out at the **Golden Gate Theatre,** where the Best of Broadway comes through every year. With the exception of *Miss Saigon* (which is headed this way in the near future), the Golden Gate has hosted just about every blockbuster musical that's ever graced a New York stage—from revivals of *Hair* and *Grease* (two different plays, mind you) to *Damn Yankees, Cats,* and *State Fair.* The other sure bet is *Phantom of the Opera,* presently in its fifth year at the **Curran Theatre.** The good thing about *Phantom* is that you can see it more than once and still enjoy it. The staging—with candelabras that rise from the mists and a chandelier that falls from the rafters—is just marvelous; and Franc d'Ambrosio, who has played the tortured phantom for three years now, has a voice so sweet and poignant it never fails to make you mad at Christine (the object of his obsession) for picking the other guy.

**CITY ARTS AND LECTURES**

Culture Vultures who live in small towns and can only hear the likes of John Updike, David Mamet, Anita Hill, or Spaulding Gray on NPR's *Fresh Air* will devour these one-on-one interviews and intimate "conversations" like it was pizza day at the cafeteria. Afterwards, walk up to **Stars,** sit at the bar and watch for celebrities.

For a naughty little musical revue, campy farce, and the occasional how'd-we-land-this-one runaway hit like Steve Martin's *Picasso at the Lapin Agile,* take them to **Theatre on the Square** or the **Stage Door Theater.**

**ACT** is of course the standard-bearer for quality repertory dramas in this neck of the woods. The caliber of the performers and the productions are consistently superior, and tickets can be hard to come by (for last-minute, day-of-the-performance seats, try the TIX kiosk on Union Square). If you're unsure of the content, try anything by Eugene O'Neill, Shakespeare, Thornton Wilder, or Tom Stoppard (his *Arcadia* a few years ago was absolutely magical).

For more alternative offerings (black turtleneck optional), the choices are varied and often hit or miss. The **Magic Theatre** in Fort Mason has championed some exceptional new playwrights over the years and has also served as a launching pad for big names looking to work out the kinks before moving on to Broadway. Sam Shepard brought many of his early works in the 1970s here; more recent offerings have included former *Saturday Night Live* regular Julia Sweeney's one-woman show and John Leguizamo's odd, funny, and disturbing character study, *Freak*.

**The Marsh** in the Mission district is a self-described "breeding ground for new performance," and a great place to catch quirky and hilarious works such as Charlie Varon's popular *Ralph Nadar Is Missing* and *Rush Limbaugh in Night School* and hilarious monologues by Josh Kornbluth.

## Buildings of Note

When it comes to architecture, San Francisco is no Chicago. Or even New York for that matter. But there's something endearing and profound about the way old and new buildings with wildly different aesthetics butt up right against each other, making unlikely alliances on the skyline. This is what my friend and fellow writer Rob Farmer has to say about the best buildings to admire from the street:

### TransAmerica Pyramid

*William Pereira and Associates (1972)*
*600 Montgomery Street*
The townspeople ridiculed Mr. Pereira when he unveiled his plans to construct a needle-like edifice that would rise above all its neighbors and pierce the sky like a great spindle. But the architect prevailed, and his building—which he would point back at the city like a huge, defiant middle finger—has become one of San Francisco's most beloved, recognizable landmarks, and certainly its most prominent. The TransAmerica Pyramid is nothing if not dramatic, and like the city it represents, it embodies a renegade, freewheeling spirit rarely found in buildings of this size. And it works so well largely because it *is* so big. If it were hidden below the nearby skyscrapers, what would be the point? The building rises 853 feet into the air, and is topped by a 212-foot spire that is lit from within. At its base it is perched on spider-like legs that make it seem as if it wants to lift off toward the sky rocket-style. Adding to its defiant character is the fact that, from a real estate standpoint, the Pyramid is a monument to inefficiency. The fifth floor has 22,000 square feet of office space, the forty-eighth has only 45. Talk about form over function.

### Former Bank of America World Headquarters
*Wurster, Bernardi, and Emmons/Skidmore, Owings, Merrill (1969)*
*555 California Street*

Nothing screams "commerce!" like the former world headquarters of the Bank of America. At fifty-two floors, it is the highest building in San Francisco (the TransAmerica Pyramid is taller, but this building, because of its location, is higher). The massive, dark, and looming edifice can be seen from parts of town as far away as Presidio Heights. It stands silently above all others, a not-too-subtle reminder that, at the core of it all, money makes the city go round. But more than a symbol of high finance, the building is a stylish example of office high-rise design—one of the finest in existence. Rising abruptly 779 feet straight up from its foundation, the simple box form is animated by faceted walls, which provide two-sided bay windows for all of the offices within. The angled walls, coupled with smoky glass and red Carnelian-granite sheathing, create an awesome display of light reflection at different times throughout the day. Rather than being an overbearing, ominous monolith that threatens the town, this building is a graceful, soaring, and luminous giant that captures the light of sunrises and sunsets and casts it back at the city in gracious fashion. It is a stark contrast to the bottom-line mentality for which it was built. The sculpture in the north plaza, a polished slab of black granite, was nicknamed "Banker's Heart" by some cynical soul. An apt description.

### 388 Market Street
*Skidmore, Owings, Merrill (1987)*

Because Market Street lies at roughly a 30-degree angle to the streets north of it, there are several "pie slice" corners along its length. These corners posed a unique problem for the early architects who endeavored to fit buildings onto the odd-shaped plots. The best solution came in the form of the oblong, nearly triangular design that came to be known as the "flatiron" shape (a name stolen from the Fuller Building in New York, which is flat and made from iron). There are several flatirons along the north side of Market Street, but only 388 is from recent times, and, strangely, this modern example is one of the best. In fact, because it so successfully fits the plot and its surroundings, 388 Market Street is one of the best modern skyscrapers of any shape. For a really neat effect, stand at the northeast corner of the building on Market Street and look up. The impossibly narrow curved-glass edge rises the height of the building like some kind of futuristic mail chute. On the other side is a cylinder, which looks to be encased within the wedge. The whole thing is covered in polished red granite; its curved windows in aquamarine metal frames—and the materials are all noticeably top quality. What's more, it's a model of mixed-use success. The first two floors are retail space, the next sixteen contain offices, and the top six are one- and two-bedroom condominiums.

## Crown Zellerbach Building

*Hertzka and Knowles/Skidmore, Owings, Merrill (1959)*
*1 Bush Street*

You'll arrive at this green-glass building and probably say to yourself, "This is worth putting in a book?" But hold on. This is where you get to impress your friends with your insider architectural knowledge. It was San Francisco's first tower to employ the glass-curtain wall, a practice that was all the rage at the time in Chicago and New York among the International-style architects. And like famous International-style buildings—such as the Seagram Building (NYC) and Lever House (NYC)—Crown Zellerbach emphasizes a tower-plaza setting, which sets the tower back from the street by placing a public plaza in front of it (very user-friendly!). But do not mistake this building with the myriad lame imitations that sprouted up in this city and others during the '60s. What places Crown Zellerbach in a league with its eastern brethren is its extravagant design and use of materials. They spared no expense, placing all the building's stairs, elevators, and mechanicals in their own solid tower—which permits the glass walls to extend from floor to ceiling on each level.

## Russ Building

*George Kelham (1927)*
*235 Montgomery Street*

It's tough to bring someone to the foot of this massive structure and try to explain that it's one of the best old buildings in San Francisco. From that vantage point, you might as well be standing at the foot of a drive-in movie screen trying to explain the intricacies of *Citizen Kane*. The hulking granite walls thrust upward and in at the first set-back, truncating your view before you get a chance to appreciate the graceful height. But from a couple blocks away (try the corner of Bush and Kearny) the complete article comes into impressive view, and it becomes apparent that what was once the city's largest and tallest building is still one of its finest. The Gothic-style tower is impressive not only for its detail and materials, but for its longevity. It's a testament to the era in which it was built, an era in which craftsmanship was not forsaken in the interest of quick construction and a quick buck. Its soaring, ornate lobby still provides an earnest anchor for its money-grubbing Financial District neighbors.

## Hobart Building

*Willis Polk (1914)*

*582 Market Street*

The legacy of Willis Polk is all over San Francisco (including in several of the city's finest residences), but perhaps his most individualistic work is at the corner of Market and Montgomery Streets. When it was completed in 1914, this was among the highest buildings on Market Street. But where this building, with its unusual rounded sides and richly ornate terminus, might have helped steer the course of large-scale architecture down a more expressionistic path, it has instead become just another of the city's architectural eccentricities. And although a neighboring building has been torn down, revealing a stark, flat side (now decorated with a monstrous Wells Fargo emblem), the Hobart still stands as a testament to a great design mind. So what if it looks a little naked and reminds you of your crazy uncle?

## SAINT MARY'S CATHEDRAL

*Pietro Belluschi, Pier Luigi Nervi, and McSweeney, Ryan, and Lee (1971)*

*1111 Gough Street*

Despite the fact that it's often likened to a giant washing machine agitator or Sister Bertrille's headgear in The Flying Nun, Saint Mary's is a fascinating study in modern church architecture. Despite what they think of the hyperbolic paraboloid on the outside, your friends are bound to be impressed by the interior: the massive marble altar, the 190-foot stained-glass cross, and those gargantuan organ pipes—one chord and they'll think it's Judgment Day.

## Pacific Telephone and Telegraph Building

*Miller/Pflueger (1925)*

*134 New Montgomery*

When Timothy Pflueger, master of the moderne style, placed his building south of Market Street, it was just one more example of his penchant for setting precedents (he had also designed some of San Francisco's most beloved, ornate, and often-imitated movie palaces). Back then, it was the only tall building south of Market, and it was the largest office building on the West Coast. Built as the headquarters for Pac Tel, the office tower was one of Pflueger's most inspired and most influential—it set the standard for several younger structures, including the Russ Building. It is clad in gray terra-cotta, and from the New Montgomery Street entrance, it seems to be a solid, towering block. But swing around behind it, and you'll see the building really has several personalities. The F shape at its rear helps break up the monotony of the more modern buildings that sprung up in the neighborhood. Pflueger also managed to make his building look sleek, in spite of the fact that the ornament is a bit eccentric. The giant thirteen-foot terra-cotta eagles at the top were completely restored during a recent six-year refurbishing. There's also a neat telecommunications museum in the lobby that displays old phone equipment and a copy of San Francisco's first telephone book.

# Other Architectural Intrigues

No exploration of the city's architectural vernacular would be complete without a perusal of Victorians. First stop should be the **Haas-Lilienthal House** on Franklin Street, the only historic Victorian in the city that is also a museum that is open to the public. The magnificent Queen Anne Victorian was built in 1886 for William Haas, whose descendants went on to own Levi Strauss and the Oakland A's, and who eventually donated the house and its original furnishings to the city. The tour is run by the Foundation for San Francisco's Architectural Heritage, which also conducts Pacific Heights architectural walking tours. From here head to the top of **Liberty Street,** where you can still see huge Queen Anne, Stick/Eastlake, and Italianate Victorians like the kind they had all over town before the 1906 earthquake. Then move on to Postcard Row, that stretch of restored Victorians on **Alamo Square** that's in all the opening credits of the TV shows. The best view of them is from the top of Hayes Street, with the downtown skyline providing a backdrop so perfect, it looks fake.

Even though it's been moved a couple of times and is now tucked safely off the street, the house at **329 Divisadero Street** is worth getting a peek at because it's purportedly the oldest house in San Francisco (built circa 1850). Around the corner at 1111 Oak Street, the **Abner Phelps House** is one of the few examples in the city of early Gothic revival style and is almost as old as the Divisadero house.

# WHERE TO STAY

Sumptuous, cozy, and just steps from the opera house, the **Inn at the Opera** was originally built in 1927 as a place to house visiting opera singers, and still is a favorite of guest soloists and cultural royalty.

Located just off the downtown theater district, the **Hotel Rex** is like an overgrown literary salon, regularly scheduling book readings and signings, and furnished like you might have envisioned Ina Coolbrith's Russian Hill flat or poet George Sterling's (the man who called San Francisco "the cool, gray city of love") North Beach haunt.

The **Albion House Inn** is a charming, low-key, moderate upstairs inn on Gough Street, right in the thick of the high-culture zone. Part of the Hayes Street scene long before there was a Hayes Street scene, the inn seems to attract a nice, middle-class, middle-aged crowd. There's a grand piano in the main room for anyone who wants to start a sing-along, and downstairs there's a cozy little continental restaurant called Charpes that'll have you wondering when the *Cheers* gang is going to show up. Friday and Saturday nights they feature jazz singers.